Adobe I..
The Official
Handbook For
Designers

Adobe Illustrator: The Official Handbook For Designers

By Tony Bove, Frederic E. Davis
and Cheryl Rhodes

BANTAM BOOKS
TORONTO • NEW YORK • LONDON • SYDNEY • AUCKLAND

Trademarks

Apple, Apple LaserWriter, Apple LaserWriter Plus and
AppleTalk PC Card are trademarks of Apple Computer Inc.
Linotronic is a trademark of Linotype Company
MacDraw, MacPaint and MacWrite are trademarks of Apple Computer, Inc.
Macintosh is a trademark of McIntosh Laboratories, Inc.
and is licensed to Apple Computer, Inc.
Microsoft is a registered trademark of Microsoft Corp.

ADOBE ILLUSTRATOR: THE OFFICIAL HANDBOOK FOR DESIGNERS
A Bantam Book/ August 1987

Cover from PAINTED LADIES: SAN FRAN'S RESPLENDENT VICTORIANS by Morley
Baer, Elizabeth Pomada, Michael Larsen. First Published, 1978, in the U.S. by E. P. Dutton.
All rights reserved under International and Pan American Copyright conventions. Reproduced
by permission of the publisher, E. P. Dutton, a division of NAL Penguin, Inc.

All rights reserved.
Copyright © 1987 Tony Bove, Frederic E. Davis and Cheryl Rhodes.
Illustrator's art cover by Pat Coleman using Adobe Systems equipment.
Page makeup by the authors; typesetting by ImageSet, Krishna Copy of San
Francisco, and Electronic Directions Group of New York

This book may not be reproduced in whole or in part, by
mimeograph or any other means, without permission.
For information address: Bantam Books, Inc.

ISBN 0-553-34471-4

Published simultaneously in the United States and Canada

Bantam Books are published by Bantam Books, Inc. Its trademark, consisting of the
words "Bantam Books" and the portrayal of a rooster, is Registered in U.S. Patent and
Trademark Office and in other countries. Marca Registrada. Bantam Books, Inc., 666
Fifth Avenue, New York, New York, 10103.

PRINTED IN THE UNITED STATES OF AMERICA

0 9 8 7 6 5 4 3 2 1

Foreword

When we started the development of Adobe Illustrator, our goal was to make a tool that would be easy to use and valuable to both the amateur and professional artist. What we didn't anticipate was how creative users would be. They are creative in the artwork they produce, and in the ways they use the program to solve illustration problems. The users of the program continue to amaze us. They have created astounding pieces of art. They have used the program in ways that we have never contemplated, and they find applications that are new, novel and innovative with each week that passes.

We have always thought that it would be great if someone would bottle the experience the early users have gained so that new users could benefit. Adobe Illustrator: The Official Handbook For Designers fills such a need.

In this book, Tony, Fred, and Cheryl explore the uses of Adobe Illustrator from the perspective of several of the more advanced users. This perspective gives the reader valuable insight into how various illustration problems are approached and solved. They also expose in detail the use of each tool. They discuss the organization and semantics of each menu item, and they discuss the structure of Illustrator files as they relate to the PostScript language. All of these portions provide a valuable reference guide to the program.

If you do not own a copy of Adobe Illustrator, then this book will give you a good idea of how powerful the program is, and what it can do for you.

If you have purchased the program, then this book will be a valuable reference to how the program works and how it is used. In any event, welcome to the creative world of Adobe Illustrator.

John E. Warnock
President, Adobe Systems Incorporated

Acknowledgments

The authors wish to acknowledge the people who helped create this book, especially Steve Rosenthal and Mike Schuster, who contributed to Chapter 6.

The authors thank the following artists for their artwork and assistance with this book: Gail Blumberg, Luanne Seymour Cohen, Pat Coleman, Gary Cosimini, Dean Dapkus, Keith Ohlfs, Sumner Stone, and John Warnock.

We also thank Robin Davis, Adelle Aldridge, Paul Brainerd, Liz Bond, ComputerWare of Palo Alto, Charles Geschke, Bill Gladstone, Brenda Hansen, Jono Hardjowirogo, Barbara Hawkins, Ric Jones, Laurie McLean, Glenn Reid, Tom Reilly, Lenny Schafer, Robert Simon, Laura Singer, Martha Steffen, Kenzi Sugihara, Keri Walker, Diane Wilde, and Paul Winternitz.

Preface

Welcome to the world of computer graphics. Adobe Illustrator is a program for designers and professional illustrators that runs on Apple Macintosh Plus, Macintosh SE, and Macintosh II computers. With it you can produce high-quality illustrations and all kinds of line art. It is unique in offering a very accurate display of PostScript graphics, and a collection of sophisticated line and curve drawing and editing tools, for a desktop computer.

This book starts with a basic introduction to Adobe Illustrator and leads you on a tour through the Gallery disk images that are supplied to customers who return their registration cards. We interviewed the artists who drew these images, and obtained rare insights into getting special effects and high-quality designs.

Chapter One is a basic introduction to Illustrator's features and to the Macintosh system. This chapter explains each icon you may encounter in a Macintosh graphics system, and how to use the SendPS program to send PostScript files directly to output devices such as the Apple LaserWriter laser printer or Linotype Linotronic typesetters and imagesetters.

Chapter Two shows how maps, charts, and clip art can be prepared with Illustrator. The artists who drew the Gallery Disk images describe how they used Illustrator to do special effects, from building reusable graphics and drawing objects with shared borders to adding paint and the illusion of three dimensions. The artists also explain some of the techniques for placing text in graphics, and how to duplicate, scale, shear, reflect, and rotate images. The chapter also covers page setup and printing.

Chapter 3 uses commercial art examples to show how an artist would start a large, complex illustration. Artists use multiple transformations and overlays, airbrush effects, strokes and fills for enclosed objects, and gray shades. Artists also show the most effective use of the New View and Preview features, and how to rotate text.

Chapter 4 uses technical illustrations to show how Illustrator can scale images with or without preserving line weights. The artists explain how they used multiple rotations, reflections, and constraints for drawing complex graphics, as well as editing techniques, such as changing straight lines into curves.

Chapter 5 is a complete reference guide to Illustrator's menus and tools. The menus and tools are presented in the order they appear in the program's display.

Chapter 6 is a brief tutorial on PostScript, the page description language used to describe the graphics created by Illustrator. PostScript files can be used with other applications that support PostScript, and can be printed or typeset on any PostScript output device. This final chapter also shows what an Illustrator art file looks like from the programmer's perspective.

Colophon

This book was written and desktop published by a dedicated group of personal computer users and enthusiasts. Chapter 1 was written by Tony Bove, Frederic E. Davis, and Cheryl Rhodes. Chapters 2, 3, and 4 were written by Cheryl Rhodes and Tony Bove, and Chapter 5 was written by Frederic E. Davis. Chapter 6 was written by Frederic E. Davis, with major contributions by Steve Rosenthal and Mike Schuster.

We used the following software to produce this book: Word 3.0 (Microsoft) for writing and editing; PageMaker 2.0 (Aldus) for page makeup; and MacPaint (Apple), SuperPaint (Silicon Beach Software), and GraphicWorks 1.1 (MacroMind) for preparing MacPaint templates.

We ran this software with the following hardware: Apple Macintosh Plus, Macintosh SE, and Macintosh II computers; Apple HD 20 and SuperMac DataFrame XP40 hard disks; the SuperMac SuperView monitor (with the Macintosh II computer); Apple LaserWriter Plus printers; Linotype Linotronic 100 and 300 imagesetters; and Datacopy Model 730, ThunderScan, DEST PC Scan Plus, and MacVision scanners.

We wish to thank the following companies for support and services in the preparation of this book: Adobe Systems, Aldus Corp., Apple Computer, Inc., AST Research, Datacopy, DEST Corp., Electronic Directions (New York City), ImageSet (San Francisco), Krishna Copy Center (San Francisco), MacroMind, Microsoft Corp., PTI Industries, Thunderware, Silicon Beach Software, and SuperMac Technology.

Table of Contents

Chapter One: Introduction to Adobe Illustrator 1
    The Role of PostScript 4
    Overview of Features 5
    Overview of the Macintosh 9
    Guided Tour of the Illustrator Display 10
        "Elephant" 11
    The Illustrator Gallery Disks 19

Chapter Two: Maps, Charts, and Clip Art 23
    Building a Reusable Graphic 24
        "U.S. Map" 24
    Drawing Objects With Shared Borders 26
    Adding Paint and Depth 32
    Text and Its Background 37
        "U.S. Weather Map" 37
    Duplicating and Rotating 38
    Page Setup and Printing 42
    Scaling, Rotating, and Duplicating 45
        "Skier" 45
    Shearing 50
        "Horse and Rider" 50
    Reflecting 56
    Summary 56

Chapter Three: Graphic Design and Illustration 59
    Starting a Large Illustration 60
        "The Golfer" 60
    Transformations 64
    Strokes and Fills 65
    Overlaying Graphics 66

Calligraphy 68
    "Artifactory" Logo 68
The Airbrush Effect 71
    "Grapes" 71
Previewing and Editing Simultaneously 75
Black and Gray Effects 76
    "Abe Lincoln" 76
Rotating Text 84
Summary 87

Chapter Four: Technical Illustrations 89
Scaling or Preserving Line Weights 90
    "Eyeball" 90
Multiple Rotations 93
Reflecting Upside Down 96
Editing Shapes 97
Editing Type 99
Drawing With Constraints 99
    "Mazda" 99
Drawing a Complex Graphic 103
Summary 104

Chapter 5: Illustrator Dissected 105
The Selection Tool 106
    Selecting, Resizing, and Moving Windows 107
    Selecting and Moving Illustrator Objects 108
    Selecting and Manipulating Illustrator Objects 112
The Hand Tool 119
The Zoom Tool 120
The Pen Tool 126
    Points 127
    Lines, Curves, and Paths 129
    Drawing with the Pen Tool 129
The Type Tool 138
    Creating Type 139
The Square Tool 142
The Circle Tool 146
The Scissors Tool 149
The Scale Tool 154

The Rotate Tool 162
The Reflect Tool 168
The Shear Tool 172
The Page Tool 177
Menu Options 181
Apple Menu 181
   About Illustrator 181
   Help 183
   Alarm Clock 183
   Calculator 183
   Chooser 184
   Control Panel 184
   Key Caps 185
   Note Pad 186
   Scrapbook 187
File Menu 189
   New 189
   Open 190
   Close 192
   Save 193
   Save As 194
   Page Setup 197
   LaserWriter Page Setup 200
   Print 202
   ImageWriter Printing 203
   LaserWriter Printing 205
   Quit 206
Edit Menu 207
   Undo 208
   Redo 208
   Cut 208
   Copy 209
   Paste 210
   Clear 210
   Select All 211
   Paste In Front 211
   Paste In Back 212
   Show Clipboard 212
   Hide Clipboard 214

    Arrange Menu 214
        Transform Again 214
        Group 215
        Ungroup 216
        Join 216
        Average 218
        Constrain 222
    View Menu 226
        Preview 226
        Artwork & Template 227
        Artwork Only 227
        Template Only 227
        Actual Size 227
        Fit In Window 230
        New View 232
        Show Rulers 233
        Hide Rulers 235
        Hide Toolbox 235
        Show Toolbox 236
    Style Menu 236
        Paint 237
        Type 243

Chapter 6: PostScript and Illustrator 247
    What is PostScript? 248
        PostScript and Output Devices 251
        PostScript Tutorial 253
        The Simplest Possible Program 255
        PostScript Graphics Commands 258
        Text and PostScript 265
        Matrices in Space 270
    The Illustrator Document 273
        The Illustrator Document Structure 275
        The Document Structure Explained 282
    The Prologue Section of an Illustrator Document 283
        Prologue Header Subsection 283
        Prologue Definition Subsection 285
    Script Section 285
        Script Setup Subsection 285

Script Body Subsection	285
Script Trailer Subsection	285
Illustrator Document Prologue Definitions	286
Graphic State Operations	286
Path Construction Operations	290
Path Painting Operations	292
Text Block Painting Operations	293
Group Construction Operations	295
Prologue Implementaton	295
The Illustrator Document Script Subsection	302
Syntax Notation	302
Script Syntax	303
Other Illustrator Document Resources	306

CHAPTER 1

Introduction to Adobe Illustrator

The touchstone of an art is its precision.

— Ezra Pound

Adobe Illustrator, from Adobe Systems, is a drawing program for professional illustrators, artists, and designers that brings a new level of precision to personal computer graphics.

Illustrator can produce an image that is not confined to the fixed resolution (measured in dots-per-inch) of laser printers. The image can be printed on almost any output device, but printers and typesetters with higher resolutions (more dots-per-inch) can do a better job of producing a smooth, yet crisp image. Illustrator has sophisticated curve-drawing techniques to make curves of any shape and size, as well as techniques for drawing any geometric or custom shape and using any pattern.

Illustrator lets you trace perfect lines, curves, and shapes using a rough image as a template, or even draw freehand (without using a template). Your display becomes the equivalent of an illuminated light table, and your tracing tools are the precise functions of Illustrator which you use by pressing keys and moving a mouse.

You can first sketch the rough image on paper and use an inexpensive desktop scanner to scan the image into the computer for use as a template. You can also use other painting and drawing programs on your Macintosh (notably MacPaint, MacDraw, or other programs that can create MacPaint documents) to create or modify a template for use with Illustrator.

Once you have the template image in a MacPaint file (either scanned or painted with a program), you can use it with Illustrator — the program displays the template as a gray-filled background image while you draw lines, curves, and shapes over it. You can at any time display only what you've drawn, only the template, or both. You can even see a preview of exactly how the artwork will look when printed.

This combination — precise drawing tools, a template for tracing on the screen, and resolution-independent images — makes Illustrator one of the best personal computer graphics tools for professional artwork and illustration in publishing and commercial graphics applications.

An excellent example of how Illustrator can make artists more productive is *The New York Times* art department, which uses Illustrator to prepare the daily weather map and four-day forecast. Illustrator graphics can be combined and edited to form new graphics, so that the art department can produce graphics faster and still get high-quality results. The Illustrator graphics files are transferred to the various daily newspapers owned by *The New York Times* — much like a wire service distributes news. Art director Gary Cosimini explains that his goal is "to automate some mechanical processes so that the artist can be creative without thinking about the processes."

Introduction to Adobe Illustrator 3

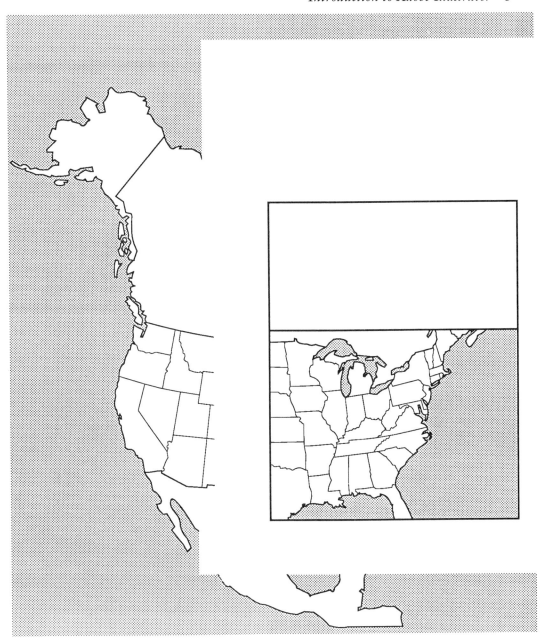

Weather map base:
Courtesy The New York Times, *used with permission.*

The Role of PostScript

The reason why Illustrator can produce resolution-independent images that can be printed on laser printers or higher resolution typesetters is that it describes the graphic image in a computer language rather than in a series of spots and spaces. The language, developed by Adobe Systems co-founders Charles Geschke and John Warnock, is called PostScript.

PostScript is generally referred to as a *page description language*. It provides a standard method of describing and transferring images, and even entire pages, which contain text (in fonts) and graphics. The language is used by an application program (such as Illustrator, or Aldus' PageMaker, or Letraset's ReadySetGo! 3) to send pages of text and graphics to a printer, typesetter, display screen, or other output device (plate maker, film recorder, etc.) that has a PostScript *raster image processor* (RIP) unit. The RIP translates the PostScript language into a raster image (a series of dots) that is ideal for the resolution of the printer, typesetter, display, or output device. Programs can use PostScript to take full advantage of the resolution of the printer or typesetter, and produce images without restrictions on resolution.

A PostScript RIP is built into the Apple LaserWriter and LaserWriter Plus; you can purchase a Linotype Linotronic laser imagesetter with a separate PostScript RIP unit (the Linotronic imagesetters can use other RIPs, such as another one Linotype manufactures, called CORA, but the PostScript RIP is the one to use for compatibility with personal computers and Illustrator). Linotype Company uses the term "imagesetter" because, unlike typesetters, their PostScript laser imagesetters can set images (graphics) as well as set type and lines.

PostScript makes it possible to "print" the same page on the 2540 dots-per-inch (dpi) resolution Linotronic 300 imagesetter (with higher quality) that you printed on an Apple LaserWriter or other PostScript printer at 300 dpi resolution — using the same computer, system, and software (such as Illustrator and PageMaker). PostScript is compatible with Macintosh system software and applications, and it is also supported by most of the page makeup and word processing programs on PCs.

Why is PostScript so important to publishing, and why does Illustrator use it to store image information? Typeset-quality output (printing with a resolution of 1000 dpi or higher) is required for most graphic design and illustration and publishing applications. With

PostScript, it is possible to automate production from creation all the way to printing, without limiting your output to the resolution of laser printers. Pages can be sent directly to a PostScript-driven plate maker for the highest possible resolution. PostScript files can be transferred over telephone lines and networks, and PostScript will also be used to send information to future color printers, four-color digital separation equipment, film recorders, slide makers, and video editing systems.

Overview of Features

Illustrator is a comfortable tool for professional artists and illustrators because it follows the paradigm of drawing with mechanical tools. It is also an excellent tool for CAD/CAM and technical line art because you can draw complex graphics and scale them to any size, yet preserve the line weights if you want (the lines will not get thicker when you resize the image to be larger).

Artists who have traditionally started with rough sketches may still work that way — the only difference is that "inking" the sketch is done electronically, with more sophisticated tools. The program lets you put inexpensive scanners to good use: converting a scanned bit map into an object-oriented, resolution-independent drawing. The least expensive scanner on the market may be used to scan an image at any resolution — no matter how rough — and bring it into the program. Then you can draw outlines, tracing the rough scanned image with precise PostScript lines, curves, and filled areas. The resulting file of PostScript code can then be sent to any PostScript device, such as a 2540 dpi Linotronic 300 imagesetter.

Illustrator runs on the Apple Macintosh Plus, Macintosh SE, and Macintosh II computers. It displays black-and-white images on the Macintosh Plus using a PostScript screen driver so that the line endings and graphic areas are perfectly aligned.

Illustrator can fill or stroke specified paths to be white, black, or a percentage of gray or any combination of percentages of process colors. You can specify process colors (magenta, cyan, yellow and black), or any PMS (Pantone Matching System) color can be approximated by mixing and specifying percentages of the four process colors. You can then generate four versions of the art (one for each process color), save those as four pages, and run them through a Linotronic typesetter, which will produce four pieces of film for a color separation.

Illustrator can create a complete PostScript page, or just the PostScript code necessary to rebuild the image when included with other page makeup, graphics, and word processing programs. You can, for example, save an illustration as a PostScript file using the Encapsulated PostScript (EPS) format and then place the illustration onto a PageMaker page for use in a publication.

If you are familiar with paint and draw programs available today, you may know about some of the problems they have. For example, what happens when you are trying to draw a map on which a complex boundary is shared between two areas? How do you change or separate those areas while retaining the shared boundary? How do you build one half of a symmetric object, clone it for the other half, and then glue the two halves together so that they are joined correctly? How can you scale an image precisely, yet preserve line weights? How can you put multiple PostScript files together and build a complex drawing in pieces? How do you edit parts of a clipping path and do other advanced PostScript effects? Illustrator is designed to handle these tasks, and its approach to drawing is subtly different from existing programs.

The drawing area can be nine 8.0-by-10.9-inch pages on the Apple LaserWriter, but page size is not restricted to this measurement. You can make drawings bigger than a page, up to a maximum drawing area of 1008-by-1008-points (14-by-14 inches). You can scale the drawing larger or smaller, using a normal Page Setup menu (the PostScript code can be edited to make an image the size of a billboard). You can zoom in on an image on as many as nine levels, with a dynamic range of 512 to 1.

When scaling, you can choose uniform or constrained scaling, preserving line weights or scaling the lines. For example, you can select everything on the page and scale it down by 33 percent of the original size with preserved line weights. For technical drawings, this is better than using a stat camera. Gray shading, when enlarged or reduced, retains its exact density, because it is repainted with the specified shading percentage.

You can control the text font (PostScript fonts, which are outlines of characters), style, size, leading (vertical spacing between lines of text), kerning (spacing between letters within a word), and alignment. With the Text tool, you can select the text and change its size; it changes the size of the outline font in fractional points and allows you to condense character width and even change the outline. For example, you can specify filled characters with 60 percent cyan and 60 percent yellow (cyan and yellow are process colors which create a shade of green when combined), and stroked with a one-point-wide black (100% black) line. Stroked and filled type is previewed with only the fill color or shade of gray, so the black outline (stroke) will not be visible on the preview screen; the letter will be filled with green (or a shade of gray, if you are using a black-and-white screen). When printed on a color printer, the image will be stroked (outlined) in black and filled with green. If your printer does not support color, the printed result will be a letter filled with a shade of gray substituted for the process colors, and outlined (stroked) in black. In preview mode, stroked only text has a gray or color fill that is the same as the stroke color you specified, but it will print properly (stroked only, and not filled). You can use the Rotation tool to rotate text by the percentage you specify, or you can rotate it freehand with the mouse.

You can select text and graphic objects together and scale them. Text and graphics are treated in a uniform manner. At any point you can edit the text (but you can't switch fonts within the text block).

Also highly useful is the constrain feature that lets you set a constraining factor according to the axis you draw. If you are doing a road map, for example, and you need to indicate buildings on the map, you can draw a direction, then place graphics to be constrained to go along in that direction.

Illustrator makes heavy use of the Option key, Command key, Shift key, and space bar. Those controls are close to one hand, while the mouse is at the other hand. You use both simultaneously — and once you learn the tricks, you can draw complex images very quickly. You hardly ever go back to the pull-down menus, the palette usually displayed on the left side, or the toolbox — you can keep your eyes and hands on the artwork. For example, to scroll around with the hand, press the space bar for the Hand tool; to zoom in and zoom out, use the Command key, the Option key and the space bar; to automatically zoom and scroll at the same time, hold down the mouse when you are in zoom mode.

As you draw a curve, you can go back and edit it by pressing the Command key, without leaving drawing mode. The program remembers its state and lets you go back and change things and then resumes without losing continuity — your hand never has to leave the mouse. That's important for an artist who is trying to concentrate on the work. To build certain types of curves you stretch the curve, press the Command key, pull back one line with the mouse (see Figure 1-1), and then go on.

This technique can be mastered to the point that it can become

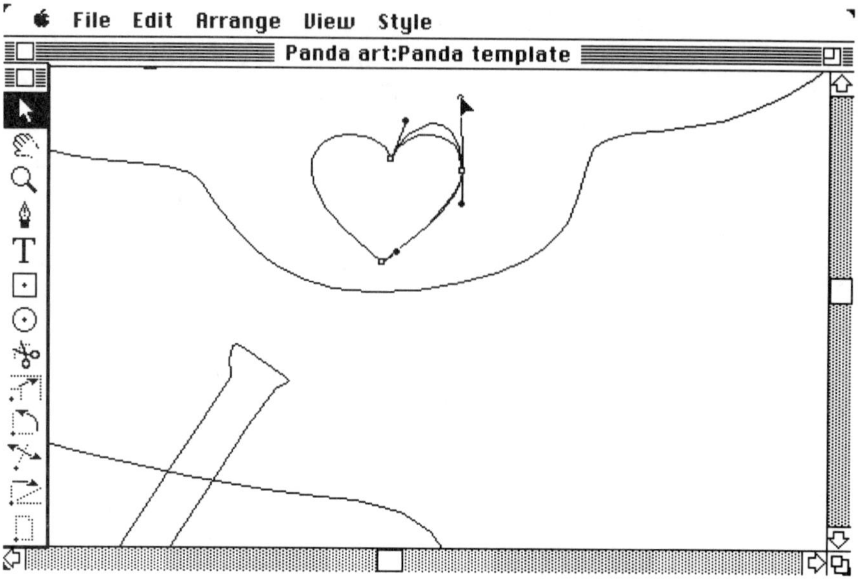

Figure 1-1.
Editing a curve by dragging a direction point.

second nature; people who are proficient can build curves much faster in this manner than by drawing them with a pencil.

There are several useful ways to select objects. The standard marquee (selection rectangle) will select every point that's within the marquee. When you select just one point, it deselects the other points unless you hold down the Shift key to extend the selection to include both the points already selected plus the new point. The Shift key lets you extend your selection to include a new point, or if the point was already selected, it will be deselected. With the marquee, you can extend the selection, even to another group of points.

Rather than trying to surround an entire path or large image with the marquee (especially if the path is larger than your screen's display area), you can point to the path, hold down the Option key, and click the mouse to select the entire path. You can then use Shift Option to extend the selection to another path. This is especially useful when you have a large number of objects — you can select them in a hurry. Option with the marquee will grab all the paths that intersect the selection rectangle. This is useful for very complex drawings; you can select everything within a certain area, and then deselect certain parts using the Shift key and clicking on them.

To paste one object between others, you can select the object, cut it, select the next object, and choose Paste In Back to paste the first object behind the selected object but in front of a third object. Any text or graphic object or group of objects can be interleaved between any other objects.

No matter how you select a group of objects, it moves as a group until you ungroup it. Build a circle or ellipse, and it is actually built as a group, with a single point in its center, plus a path. Hold down the Shift key (constrain key) to draw a perfect circle rather than an ellipse. You can build a circle or ellipse from center-to-edge rather than from edge-to-edge by using the Option key to constrain. Ellipses are created to align to the x and y axes settings; they align to whatever degree of rotation is set. Select a circle and ungroup it, so you can select a point on the circle, then cut it; the circle becomes four Bezier curves that can then be edited. Or use the Scissors tool to cut the circle into segments for precise arcs.

Those who can program in PostScript will also find Illustrator useful. You can select any point and insert a comment, and the program inserts the comment in the PostScript file, so you can later find that area and edit the PostScript code.

Overview of the Macintosh

The Macintosh computer displays an electronic desktop with icons for disks, files, and folders that hold files. The files may be application programs (like Adobe Illustrator) or data files (such as drawings or text).

The following are icons you might see on the Macintosh screen:

Adobe Illustrator™ 1.0   This is the icon for the Illustrator program. To start up the Illustrator program, you point to this icon and double-click the mouse button.

Illustrator document   This icon represents an Illustrator artwork document, which should be named to describe its contents. The Practice folder on the Tutorial disk that came with Illustrator includes Illustrator documents named "Panda art," and "Elephant art." An Illustrator document is a text file which contains the PostScript description of the artwork. An Illustrator document can be opened by either the Illustrator program, or it can be opened by a word processing program if you want to edit the PostScript code. If you point to an Illustrator document icon and double-click the mouse, the Illustrator program is automatically started and it opens the Ilustrator artwork document and any template document associated with that Illustrator artwork document.

Mac encaps. PostScript   This icon represents a Macintosh Encapsulated PostScript document. These documents are used when you want to use Illustrator-created artwork with another Macintosh program such as a page layout program. For more information about creating a Macintosh Encapsulated PostScript document (or PC Encapsulated PostScript document) see the File menu's Save As command description in Chapter 5. See Chapter 6 for a detailed discussion of Illustrator and Encapsulated PostScript.

folder   The folder icon represents a group of files and/or folders that are inside the folder. Folders are useful for organizing icons (files) on the Macintosh desktop. Folders are the equivalent of what are called subdirectories on other computer systems. When you create a new folder, it is automatically named "Empty Folder." Folders usually contain a group of related items, so you should rename your folder to describe the folder's contents. (See your Macintosh manuals for a description of how to create, rename, and move files into and out of folders.)

MacPaint document   This icon represents a MacPaint document. MacPaint documents and PICT files are the only type of documents that can be used as templates for tracing over with Illustrator. Do not confuse MacPaint documents with the documents of other painting programs which look similar, such as FullPaint. If you plan to use a paint program other than MacPaint with Illustrator, it must be able save its files as either MacPaint documents or PICT documents; virtually all painting programs allow you to do this. MacPaint documents have a resolution of 72 dpi (dots per inch).

Introduction to Adobe Illustrator   11

MacDraw (PICT) document   This icon represents a MacDraw document saved in the PICT format. MacDraw documents in the PICT format and MacPaint documents are the only documents that can be used as templates for tracing over with Illustrator. Do not confuse MacDraw PICT documents with other types of MacDraw documents, or the documents of other drawing programs which have a similar appearance. If you plan to use another drawing program, it must save its files as either MacPaint documents or PICT documents; virtually all of the drawing programs allow you to do this. MacDraw PICT documents have a resolution of 72 dots per inch when used as templates with Illustrator.

Guided Tour of the Illustrator Display

When you first start the Illustrator program by double-clicking on the Illustrator icon, an almost empty screen called the Illustrator desktop is displayed. The familiar Apple icon and other Menu titles appear at the top of your screen, but no tools or windows are visible, because no documents have been selected.

Most Illustrator commands are not available unless a document is open. Unavailable commands appear as gray text in the menus; available commands appear as black text. The only commands you can use from the Illustrator desktop are New, Open, and Quit from the File menu and Show Clipboard from the Edit menu. No commands can be selected from the Arrange (Figure 1-2), View, or Style menus.

Select "Open from the File menu (see Figure 1-3). (The three dots after a word in the menu indicates a dialog box will appear to request further information.) Use the Open command to either resume work on an existing Illustrator document or to create a new Illustrator document by tracing over an existing MacPaint file or PICT file that you want to use as a template. Use the New command to create a new Illustrator document without using a template for tracing.

Select Open from the File menu and the Get File dialog box appears (see Figure 1-4). Use the scroll box if necessary to select any Illustrator document, MacPaint document, or PICT document. If you select an Illustrator document that has a template associated with it, the template is automatically opened. (A template used to create

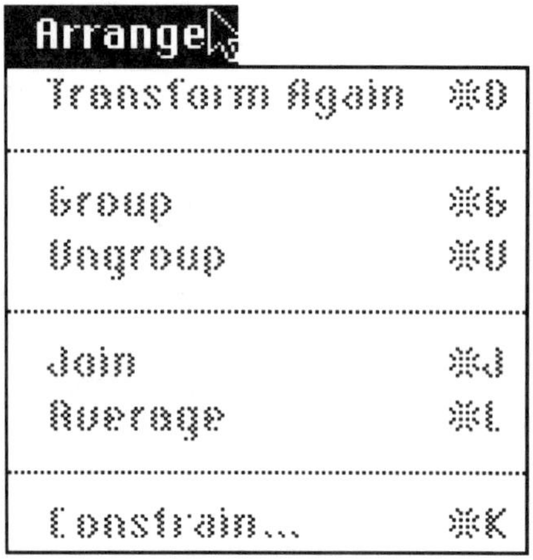

Figure 1-2.
The Arrange menu, with the command options as gray text, indicating that no command options are currently available.

Figure 1-3.
The Open option is selected from the File menu.

an Illustrator document becomes associated with that document.) If you select a template document (MacPaint or PICT file) a new, untitled Illustrator document is opened on top of the template.

Select the document you want to open, then point to the Open button in the dialog box and click the mouse button. In the example

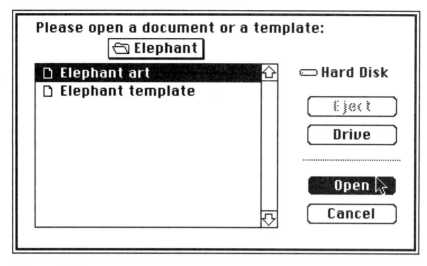

Figure 1-4.
The Get File dialog box with the Open option selected for the document "Elephant art."

above, the Illustrator document named "Elephant art", located in the folder named "Elephant" (on the Tutorial disk supplied with Illustrator) is opened. The template document named "Elephant template" is a MacPaint file created by using a scanner to digitize a hand sketch of an elephant.

When the Illustrator document and its associated template are first opened you see the artwork at its actual size (the size at which it will be printed) with the Illustrator document placed directly over the MacPaint template (see Figure 1-5). Since Illustrator is often used for tracing over existing templates, the background of the Illustrator document is transparent. Another way of thinking of it is that the template document is printed on opaque paper and the Illustrator document is printed on a piece of glass (or mylar) that is placed over the template. The Illustrator document is a 14-by-14-inch workspace; due to the small size of the Macintosh Plus and Macintosh SE screens, it is often impossible to fit the entire image in the active window when the document is viewed at its actual size. Larger video screens (if you can afford one) — available for the various models of Macintoshes — let you see more of the Illustrator document at once and save scrolling time.

To find out what view is displayed in the active window, check the View menu. In Figure 1-6, the check mark in front of the Artwork & Template option means that both the Illustrator document (the

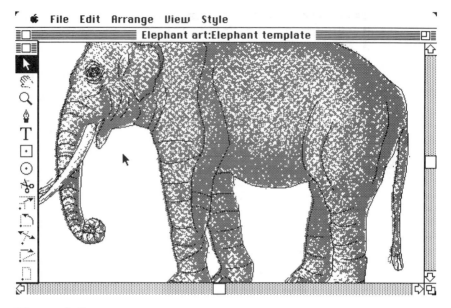

Figure 1-5.
The Illustrator document "Elephant art" and the associated template "Elephant template" are both displayed.

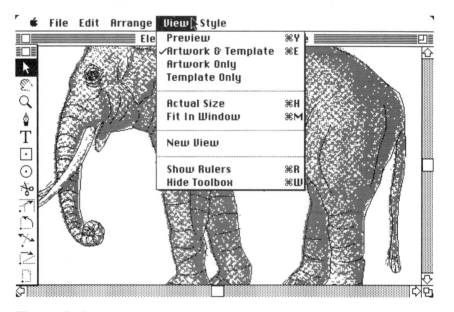

Figure 1-6.
The Illustrator artwork document overlaid on the MacPaint template document.

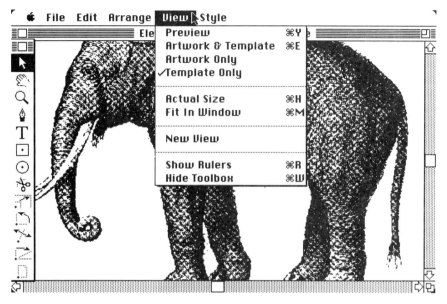

Figure 1-7.
The template document is displayed without the artwork.

artwork) and the MacPaint document (the template) underneath it are displayed in the active window. (If your screen shows more than one window, only one window is the active window; click the mouse in a window to make that window the active window.)

Other views of the active window can also be selected from the View menu. To see the template without the artwork, select the Template Only option from the View menu (see Figure 1-7).

Likewise, to display the Illustrator artwork without the template, select Artwork Only from the View menu (see Figure 1-8).

The Artwork Only view displays the points, lines, and curves created with the Illustrator program. These points, lines, and curves do not exactly match the printed artwork because the Artwork Only view — and the Artwork & Template view — do not display line weight, gray-scale values, color values, and other characteristics of the printed artwork.

To better approximate the printed artwork, select the Preview option from the View menu. However, even the Preview display is not exact. For an accurate view of the printed artwork, you must actually print it on a PostScript printer or PostScript imagesetter (laser typesetter). In Figure 1-9 the Preview option displays line weights different from the Artwork Only and Artwork & Template

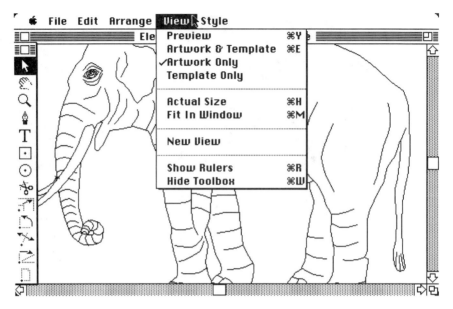

Figure 1-8.
The artwork document is displayed without its associated template.

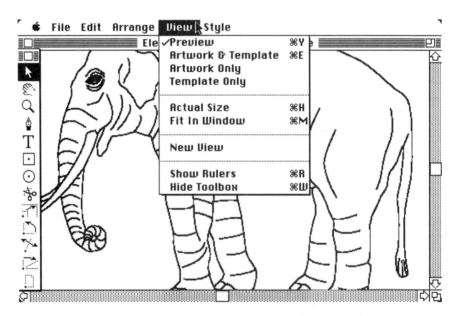

Figure 1-9.
The Preview view of the Elephant artwork is a very close match, but is not an exact representation of the printed document.

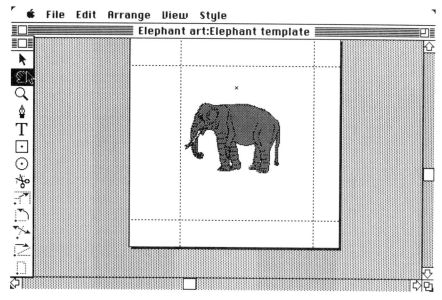

Figure 1-10.
The elephant artwork and template fit in the window.

views; the heavy line weights were specified when the artwork was drawn.

Not only can you view the Illustrator document and template in a variety of ways, you can also view them in a variety of sizes. If you want to shrink the entire 14-by-14-inch Illustrator document down in order to fit it in the active window, you can either select Fit In Window from the View menu, or you can point to the hand tool in the toolbox palette and double-click the mouse button. The elephant artwork and template in figure 1-10 fit entirely within the active window.

Illustrator provides ways to shrink the document for seeing the big picture, and also provides ways to enlarge the document for doing detail work. To zoom in on an area of the document, click on the zoom tool in the toolbox palette, position the zoom tool over the area you want to inspect more closely, and click the mouse button (see Figure 1-11).

Each click of the mouse enlarges the document by a factor of two. In Figure 1-12 the mouse button was clicked four times in order to enlarge the document 800 percent. The maximum enlargement possible with Illustrator is 1600 percent. The + disappears from the

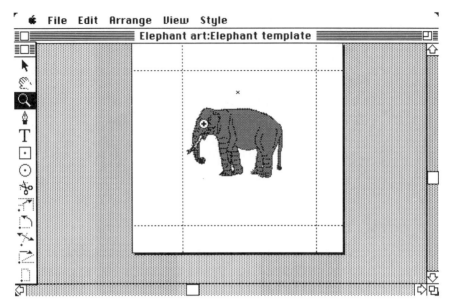

Figure 1-11.
The zoom tool is positioned over a portion of the artwork. Click for a closer look.

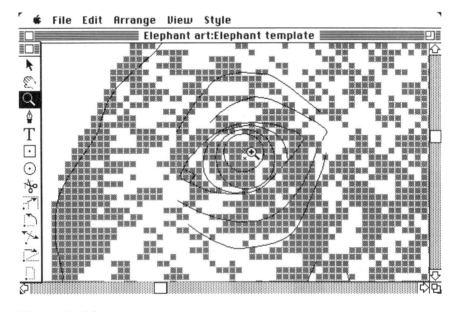

Figure 1-12.
A detail view of the elephant artwork enlarged 800 percent. The + in the zoom tool (magnifying glass) indicates the artwork can be magnified further.

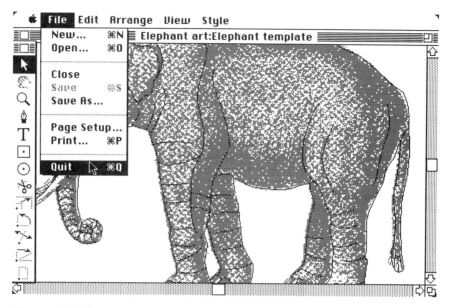

Figure 1-13.
Use the Quit option from the File menu to close the elephant artwork document.

magnifying glass when you have reached the maximum enlargement, but you can hold down the Option key and click the mouse button to zoom out (a - in the magnifying glass indicates you are zooming out to reduce the view).

To end this quick tour of Illustrator, select Quit from the File menu to exit from the Illustrator program (Figure 1-13), and don't save any changes. (Watch the supplied videotape and read the Adobe Illustrator *User's Manual* for a complete tutorial.)

The Illustrator Gallery Disks

When you send in your Adobe Illustrator registration card, you will receive three disks. One disk contains a non-copy-protected version of Illustrator, and two disks: "Gallery I" and "Gallery II". These disks are collections of Illustrator artwork. The non-copy-protected version of Illustrator makes it easier to use the program with a hard disk (refer to the installation procedures in the Adobe Illustrator *User's Manual*).

The "Gallery I" disk also includes a useful utility program called SendPS that allows you to print Illustrator files (or any other

PostScript file for that matter) on any PostScript printer without the need for the Illustrator program. SendPS also performs several other handy functions such as printing the PostScript file as a text file, and giving you a list of the PostScript typefaces (fonts) available in the printers connected to your Macintosh via AppleTalk.

SendPS was written by Glenn Reid of Adobe Systems, but the program is "distributed without explicit support" from Adobe, instead the program is intended as a "shareware" PostScript utility program. Adobe encourages people to "use it, distribute it, but don't sell it." By allowing you to give SendPS away, Adobe is providing you with a way to give people disks with your Illustrator artwork that can be printed using the SendPS program. This allows a service bureau, or other people in your organization, to print your artwork on a PostScript printer even if they don't have the Illustrator program.

Here's how to print an Illustrator file with SendPS: First, use the Chooser desk accessory from the Apple menu to choose a PostScript printer that is connected to your Macintosh. Next, point to the SendPS icon on your "Gallery I" disk (or on your hard disk if you have copied the files onto your hard disk already) and double-click the mouse button. Then, select Add 'showpage' at end from the Option menu. Next select Download POSTSCRIPT File from the File menu. Now choose any Adobe Illustrator document that you wish to print from the File Dialog Box, and print it by clicking on the Download button.

Please note that the SendPS program doesn't work properly with Illustrator documents that are formatted for horizontal printing. By selecting "landscape" on the Page Setup option on the File menu, the artwork on these documents may look "cut off" and only part of the artwork may print. In this situation the only thing to do is to reformat the artwork for vertical printing by selecting the "portrait" page setup option rather than the landscape Page Setup option.

The two gallery disks are intended as examples of artwork created using Illustrator. Only the Illustrator artwork is contained on the Gallery disks; the templates used to create the artwork are not included.

We interviewed several of the artists who created artwork for the Gallery disks to gain insight on how they created their artwork; Chapters 2 through 4 describe how the artists used Illustrator to draw the artwork supplied in the Gallery Disks. Illustrator's various tools and menu options were used to easily create special effects that are often difficult to achieve with other programs, or that would be difficult to duplicate with traditional art methods.

Return your Illustrator registration card for a free subscription to Adobe's *Colophon*; you will receive more tips and techniques from artists using Illustrator.

Chapters 5 and 6 comprise a reference section. Chapter 5 contains a complete description of each tool in the toolbox palette (from top to bottom) and all the selections and commands on the pull-down menu items (from right to left, top to bottom). Chapter 6 contains further information on using Illustrator with PostScript.

CHAPTER 2

Maps, Charts, and Clip Art

The best way to learn Illustrator is to practice. Dean Dapkus, an artist from San Jose State University, knew nothing about computers when he started: "The rate with which you increase your efficiency is incredible. I began by doing simple symbols such as the men and women on bathroom doors and other international sign symbols. For my first drawing, I spent about three days doing a simple coffee cup.

"By the time I did the Gallery artwork, I was able to complete those drawings in 10 to 20 hours. By now, I could cut the time it took to do those images by half again. You really build your skills as you go along, and you can apply the techniques you learn to each new drawing."

Learning how to use Illustrator is different than learning most computer programs because the program has so many features. Illustrator can be difficult to learn at first, but it is not difficult to master if you know something about design. You learn how to become more productive with the program, and you find out that once you know how to do something, you don't have to keep reinventing the solution. Pat Coleman, a free lance graphic designer at Adobe Systems, is well adapted to using what is readily available: "Once you create an image, it can become a piece of clip art and you can borrow from it to create new images."

Drawing with Illustrator is much different than drawing with other graphics programs. Other programs create a line or curve based on the actual movement of the mouse — you actually draw with the mouse as if it were a pencil or paintbrush, even though the shape of the mouse makes it very hard to draw with precision (as John Warnock, one of the inventors of Illustrator, described the process, "It's like drawing with a brick.").

The pen tool in Illustrator does not draw lines as other programs do; you use it to establish points, which can be very precisely placed, and Illustrator draws the line or curve segment to connect the points. The process is more like a connect-the-dots puzzle, with one important difference: you can use the mouse to move the points, lines, and direction pointers, to change the shape of a curve.

Building Reusable Graphics

You build an illustration by establishing the points along a path and linking those points with straight lines or curves. You can also draw rectangles and ovals (including perfect squares and circles) in much the same manner as other graphics programs — dragging the mouse to describe the area to be enclosed by the rectangle or circle. But other polygons and arbitrarily enclosed shapes are really just paths of points. The more points you use, the finer the control you have over the shape.

A map is an excellent example of a piece of line art that can be manipulated easily with Illustrator. You can quickly scale a complete map to any size and either keep the line weights the same (each line remains exactly the same width but changes length to accommodate the resizing), or let the line widths change with the same ratio as everything else.

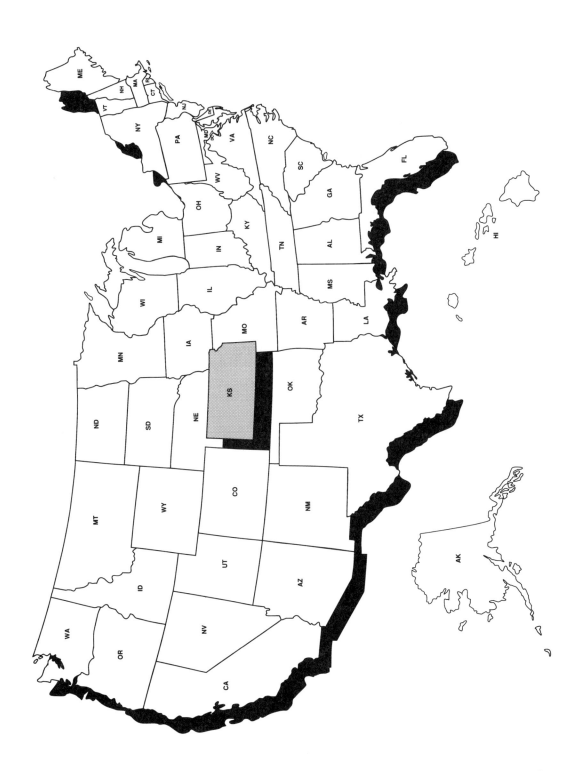

A newspaper, for example, can take a large weather map and reduce it to use the map as a background for a four-day forecast, reducing the line weight as well so that the smaller versions do not have heavy lines. You can also make the map be very large (the size of a poster) but leave all of the lines the same width as the actual size.

Maps or portions of maps can be reused for other purposes, and patterns (for example, rain and snow patterns) can be overlayed on top of a copy of the map to produce a different weather chart for each day. The benefit over manual methods is that once a state is drawn, it never has to be drawn again — it can be scaled to any size and reused by itself or as part of the entire weather map.

Drawing Objects With Shared Borders

Pat Coleman drew the United States map found in Gallery Disk #1. Figure 2-1 shows the map template ready for use as a drawing aid, and Figure 2-2 shows how she drew more precise curves in areas where the template did not show enough detail.

To start drawing the map, Pat concentrated on each state and drew its outline separately. California, for example, combines curved

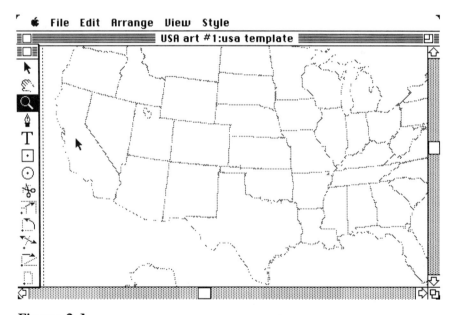

Figure 2-1.
A MacPaint file brought into Illustrator as a template for drawing the map. This file was created by scanning a map from an advertisement.

Maps, Charts and Clip Art 27

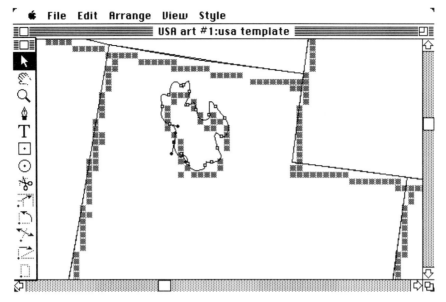

Figure 2-2.
The Great Salt Lake is just a pattern of dots in the MacPaint-formatted scanned image used as a template, but you can enhance it considerably by drawing more precise curves.

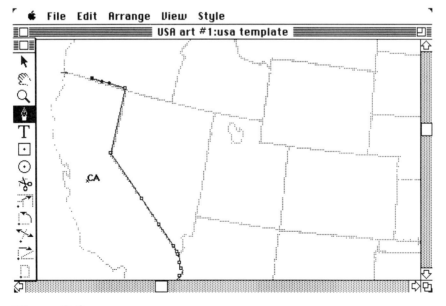

Figure 2-3.
Drawing a state using curved and straight segments to form a complete outline. Each state can be moved or used by itself.

segments with straight segments (Figure 2-3). It takes a lot of small curved segments to draw the outline of the Bay Area, so she used the zoom tool to zoom into the area and see more detail (Figure 2-4). You can use the zoom tool to magnify the graphics (Figure 2-5) and still use all of the tools to draw very small segments.

Each state was drawn as one continuous enclosed path. To form a boundary where two states join (and thereby start the outline of the next state), Pat first selected the anchor points that defined the segments of the common border, and copied the segments to the Clipboard (Figure 2-6). Then she used the Paste In Front command, which placed the segments in the Clipboard in the same location and on top of the segments copied. She switched to the pen tool and continued drawing the rest of the state (Figure 2-7). "I used that technique for all of the common borders, so I had a head start in creating each new state, and it went fairly quickly."

Each state's border overlapped other state borders, so she made it easier to select a state by using the state's abbreviation as a handle. She typed the abbreviation with the Text tool, specifying the appropriate font, style, and size. Then she selected the outline path by holding down the Option key while pointing to a segment of the outline, and held down the Shift key to point at and include the state abbreviation in the selection. Finally she used the Group command

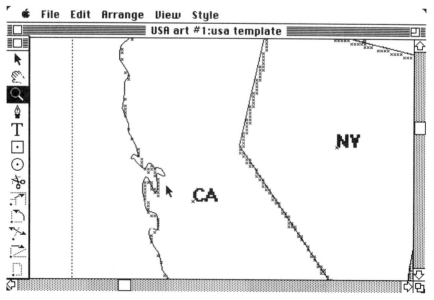

Figure 2-4.
Using the zoom tool to see more detail.

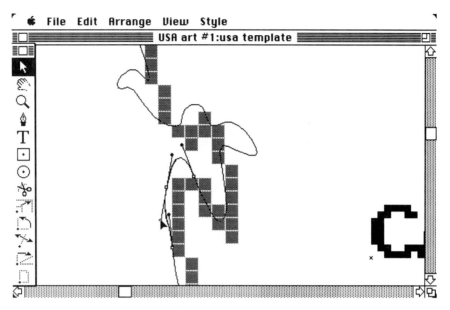

Figure 2-5.
The magnification can be as high as 1600% of the actual size.

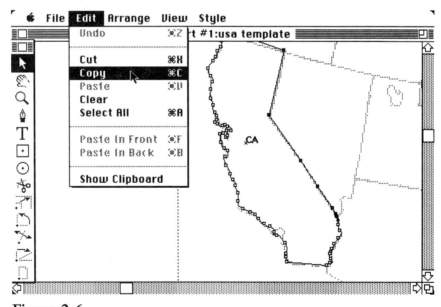

Figure 2-6.
To copy a boundary, select the segments of the boundary (hold down Shift to include another segment in the selection), and copy to the Clipboard.

in the Arrange menu to combine the selected items into one group. Anyone can now point at the state's abbreviation and click the mouse button to select the entire state (Figure 2-8).

Colorado was the easiest state to draw. First she drew all of the states that border it and added the Colorado state abbreviation in the proper place; then she selected the segments for the borders (holding down Shift to add segments to the selection), copied the borders to the Clipboard, and used the Paste In Front command while the borders were still selected (Figure 2-9). The borders joined to form an enclosed path; she selected it by holding down the Option key while pointing to a segment, and then held down Shift and selected the state abbreviation (CO), and finally grouped them to form one unit.

It is very convenient to select the state abbreviation and get the entire state. However, if you select a common border and get the neighboring state by accident, you can paste it behind the one you want by typing Command-B. You can then select the state you want because it would be on top. You can always flip the order of the segments with this shortcut.

Important Tip: At any time during the process of creating the map, you can save your work so that if a power outage occurred you

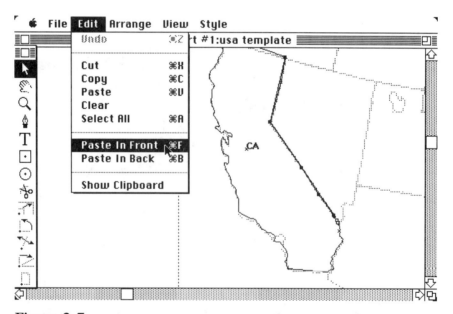

Figure 2-7.
After using the Paste In Front command to paste the copied boundary on top of the existing boundary, you can continue to draw the outline of the adjoining state.

Maps, Charts and Clip Art 31

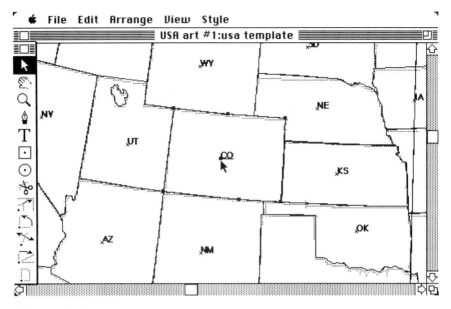

Figure 2-8.
Selecting the path for the entire state by selecting the state abbreviation, which is grouped to the path serving as the outline of the state.

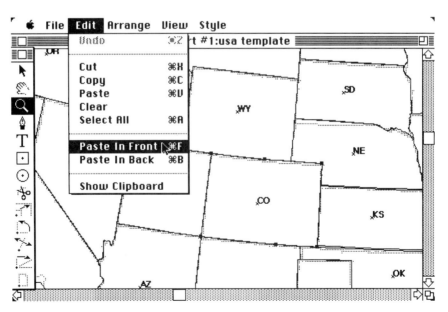

Figure 2-9.
Select the borders of the other states and copy them to the Clipboard, then Paste In Front the contents of the Clipboard to make Colorado's border.

would not have to redo the work. Save the map continually while you work, but when it is finished and you want to edit a copy while leaving the original intact, use the Save As command to create a new illustration based on the original. The illustration's name changes to the new name (leaving the original name and illustration untouched), and subsequent Save commands save the work under the new name.

Adding Paint and Depth

To give the map a three-dimensional look, Pat Coleman added a shadow behind it, painted in gray. The outline of the entire country consisted of so many anchor points that the program could not move and duplicate all of them at once. (If the Clipboard is full, the Mac can't move things, because it runs out of memory.) Pat had to divide the shadow outline in half: one for the East Coast and one for the West. "I wanted to demonstrate that each state was independent and could be lifted out, moved around, and used as an independent state. So each state is a path by itself. That's why I had a challenge in creating the shadow — I had to redraw the outline around the states,

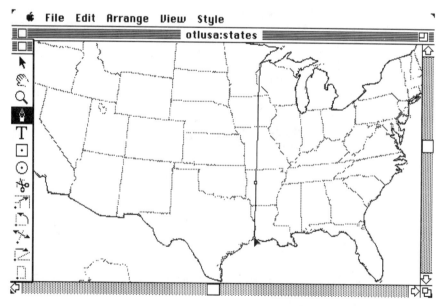

Figure 2-10.
Drawing another outline (using the same template) which will be used as a shadow behind the map.

and that's how I discovered that I had exceeded the memory with too many points. So I drew two outlines."

On the map there are many segments meticulously defining the coastlines, so Pat decided to draw another, less detailed outline using just the map's template. First she closed the artwork file and saved it, then she opened the template by itself, creating a new artwork file, and drew one outline around the West Coast, and one around the East Coast. To join the endpoints of the East Coast shadow (to keep it separate from the West Coast shadow), she clicked with the pen tool a point on top of the first endpoint, and clicked on top of the other endpoint — Illustrator drew a straight line (Figure 2-10). She created the same type of line for the West coast shadow by copying it to the Clipboard, then using the Paste In Front command to place the copy on top of the original line.

After finishing the outlines, she selected the first one by holding down the Option key while selecting a segment (which selects an entire path); then while holding down the Shift and Option keys, she selected the other path. The Group command combined the two paths, defining the shape of the country into one unit (Figure 2-11). She was then ready to copy the entire group into the Clipboard, and save the new art file containing the U.S. profile (no states).

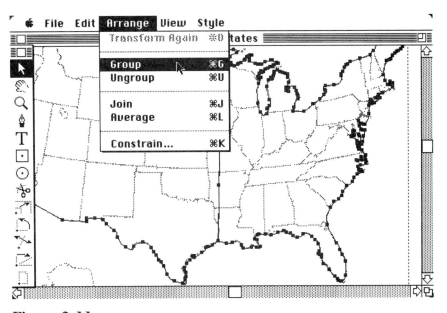

Figure 2-11.
After selecting all of the paths (hold down Shift to include another path with a selection), use the Group command to treat them as one object.

Using the Open command, she opened the original U.S. art file without its template, and used the Paste In Back command to paste the group of paths from the Clipboard behind the U.S. map (Figure 2-12). The group remains selected, so she took the opportunity to specify the shadow using the Paint command in the Style menu — an 85% shade of black (dark gray) for the pattern, and no stroke (line outlining the paths), as shown in Figure 2-13.

Returning to the art window, she started dragging the selected paths defining the shadow and then held down the Shift key while dragging. When she released the mouse and then released the Shift key, the shadow's outline had moved in a 45-degree angle below and to the right of the U.S. map (Figure 2-14).

The final step was to select a state, then hold down the Shift key and add all of the states to the selection, so that she could use the Paint menu again and apply the setting to all of the states at once. She switched the shade from black (the default setting) to white (Figure 2-15). The white shade makes the enclosed path white so that nothing underneath shows through.

To see what the map and shadow would look like if printed (and to see an approximation of the shadow's pattern), use the Preview command in the View menu (Figure 2-16). Preview displays the

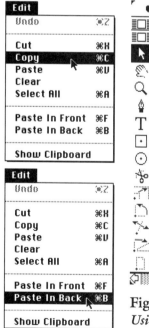
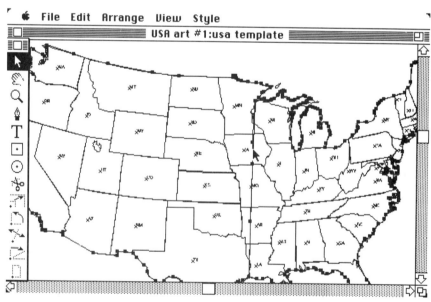

Figure 2-12.
Using Paste In Back to place the object in the Clipboard behind the object in front; in this case it places the outlines behind the map.

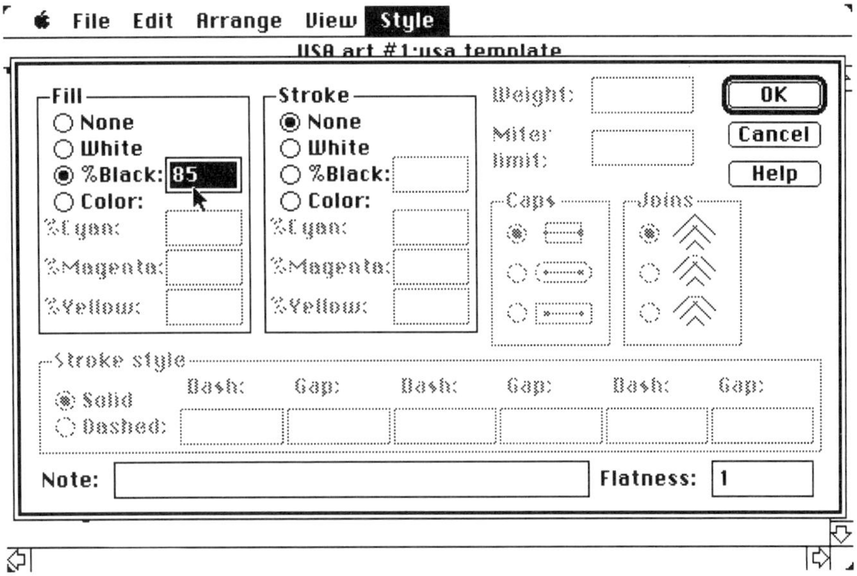

Maps, Charts and Clip Art 35

Figure 2-13.
When an enclosed path or set of paths are selected, you can paint them with various shades of gray or color, and define their strokes (outlines), by using the Paint command in the Style menu.

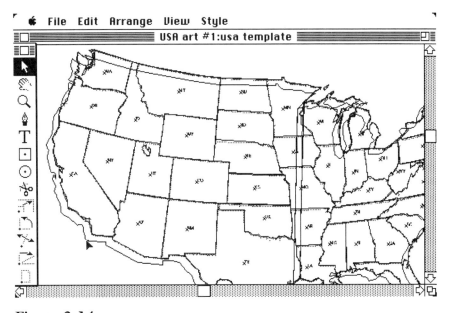

Figure 2-14.
Moving the shadow paths, constraining the movement along 45-degree angles by holding down the Shift key after starting to drag the paths.

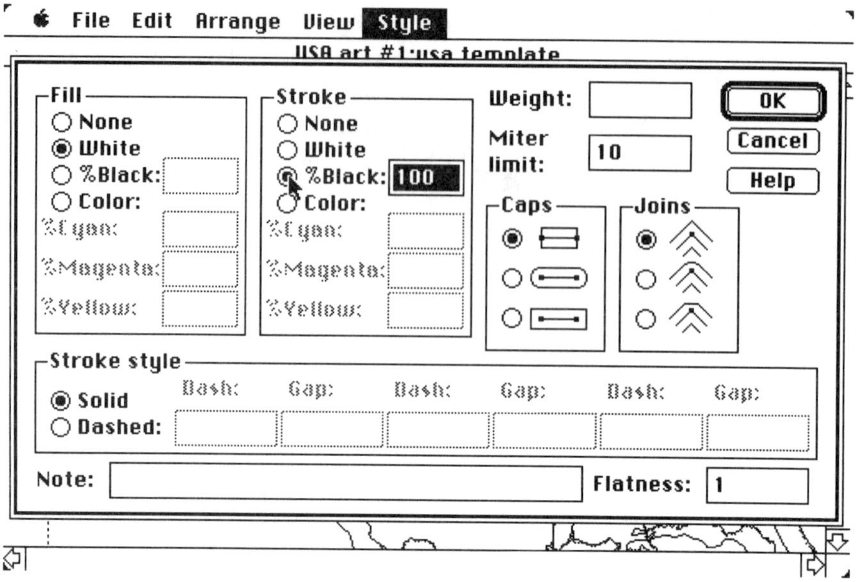

Figure 2-15.
The Paint dialog box with the background shade for the states set to white.

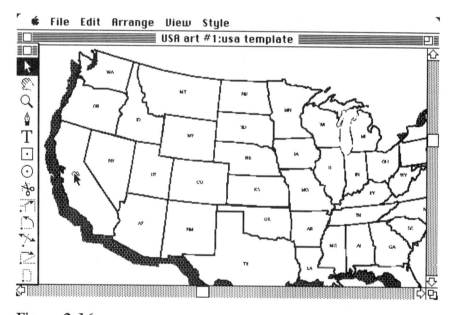

Figure 2-16.
A Preview of the artwork as it will look when printed (as best the screen can display).

closest view of what the artwork will look like when printed, but takes some time to perform. You can't use the drawing or editing tools while using Preview — you must switch back to an artwork view to draw or edit the artwork. A better solution is to split the display screen so that one half displays the preview, and the other half displays an artwork view. Then, as you continue working on the artwork side of the screen, the updates will appear in the Preview half of the screen.

Text and Its Background

Dean Dapkus borrowed the U.S. map to create a weather chart. First he ungrouped each state and deleted the state's abbreviation; then he added small black circles and city names for the prominent cities in the country. The circles are easily drawn by selecting the ellipse tool, dragging from edge to edge, and holding down the Shift key to constrain the ellipse into a perfect circle.

Dean explains how he placed city names on top of state lines: "I wanted the text of the city names to go over existing state lines, but

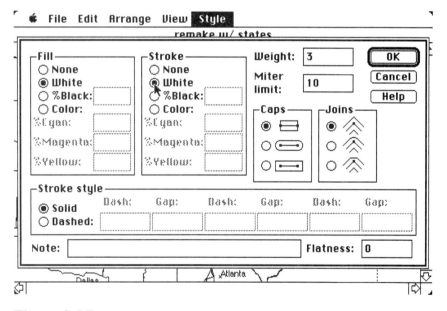

Figure 2-17.
Creating a white background behind a word by first defining the word with a white fill and stroke, then defining a black version and pasting the black version on top of the white version.

rather than drawing a white box behind the text to create a blank space behind the name to cover the state line, I typed out the name of the city, such as Minneapolis, gave it a line thickness of three, painted it white, and gave it a white fill (Figure 2-17).

"I then copied the name to the Clipboard, then used the Paste In Front command to paste the name on top of the white name, and changed the copy to have no stroke and a black fill. I then had Minneapolis in black, with a white outline around it. That's something you can't do with other graphics programs — they don't let you treat text as graphics."

Duplicating and Rotating

Dean Dapkus also designed the curved weather front that overlays the weather chart. The curved weather front comprises a lot of small triangles whose baselines are matched to a long curve. Dean started thess graphics by first making a triangle, then duplicating it quickly. To make the triangle, Dean used the pen tool to define three points and to link them with straight lines (Figure 2-18). The enclosed path

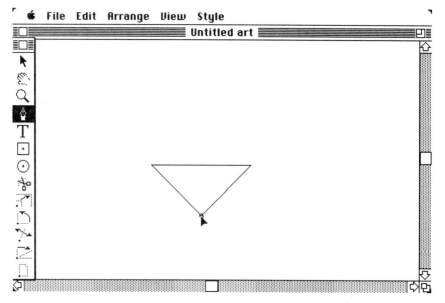

Figure 2-18.
Drawing a simple triangle path that will be duplicated and rotated to form a weather-front graphic.

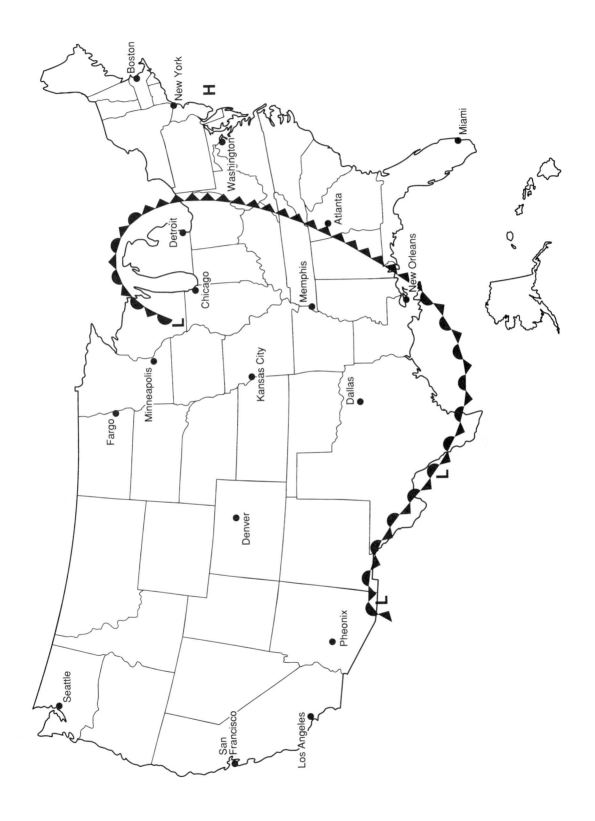

is automatically filled with black as the default shade, and its stroke is also black.

To duplicate the triangle, Dean selected the first triangle by holding down the Option key while selecting a segment; this action selects the entire path. He started to drag the path, then held down the Option key so that he would create a copy (Figure 2-19), and held down the Shift key so that the movement would be constrained horizontally. When he had the second triangle next to the first and touching at the baseline, he let go of the mouse, then let go of the Option and Shift keys. He could then repeat the duplication many times by pressing Command-D (or selecting the Transform Again command in the Arrange menu) for each duplication.

Dean had a string of triangles but they were in a straight line. To make curved weather-front graphics, Dean drew a curve to simulate the weather pattern, and selected all of the triangles. Dean then used the rotation tool to rotate the triangles into position to match the curve. He first selected the rotation tool, then clicked one end point of the first triangle to be the center of rotation (sometimes called the *locus point*), then dragged the corner of the baseline of any triangle up to the curve (Figure 2-20).

After releasing the mouse and finishing the rotation, Dean held down the Shift key and clicked a path of the first triangle to remove

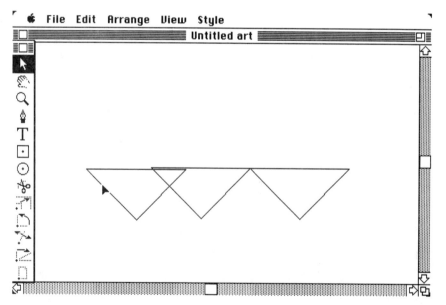

Figure 2-19.
Duplicating the triangle to form a string of triangles.

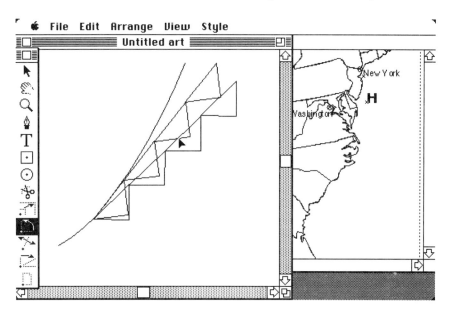

Figure 2-20.
Matching up the first triangle's baseline with the curve of the weather front using the rotation tool on the entire set of triangles.

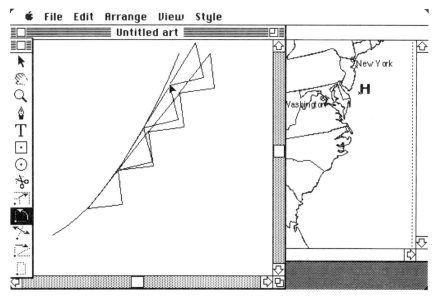

Figure 2-21.
Matching up the second triangle's baseline with the curve of the weather front after deselecting the first triangle and then using the rotation tool.

it from the selection of triangles to be rotated. This left the subsequent triangles still part of the selection, which could then be rotated into place (Figure 2-21), removed from the selection, and so on. "I just rotated every time I needed a curve," said Dean, explaining his technique for treating a group of paths as one object, and rotating it.

To draw the part of the weather front around the Great Lakes, Dean drew a half circle next to a triangle, then selected both the half circle and triangle and duplicated them by dragging and holding down both the Shift and Option keys, as described above when duplicating the triangle, then using Command-D (Transform Again) to repeat the duplication. To align the string of half circles and triangles, Dean used the same rotation technique described above, removing from the selection each triangle and half-circle that was properly aligned with each rotation.

Page Setup and Printing

The drawing area in Illustrator is 14-by-14 inches, which is much larger than a standard 8 1/2-by-11-inch page printed by the LaserWriter and other laser printers. The Linotype Linotronic typesetters, however, can typeset an image the width of the paper or film path — that is, less than 12 inches in one dimension (L100 and L300), or 18 inches in one direction (L500). Illustrator lets you control how large a page size to use, and where the image falls on the page or pages.

Illustrator divides the drawing area into pages that match the dimensions you set for page size in the Page Setup dialog box (in the File menu). The program assumes you want a vertical page, also called *portrait mode*, where the longest edge of the page is vertical. Figure 2-22 shows the drawing area divided into pages that are the standard size for the LaserWriter. With the page tool (the last icon on the palette) you can move the page dividers to control how much of the image prints on each page. You can change the page orientation in the Page Setup dialog box to be horizontal, or *landscape mode*.

The weather chart would print vertically if Dean had just used the Print command, and only a portion of the chart would print on one page. Before printing, Dean opened the Page Setup dialog box to change the page orientation to horizontal (Figure 2-23), and then used the page tool in the Fit In Window view to fit the entire chart on one page (Figure 2-24).

Maps, Charts and Clip Art 43

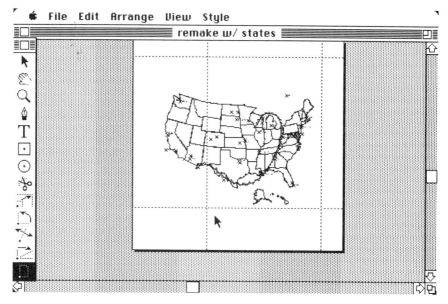

Figure 2-22.
The drawing area is divided into pages that are the standard size for the Apple LaserWriter. With the page tool you can move the page dividers to control how much of the image prints on each page.

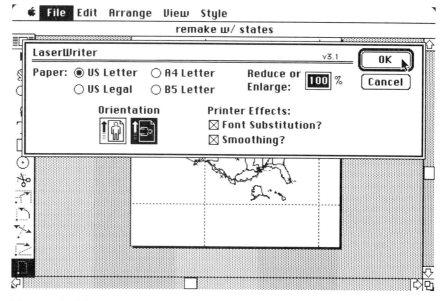

Figure 2-23.
Changing the page orientation to horizontal (landscape mode) in the Page Setup dialog box for the LaserWriter. You can also specify a percentage enlargement or reduction.

Illustrator numbers the pages (but does not print the page numbers) so that you can specify one page or a range of pages when printing. Although the corner areas do not display as full-sized pages, they are numbered so that page 1 is the top left corner, page 2 and 3 are the top center and top right, page 4 is the left middle edge, page 5 is the center of the 14-by-14-inch page (which holds the chart), and so on, up to page 9 at the bottom right corner. Illustrator will print only those pages that contain part of the graphic or its *bounding box* (the area that represents the smallest rectangle surrounding all points of the graphics). If your shape has curved edges, for instance, the bounding box that encloses the shape could extend across an extra page that will print as a blank page. If a *direction point* extends across a page boundary, the printer could print a blank page for that reason. (The direction point determines the shape of a curve, and is connected to an anchor point.)

The LaserWriter Page Setup dialog box (see Figure 2-23) lets you specify a percentage reduction or enlargement. You can specify a percentage in the range of 25% reduction to 400% enlargement with a LaserWriter. The LaserWriter and LaserWriter Plus print only in an area that is 8.0-by-10.9-inches because the LaserWriter doesn't print all the way to the edge of the paper. The Linotronic typesetters from Linotype Company do not have this limitation since you can run 12-

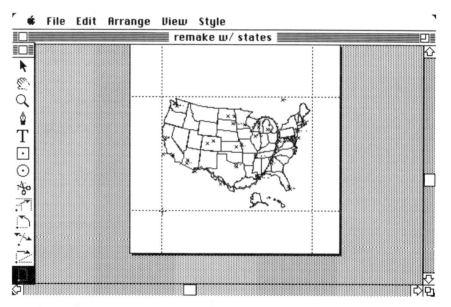

Figure 2-24.
The artwork is changed to landscape mode and takes up only one page.

inch (L100 and L300) wide film or paper, and print large images in landscape or portrait mode. Illustrator ignores the smoothing effects for the Apple LaserWriter, and font substitution does not affect appearance; however, you should leave font substitution on to conserve LaserWriter memory.

Illustrator saves the page setup settings you chose for your artwork file, so that when you open the artwork file again, the program will use the same settings if the same printer is chosen with the Chooser desk accessory. If, however, you have chosen a different printer, the program adopts default settings for that type of printer.

Scaling, Rotating, and Duplicating

Keith Ohlfs, a freelance artist and a student at San Jose State University, drew "Skier" and "Horse and Rider," as well as several other pieces on the Gallery disks. "Skier" is an example of how you can take one image, change its shape and size by scaling, change its orientation by rotating, and then duplicate it many times to form a succession of images suggesting movement.

Keith started the skier illustration by scanning a photograph of a skier, and using it to trace the basic shape (Figure 2-25). He drew the

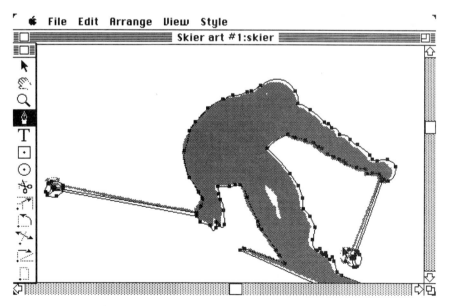

Figure 2-25.
Drawing the shape using a scanned photo of a skier as a template.

spokes of the ski poles by zooming in to see the detail of the template. After drawing several paths to make up the image of the skier and poles, he selected all of them and grouped them so that the rest of the operations worked on the entire group.

The image was too big for the LaserWriter page, so Keith used the scaling tool to manually rescale the artwork. He scaled it by clicking a focal point for the reduction that was below and to the left of the image (Figure 2-26), and dragging to the left and down, holding the mouse button while watching the outline of the graphic change shape. He let go when he liked the way the image had been slightly stretched and contorted (Figure 2-27). Keith then selected the rotation tool, clicked a focal point for the rotation, and dragged downward clockwise. He then changed his display to view artwork only, to touch up the curves and lines and make the image look better.

To create the first duplicate skier, he started dragging the selected group up and away from the original position, then held down the Option key (while dragging) so that he would be moving a copy of the image, not the original. He also held down the Shift key (while dragging), so that the copied outline moved in a 45-degree angle (Figure 2-28). Having done this simple transformation (actually just

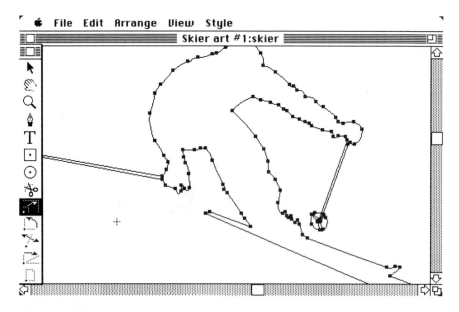

Figure 2-26.
After selecting the scaling tool, you click a focal point for the reduction, then drag in a direction toward (reduce) or away (enlarge) from the point.

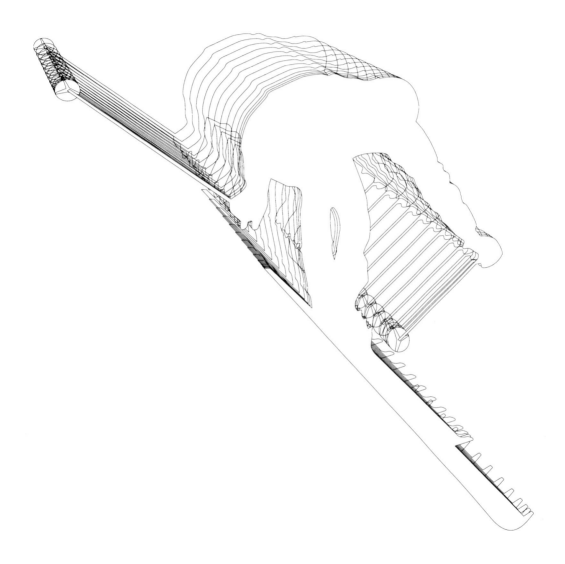

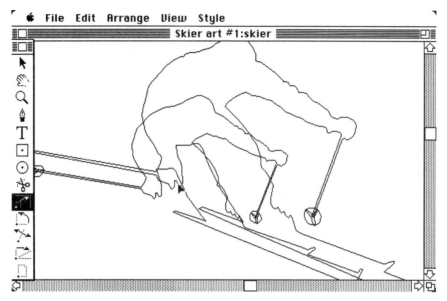

Figure 2-27.
The scaling tool lets you stretch and compress an image; with the Shift key you can scale proportionately.

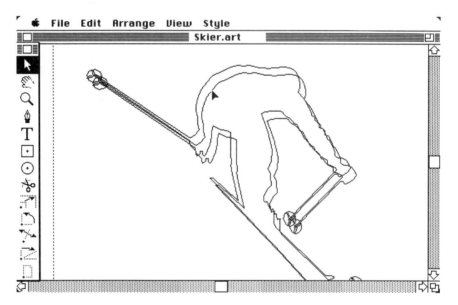

Figure 2-28.
Dragging the selected outline while holding down the Option key, to create a duplicate that is offset from the original. Holding down Shift also constrains the movement to 45-degree angles.

a move and copy) once, he could repeat it over and over very quickly (Figure 2-29) by pressing Command-D or selecting the Transform Again command in the Arrange menu. The result is an image that simulates movement when the outlines are properly painted. The skier image and its copies are painted black by default.

Important Tip: By holding down Shift after starting the drag, you can move things straight up/down, sideways, or in 45-degree angles. You can also change the axes orientation that determines these angles by using the Constrain command in the Arrange menu. The horizontal and vertical (x and y) axes are usually parallel to the sides of your window, but you can change them to any orientation, then constrain all movements to that orientation. We show an example of constraining along a different axis in Chapter 4.

If you wanted to be more precise about the movement, you could hold down the Option key while using the Pointer tool (after selecting all of the segments of the outline), and bring up a Move dialog box (Figure 2-30) which lets you specify a measure of space in points (there are 72 points, or 6 picas, to an inch).

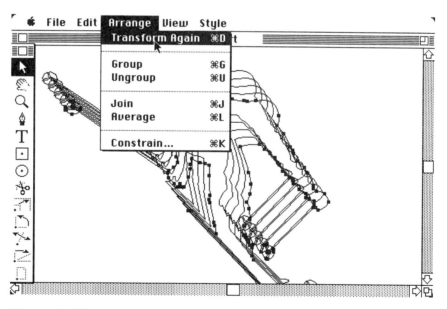

Figure 2-29.
Having performed the previous copy and move (a transformation), you can repeat the transformation over and over by pressing Command-D or using the Transform Again command in the Arrange menu for each transformation.

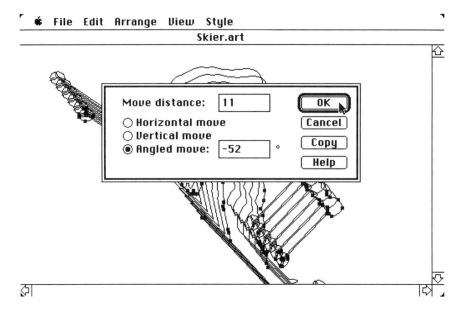

Figure 2-30.
After selecting the group of paths comprising the skier, hold down Option and click the selection (arrow) tool to bring up this Move dialog box, which lets you enter measurements in points.

Shearing

"Horse and Rider" shows how you can create a slanted shadow of an object. You can slant an image along an x and y axes by using the shearing tool. "Horse and Rider" started as a tracing of a template (Figure 2-31), which took about 15 minutes to draw.

To create the slanted shadow, Keith drew a marquee around the entire object by clicking the selection (arrow) tool and dragging from one corner of the object to the other corner (Figure 2-32). Everything inside the marquee's dotted lines is selected, even though the paths are not grouped. You can group the paths after they are selected by using the Group command in the Arrange menu.

Then Keith clicked the Shear tool, and the pointer turned into a crosshair. He moved the pointer to the horse's hind foot to define the intersection of the x and y axes for shearing (Figure 2-33). The pointer changed from a crosshair to an arrowhead, and he then dragged in a horizontal direction away from the intersection of the x and y axes, and held down the mouse button to wait for the program to redraw the sheared graphic. He then held down the Option key

Maps, Charts and Clip Art 51

Figure 2-31.
The template for the "Horse and Rider" illustration.

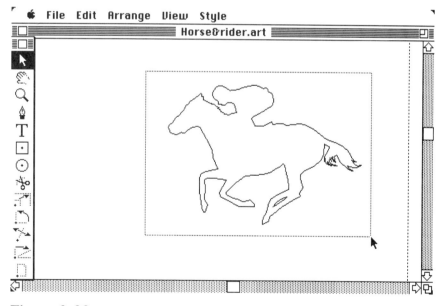

Figure 2-32.
Selecting the entire object by drawing a marquee with the selection tool. Everything inside the marquee's dotted lines is part of the selection.

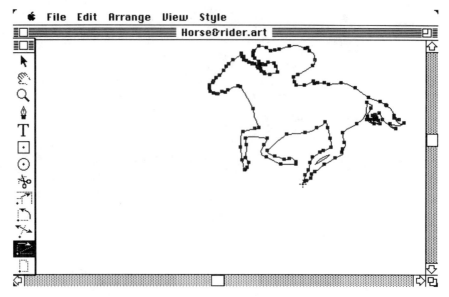

Figure 2-33.
Clicking a point to establish the x and y axes on which to base the shearing operation.

to make a duplicate image for shearing (leaving the original image unsheared), and continued dragging back and forth slightly to adjust the shearing. When he had the image properly sheared, he released the mouse button, then released the Option key (Figure 2-34).

Shearing is best understood if you imagine that there is a horizontal (x) or vertical (y) axis that is either parallel to the sides of the window (the usual case), or angled from that position (if you've changed the axes with the Constrain command in the Arrange menu). You pick the intersection of the x and y axes, and you drag in either the horizontal (x) or vertical (y) direction (parallel to an axis) to shear the image in the direction of that axis. All points in the image that lie along the chosen axis do not move; all other points in the image move in the direction of that axis. So, as you drag horizontally, the image is slanted horizontally (along the x axis); as you drag vertically, the image is slanted vertically (along the y axis).

If you have trouble with the Shear tool — for example, if the shearing is too drastic, flattening the graphic into a line — you can start your dragging farther away from the intersection point of the x and y axes, and have finer control over the shearing so that the changes are not so drastic.

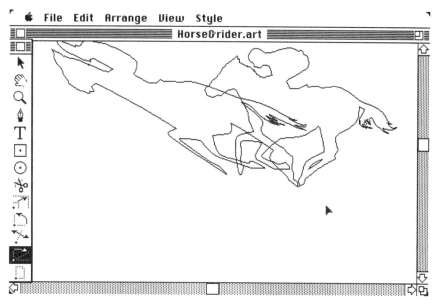

Figure 2-34.
Dragging horizontally shears the image along the x axis; holding down Option after starting the drag creates a duplicate graphic for shearing (leaving the original unsheared). First release the mouse button, then release the Option key, to complete the shear.

After shearing in one direction, the pointer turns again into a crosshair so that you can establish another *x-y* intersection and drag along the *x* or *y* axis to shear the object again. You can also shear along angles that are multiples of 45 degrees (relative to the *x* and *y* axes) by holding down the Shift key while dragging the arrowhead pointer.

To specify the exact shear angle in degrees rather than dragging the arrowhead pointer, click the Shear tool (with the image already selected), then hold down the Option key while clicking the shear axis point, and Illustrator displays a dialog box for specifying the shear angle and the type of shear (horizontal, vertical, or angled by a specific degree (Figure 2-35). A positive shear angle slants the image clockwise, and a negative shear angle slants the graphic counterclockwise (as in "Horse and Rider"), both relative to the original position. (This differs from other functions, such as rotation, where a positive angle produces a counterclockwise rotation.)

If you click the OK button, the program uses the specifications to perform the shear. To shear a copy of the image rather than the original image, click the Copy button rather than the OK button in

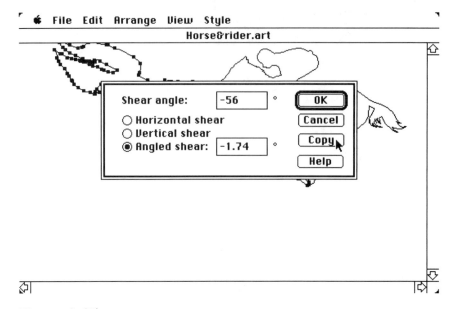

Figure 2-35.
To specify the shear angle in degrees, hold down the Option key when clicking the shear axis point to display this dialog box.

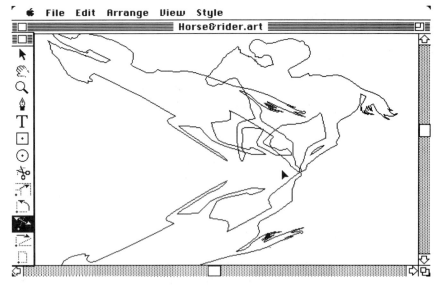

Figure 2-36.
Using the reflection tool to make a mirror image of a shape.

Maps, Charts and Clip Art 55

Reflecting

For the final transformation, Keith used the reflection tool to produce a mirror image of the sheared copy. First he selected the reflection tool, then he clicked a point of reflection on the same hind foot that served as the point of shearing. Dragging downward away from the reflection point caused the image to be reflected into a shadow (Figure 2-36). In this case Keith did not hold down the Option key, since he was not making a duplicate image — he wanted to keep only the reflected version.

The "Horse and Rider" image and its sheared copy are both painted black, which is the default setting.

Summary

With "U.S. Map," Pat Coleman showed how to draw objects that have common borders; how to copy and paste a segment, path, or group; and how to set up a shadow behind an object to make it appear three-dimensional. She also explained how she grouped the path outlining each state with the state's abbreviation, for easy selection of individual states. She drew a map that could be used whole, or in part; each state or group of states could be used individually and with other artwork files.

Dean Dapkus took Pat's map and created a weather chart. Dean showed how he duplicated paths and used the rotation tool to form a weather front. He also explained how he used the text tool with a white stroke and fill to place text that extends over areas of the image. Dean changed the page setup to horizontal (landscape) in order to print the entire chart on one LaserWriter page, and discussed how you might scale a complete illustration by a percentage reduction or enlargement in the Page Setup dialog box.

Keith Ohlfs showed his technique for transforming and then duplicating an image in the "Skier" illustration. Keith showed how you can repeat a duplication (or any tranformation) over and over to achieve a special effect such as the skier that appears to be moving.

Finally, Keith showed a simple example of shearing and then reflecting a duplicate of an image (the horse and rider) to make a shadow.

A wide range of tools for creating graphics are described in this chapter; including tools for selecting, scaling, zooming, rotating and shearing an inamge, as well as the type, pen, page, and ellipse or circle tool. The chapter also described the Open, Save, Save As, Print, and Page Setup commands in the File menu; the Cut, Copy, Paste, Paste In Front, and Paste In Back commands in the Edit menu; the Transform Again, Constrain, Group, and Ungroup commands in the Arrange menu; the Preview and other display modes in the View menu, and the Paint command in the Style menu.

CHAPTER 3
Graphic Design and Illustration

The largest category of artwork produced using Illustrator is graphic design and illustration. Andy Warhol is one artist who would have especially liked the program; his Campbell Soup cans would have been a perfect subject for Illustrator. He could have outlined the cans quickly, added text for the label, and specified exact shades of gray and process colors.

Illustrator gives you a better chance of getting a representational image because it is a versatile program for duplicating, reducing, stretching, compressing, and reusing graphic objects to form illustrations. The effects take some time to create, but once they are created, they can be reused over and over, and modified very quickly for custom work. Keith Ohlfs, a freelance artist who drew many of the Gallery pieces, compared the use of Illustrator for the images he drew with the use of conventional methods: "These effects could be done in an ink drawing, but Illustrator makes them much easier, and you can vary copies of them again and again for use in other drawings, which saves a lot of time and effort."

Starting a Large Illustration

"The Golfer," by Luanne Seymour Cohen, a graphic designer for Adobe Systems, is an excellent example of the type of commercial art that is easily rendered by using Illustrator. Luanne started with a scanned image of a photocopy of an old advertising poster. She scanned a photocopy because the original, which was in color, scanned too dark. The goal was to get as much detail out of the poster as possible, and not to worry about the quality of the scanned image (Figure 3-1).

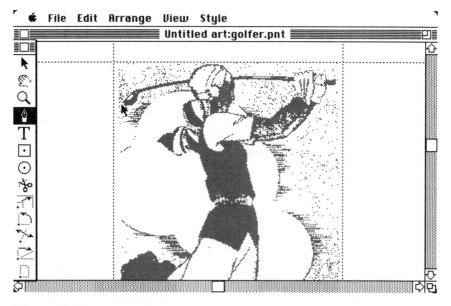

Figure 3-1.
Starting with a low-quality scanned photocopy in order to get as much detail as possible (the original color image, when scanned, was too dark to see details).

ARTWORK CREATED USING ADOBE ILLUSTRATOR. ADOBE ILLUSTRATOR IS A TRADEMARK OF ADOBE SYSTEMS INCORPORATED.

Luanne started the artwork by drawing the background because, she says, "I think of [Illustrator artwork] as layers of paper." She drew the background square first, then the circles for the clouds, then the lines on top of the circles, then the golfer's clothing, and finally the overlays, such as the golfer's bracelet. She worked on the face before the hair because she knew the hair would cover the head and therefore she didn't have to draw a perfect head shape (Figure 3-2).

Luanne explains how she drew the face: "When it was scanned, a lot of detail disappeared. I wanted the golfer to have a modern face, so I sketched my office mate, but changed her hair." Figure 3-3 shows that although the scanned image has very little facial and hairstyle detail, Luanne used the image as a guide to help draw a new face and hairstyle. "There was no eye, or any facial detail in the scanned image, so I drew the eye from a sketch, and moved it around by selecting until I had it where I thought it should be." The selection tool lets you draw a marquee by dragging; you can drag the marquee around the part of the image you want to select, and the program selects any path intersected by the marquee (Figure 3-4).

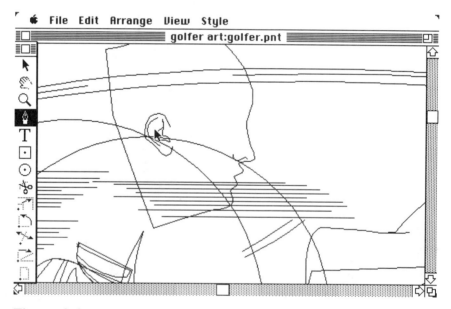

Figure 3-2.
Only the front part of the head image has to be sketched by the artist; the rest of the head image can be left in rough form, since it will be covered by hair.

Graphic Design and Illustration 63

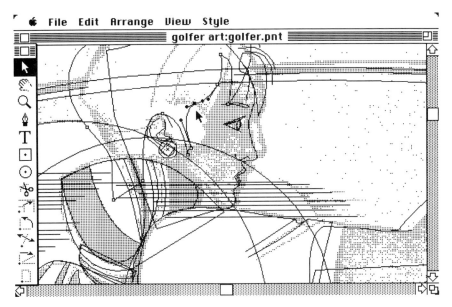

Figure 3-3.
Drawing a new face and hairstyle with the help of a scanned image for placement.

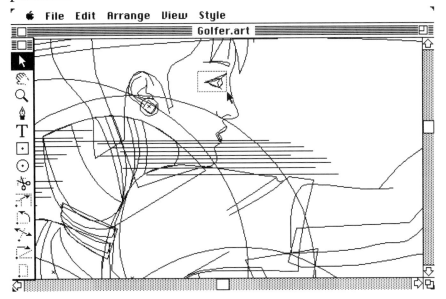

Figure 3-4.
Selecting the eye by dragging a marquee around it with the Selection tool, which selects any path intersected by the marquee.

Transformations

To draw the belt, Luanne drew one square and sheared it into a diamond shape by using the shear tool, clicking an *x-y* axes point for the shear on the lower left corner of the square, and dragging vertically upwards along the *y* axis (Figure 3-5). The axes point and the vertical drag keeps the left side of the rectangle from moving as the other points of the shape are sheared into a diamond.

Luanne then created a copy of the shape by holding down the Option key while dragging to rotate the shape slightly (Figure 3-6). She repeated the copy and rotation (a *transformation*) with a Command-D (Transform Again). She then used the rotation tool (and held down Option while dragging) to create the next shape (another transformation that can be duplicated by typing Command-D or selecting Transform Again from the Arrange menu).

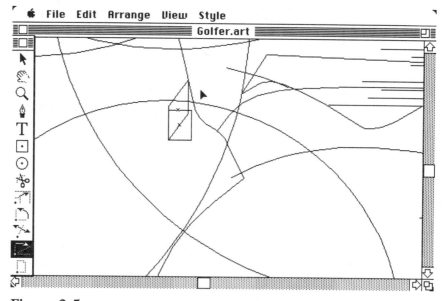

Figure 3-5.
Shearing a rectangle into a diamond by first clicking an x-y axes point on the lower left corner of the rectangle (to keep all points on the y axis from moving), and dragging upward to shear along the y axis.

Strokes and Fills

To draw the folds in the tunic, Luanne drew lines and turned their strokes to white (Figure 3-7). She drew them last so that they would be placed on top of the 100% black tunic (she could also have used Copy and then Paste In Front to place the line in front of the selected objects). To get the soft fold look in the golfer's skirt, she drew lines with strokes set to a shade of gray. However, the white line on the bracelet is a white-shaded shape, not just a line.

The cloud behind the golfer comprised many circles filled with white that have no stroke, so they blend together without seams. She drew one circle and set the Paint attributes (white, no stroke), then those attributes were used automatically for the shapes drawn afterwards (until she changed the Paint settings).

The white circles are drawn on top of a large rectangle for the entire page, which is set to have a 10% black screen (gray), and a 100% black

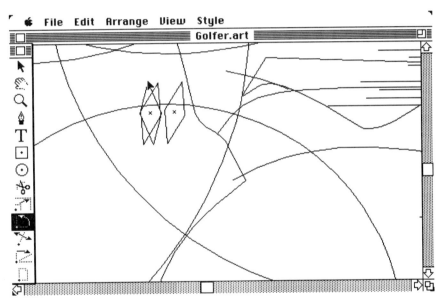

Figure 3-6.
Drawing the belt by shearing a square into a diamond shape, and rotating it by hand with the rotate tool.

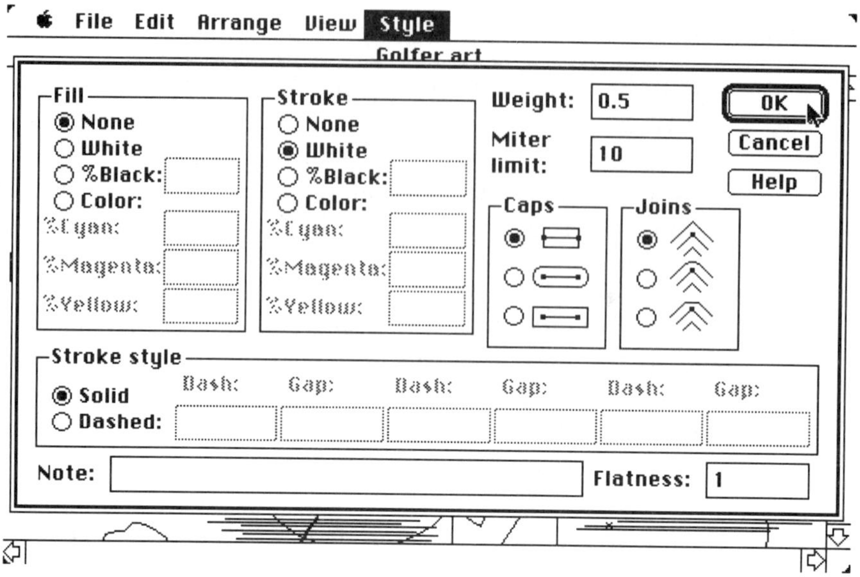

Figure 3-7.
Creating white-stroked lines to represent the folds in the golfer's tunic.

stroke whose weight is one point. Another box was drawn on top of the gray box with the same dimensions, but with a heavier line (three points) and no fill.

Overlaying Graphics

The lines on the clouds were drawn first, and then pasted in back of the clouds (first she copied the lines to the Clipboard, then she selected the clouds, then used the Paste In Back command). Luanne drew a few lines of random length, moved them into position, grouped them, then copied the group, moved the copy into position, and grouped the first group with the copy. She could then copy the bigger group, move this copy into place, and form one large group. When she was finished, she had seemingly random lines joined into a group that could be moved anywhere on the page.

Luanne added the sailboats on top of the sea pattern at the bottom of the page by drawing one sailboat, painting it white with no stroke, and copying it while scaling the copy to a smaller size. First she selected a fixed point as the scale origin (Figure 3-8), then she

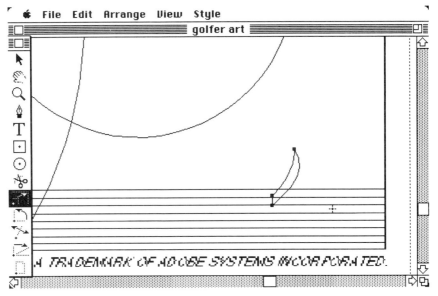

Figure 3-8.
Selecting an origin (fixed point) for the scale to reduce the shape.

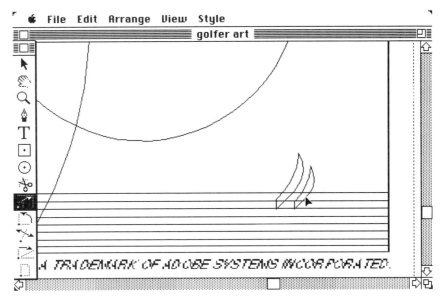

Figure 3-9.
Holding down the Option key while dragging the shape to make a duplicate shape that is scaled down.

dragged while holding down the Option key to make a duplicate shape that is scaled down (Figure 3-9).

The last object drawn to complete the figure of the golfer was the sleeve, which covered some of the rough edges of the other objects. The sleeve was given a fill of 20% black (gray) with a 100% black stroke with a weight of 0.2 points. The fill makes it a solid shape; no fill would have made it transparent. "I really think of drawing with Illustrator as layers of paper," says Luanne, "perhaps a collage of objects. I think about things as being in front, or behind... When you are working with a complex drawing with a lot of lines and pieces, you might not be able to keep track of what's in front and what's behind. You can use Cut and Paste In Front or Paste In Back to move things behind or in front of other selected objects. There are times when even if you know the order to draw things, circumstances dictate that you can't follow that order. I have to draw the golf club in front of her head, but I can cut and paste to layer it in the correct order."

Calligraphy

Illustrator can turn the skill of calligraphy into a piece of cake. The original calligraphy for the Artifactory logo — the original name choice for Adobe Illustrator — was drawn by hand using calligraphy techniques by Sumner Stone. Pat Coleman scanned the hand-drawn image to use as a template for drawing with Illustrator (Figure 3-10).

To get the thick and thin lines of calligraphy, Pat treated each pen stroke as an enclosed polygon, not as a single pen stroke, and drew around the characters to get the filled paths. Pat described how Illustrator compares to a calligraphy pen or brush: "The program fills any enclosed space. It's a different technique than calligraphy, but you actually have more control than with a calligraphy brush or pen, and you can zoom in to get the thick and thinness of each stroke exact." (Figure 3-11 shows how she could zoom into the artwork and work on the serifs and strokes.)

Pat duplicated an already-drawn pen stroke and used the copies to make other strokes, making the strokes consistent. She could also point to a stroke and adjust its direction points to change the curve.

To create the reduced versions, Pat selected all of the paths in the logo by using the selection tool and drawing a marquee around the image (Figure 3-12). She then selected the scaling tool, clicked a point of origin for the scale (upper right corner to scale downwards), and dragged down and to the right in a diagonal. "Scaling is another

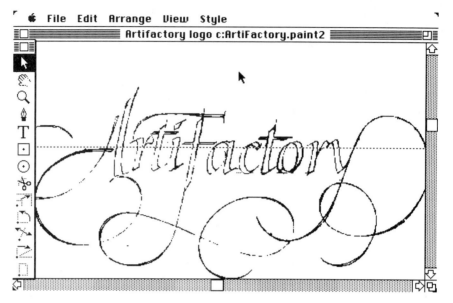

Figure 3-10.
Using a scanned sketch of the Artifactory logo (drawn with calligraphy techniques) as a template.

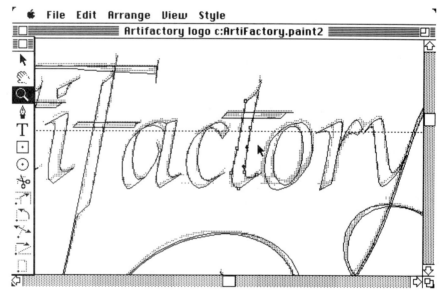

Figure 3-11.
Zooming in to work up close on the serifs in a letter.

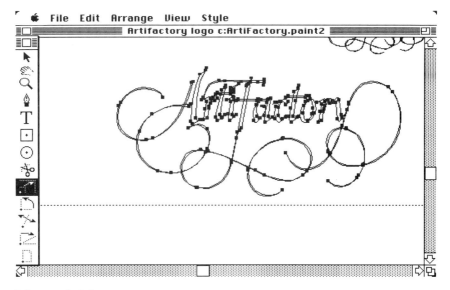

Figure 3-12.
To select a graphic composed of many small paths, draw a selection marquee around the object by dragging with the Selection tool.

feature that makes Illustrator useful for calligraphy and logos. The image doesn't lose quality when it's reduced, and it doesn't fill in and get muddy, like bit-mapped graphics do when they are reduced."

The Airbrush Effect

Keith Ohlfs' "Grapes" shows how you can create a gray or color airbrush effect. Keith created one grape using concentric circles on the grape to simulate gradations in shading. He drew several concentric circles at once by drawing one circle, selecting the Scaling tool, clicking the edge of the circle as the fixed point for scaling, and holding down the Option key while dragging the circle, creating a second circle that still touched the first circle on the fixed point. He repeated this transformation (duplicating and scaling an object) by typing Command-D (or selecting Transform Again). He then went back to adjust each circle for positioning.

Each circle has no stroke and a fill of a certain percentage of black (or of a color) relative to its position on the grape; for example, the

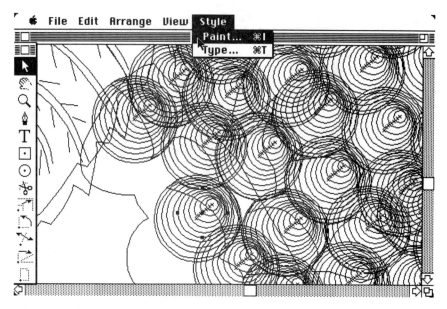

Figure 3-13.
Selecting a concentric circle on the grape to display or change its paint characteristics.

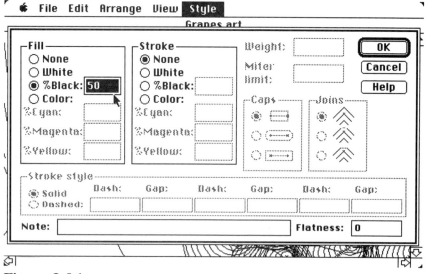

Figure 3-14.
The paint characteristics of that circle: 50% black fill (gray) and no stroke, which allows it to blend into the next circle.

middle circle (Figure 3-13) has a fill of 50% black and no stroke (Figure 3-14), which makes it easier to blend the circles into a pattern. The innermost circle is white.

After creating one grape, Keith duplicated it by using Copy and Paste In Front or Paste In Back, so that some grapes were overlapping others.

To create the more pronounced gradations of gray in the branch (Figure 3-15), Keith painted the branch path with a 10% gray fill, then drew white-stroked and black-stroked lines and white shapes on top to intersperse white and black in the gray pattern.

Keith saved a grape in a separate file by using Copy, then selecting a New file, then using Paste. The new file could then be opened whenever he needed a group of concentric circles with a gradation of shades. Eventually Keith had made several of these files containing pieces of the image with well-defined gray scales.

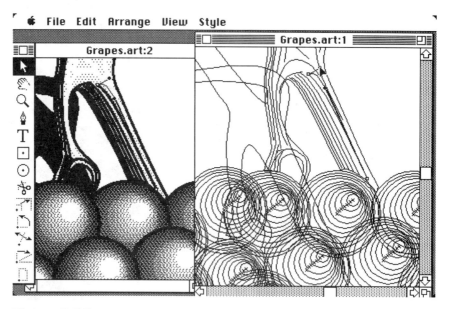

Figure 3-15.
The branch was painted with a 10% black (gray) fill, then white-stroked and black-stroked lines and white shapes were drawn on top. The second view was created with the New View command, and the windows were resized to be next to each other.

Previewing and Editing Simultaneously

To see how the artwork will look when printed, at the same time that you are editing the overlaid graphics, create another window display of the same artwork with the New View command in the View menu, and then select the Preview command to make the new (active) window the preview. You can resize both windows to fit side by side on the screen (see Figures 3-15 and 3-16), and either window can be the preview window.

Using the New View and Preview commands, Keith set up two windows in order to adjust the background shadow (Figure 3-16). To create the leaf shadow, Keith selected the path of the outline of the leaf, and held down the Option key while dragging it, to create a duplicate outline. Keith then painted the duplicate 100% black, cut it from the artwork, selected the path of the outline of the leaf again, and used the Paste In Back command to place the 100% black outline behind the leaf. The branches and the grapes were just as easy to create.

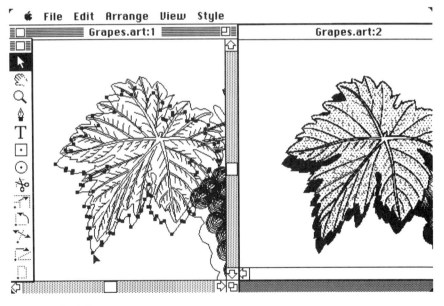

Figure 3-16.
Adjusting the leaf shadow using two views.

Black and Gray Effects

Dean Dapkus' "Abe Lincoln" is an example of an image that would ordinarily be drawn with a paint-type graphics program because it has so much irregular detail that could only be drawn with dots. (Paint-type graphics are called "bit-mapped graphics" because they comprise many single pixels of the display, which correspond to specific dots on paper when printed.) However, since paint-type graphics cannot change in resolution (the number of pixels and the number of dots per inch can't be reduced to achieve higher resolution), artists have always wanted a program that could be as precise and flexible as Illustrator for defining very tiny line and curve segments that are resolution-independent.

Dean drew "Abe Lincoln" using large black silhouette shapes. He then magnified areas and drew segments with very thin line weights and white strokes. First he drew one segment and changed the default paint specifications (with the Paint command in the Style menu, or Command-I) to have no fill, a white stroke, and a thin line weight (Figure 3-17). After clicking OK, those specifications were

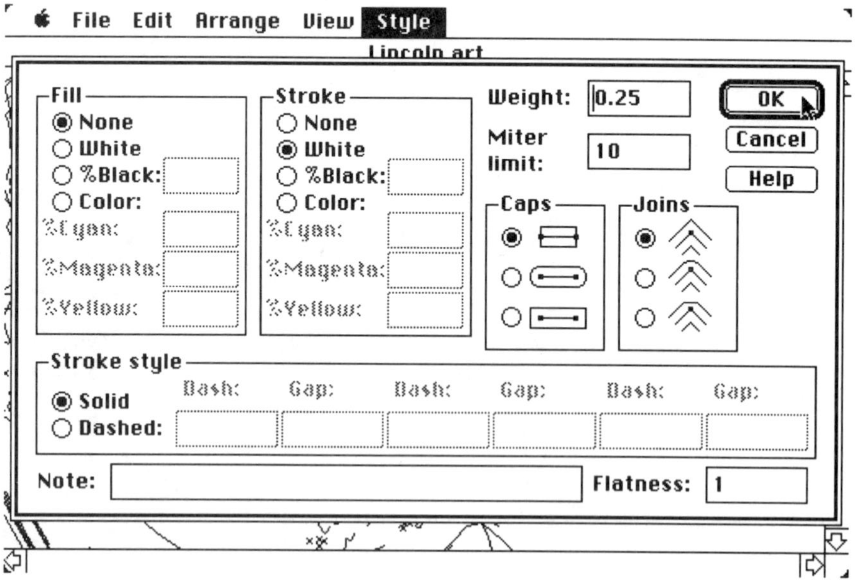

Figure 3-17.
Changing the default specifications in the Paint dialog box to no fill and very thin white strokes.

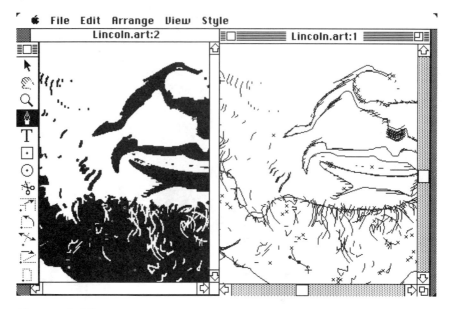

Figure 3-18.
Drawing white-stroked segments in the black silhouette of Lincoln's beard.

used for drawing subsequent segments until he changed them again with the Paint command. Figure 3-18 shows a magnified view of segments Dean drew in Lincoln's beard. Dean explains: "This technique is similar to one that a lot of artists are familiar with, called scratchboard. You start with a black artboard, and you scratch or etch in white shapes."

The effect of a simulated halftone with gray shades can be done by drawing paths close together and using increments of gray shading for fills (for example, 5%), and no strokes.

The strawberries in the label of "Jar of Preserves" (by Gail Blumberg, a graphic designer for Adobe, and Keith Ohlfs) were drawn with one basic shape (Figure 3-19) that was duplicated and scaled (Figure 3-20). You can very quickly make duplicate scaled images by repeating the first scale transformation with Command-D or Transform Again (Figure 3-21).

The artists assigned a different percentage of black (gray) to fill each shape, and set no stroke (Figure 3-22). Small ovals were drawn to look like seeds on top of the layers of gray.

Keith created a file of standard gray shaded images that can be scaled in any direction and used for filling areas of other illustrations

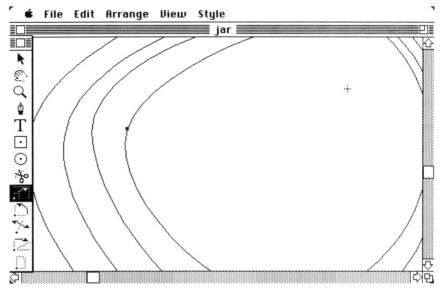

Figure 3-19.
Each strawberry is a series of scaled versions of the basic shape, with the scale origin point set to make the shapes closer on one edge.

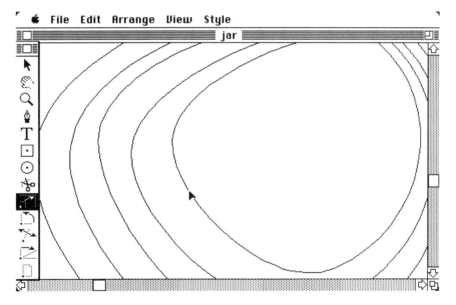

Figure 3-20.
Duplicating and scaling the shape by holding down the Option key while dragging with the Scaling tool.

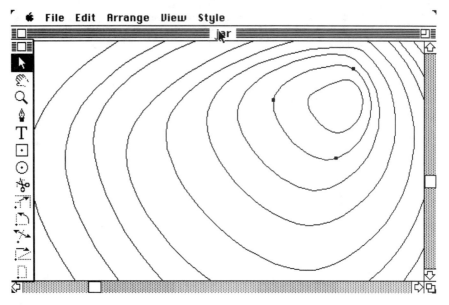

Figure 3-21.
Repeating the scale transformation with Command-D (or Transform Again).

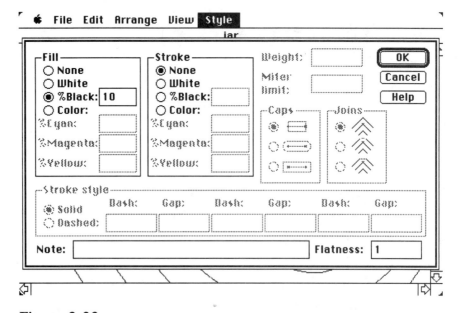

Figure 3-22.
Each scaled shape is filled with a different percentage of black and has no stroke.

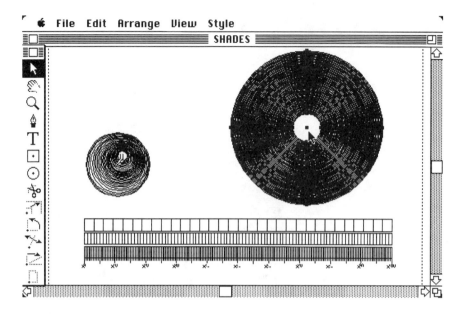
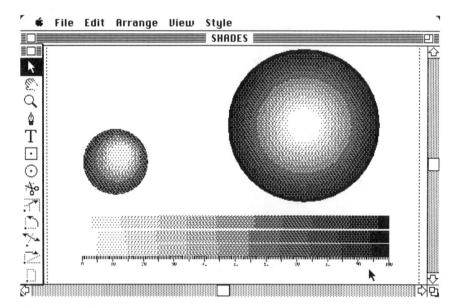

Figure 3-23.
A file of reference shades (by Keith Ohlfs) that can be copied and pasted into other illustrations and adjusted to fill shapes.

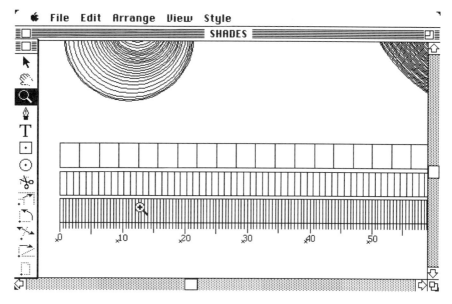

Figure 3-24.
The three shaded rectangles represent (from the top) shades for use with the LaserWriter at 300 dpi, the Linotronic 100 at 1270 dpi, and the Linotronic 300 at 2540 dpi.

(Figure 3-23). The shaded circle and the first long shaded rectangle are designed for 300 dpi laser printers (such as the LaserWriter) and have 33 steps, each with a different percentage of black to simulate a gray tone. The middle rectangle is designed for 1270 dpi typesetters (such as the Linotronic 100), and has 100 steps. The lower one is designed for 2540 dpi typesetters (such as the Linotronic 300) and has 200 steps (Figure 3-24). "Although each one takes up a lot of disk space," says Keith, "when I want to have an airbrush effect, I can copy and paste the appropriate shape and then stretch it to whatever size I need."

The shaded objects can be adjusted properly because they consist of grouped paths — Keith could select anywhere on the object and get the entire object. He then used Copy and Paste to copy the shade to the jar artwork, where he dragged in the edges until it lined up (Figure 3-25), then used the reflection tool to mirror it to the other side of the jar. He added points to segments with the scissors tool in

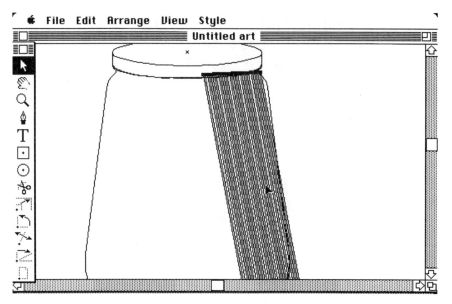

Figure 3-25.
Stretching and shearing the shaded rectangle to fit the shape of the jar.

order to bend them. "Using the shades reference saves a lot of time," he says, because he can use them over and over in many different illustrations, no matter what the final shape is.

Rotating Text

To add the text to the label of the jar of strawberry preserves, Gail used the text tool and clicked a starting point for the first letter, typed the letter, and set its type characteristics (Figure 3-26). Then she selected the rotation tool, clicked the point of rotation at the center of the label (Figure 3-27), and dragged with the Option key to create a rotated copy of the first letter (Figure 3-28). To rotate more letters to form a word, she repeated the transformation by pressing Command-D (Transform Again).

After rotating the same letter around the label into the positions she wanted, she went back and selected each letter with the pointer tool and used the Type command in the Style menu (Command-T) to change the letter to the appropriate letter for that word.

Graphic Design and Illustration 85

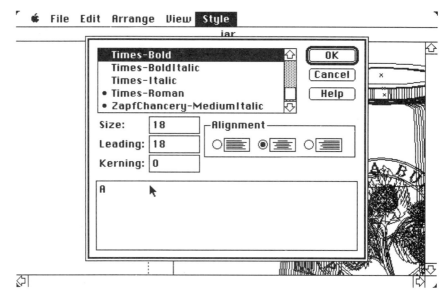

Figure 3-26.
The Type dialog box for each letter of the label.

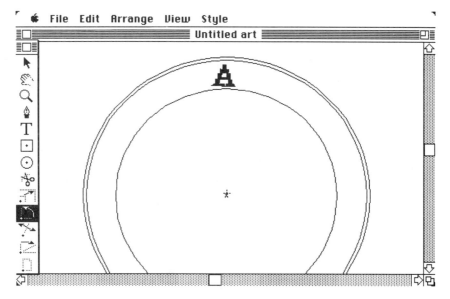

Figure 3-27.
Clicking a center of rotation for the letters in the label.

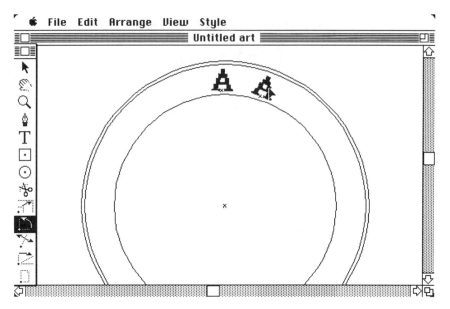

Figure 3-28.
Dragging with the Option key to create a rotated copy of the first letter.

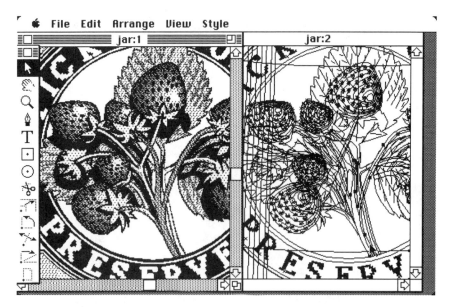

Figure 3-29.
Using the Paste In Front and Paste In Back commands, with the help of New View and Preview, to paste the strawberries in front of the label and the stems behind.

Through careful use of the Paste In Back and Paste In Front commands, Gail was able to place the strawberries in front of the text on the label, while the stems of the berries are behind the label, providing the illusion of three dimensions. It is helpful to work with two views (Figure 3-29) when overlaying complex images.

Summary

This chapter showed examples of using nearly every tool in Illustrator's arsenal and provided tips and techniques for drawing almost any type of illustration.

"The Golfer" started with a dark scan as a template and Luanne Seymour Cohen, the artist, used numerous overlaying graphics to hide all the rough spots. She was able to select all of the paths that make up an object (the golfer's eye) by dragging across the object with the pointer tool, creating a marquee rectangle that selected everything inside it and every path it intersected. Luanne also showed how to perform simple transformations — shearing and rotating — to draw the diamond-shaped belt. To repeat a transformation, you can use the Transform Again command or type Command-D. She used the scale tool to transform several sailboat images.

"The Golfer" provided examples of drawing white-stroked lines and pasting them on top of a black-filled shape using the Paste In Front command. White-filled circles (with no stroke) were used to simulate clouds, and a 10% black screen was applied to the background.

The "Artifactory" example showed how you can simulate the thick and thin pen strokes of calligraphy by drawing lines that enclose the pen strokes to form individual shapes that can be manipulated to simulate the thick and thin of the calligraphy stroke. The zoom tool comes in handy for working on details. The example also demonstrated how an image that has been worked into perfection can be copied and used for other areas in the artwork. Illustrator calligraphy can be reduced or enlarged without any loss in quality.

The "Grapes" artwork demonstrates the airbrush effect you can achieve by drawing one shape, scaling it slightly, and using Transform Again (Command-D) to repeat the transformation many times, then assigning to the shapes a gradual range of percentages of black or color (and no stroke, for smoothness). By drawing paths close together and using close percentages in sequence of black or color for fills, you can achieve an airbrushing effect.

You can also draw white-stroked lines to place on top of black areas, or black-stroked lines and white shapes on top to intersperse white and black in the gray pattern. To see two views of the artwork while working — a preview and a view of the artwork only — you can use the New View command.

The "Abe Lincoln" portrait was drawn by mimicking a conventional process called scratchboard, where an artist scratches or etches white shapes on a black artboard. After setting up white strokes for lines with a certain line weight, those specifications are used for drawing subsequent segments until changed again with the Paint command.

"Jar of Preserves" demonstrates many features, from quickly performed successive transformations to the use of Paste In Front and Paste In Back to simulate three-dimensional graphics. The artist (Gail Blumberg) also used the rotation tool with individual letters to rotate them around the jar's label.

The example also includes the use of a file of standard gray shaded images that can be scaled in any direction and used for filling areas of other illustrations. Gray shading was accomplished with a one-time use of the airbrush technique with finer gradations used in gray-shade templates designed for the LaserWriter printer and the Linotronic 100 and 300 typesetters.

CHAPTER 4

Technical Illustrations

Illustrator can make engineering and scientific art departments and technical publishing efforts far more productive than they have ever been. Illustrator not only provides the power to make complex drawings, it also provides the flexiblity to incorporate pieces or entire drawings in other drawings, to let artists sketch or scan images and trace them accurately, and to make the archival recording of drawings routine and less prone to casualties.

Illustrator is the first personal computer program to provide both the flexibility of drawing of Bezier curves and transforming with the mouse with the precision of specifying angles in degrees, percentages for scaling, and the option of scaling or preserving the line weight (the line's thickness). Combine these capabilities with the ability to trace over templates that can be scanned images or sketches, and the ability to add formatted text in fonts and perform PostScript effects, and you have a fantastic tool for technical artists, designers, and illustrators.

Technical publications departments will especially like the feature of tracing over scanned images, because this method may be the best way to convert old graphics into Illustrator graphics. All of the previous examples were based on scanned templates. However, you can also draw without using a template simply by measuring points in your sketch or original image and using the ruler in Illustrator to precisely place those points.

Dean Dapkus drew "Eyeball" from thumbnail sketches derived from biology texts. "Once you know how to use the zoom tool to analyze and edit details, and the shortcuts for drawing [the reflection, rotation, shearing, and scaling tools], there isn't anything difficult about working without a template."

Scaling or Preserving Line Weights

In traditional technical art drawing, artists have to draw diagrams and illustrations very large and then reduce the art photographically. Line weights are automatically scaled with the rest of the art. This means that you have to take the final reduction percentage into consideration before drawing a single line.

With Illustrator, you can scale either one path, a group of paths forming an object (or part of an object), or an entire illustration, and have the choice of scaling or preserving the line weights. Artists especially want to be able to preserve line weights on miniscule drawings so that when they are reduced, the lines don't disappear. On the other hand, with a finished drawing that looks good the way it is, scaling the line weight with the art will preserve the look of the drawing.

When you drag to scale, the line weights are preserved (not scaled). To get the option of scaling or preserving line weights, you must use the Scaling dialog box rather than the drag method of scaling. After selecting the scaling tool, hold down the Option key while clicking a scale origin point. The dialog box for scaling requires a scale factor as a percentage for uniform scaling (scaling in proportion), and the choice of preserving or scaling line weights by the same percentage. You can't scale line weights with non-uniform scaling, in

The Eye

1. Lens
2. Conjuctiva
3. Iris
4. Pupil
5. Cornea
6. Sclera

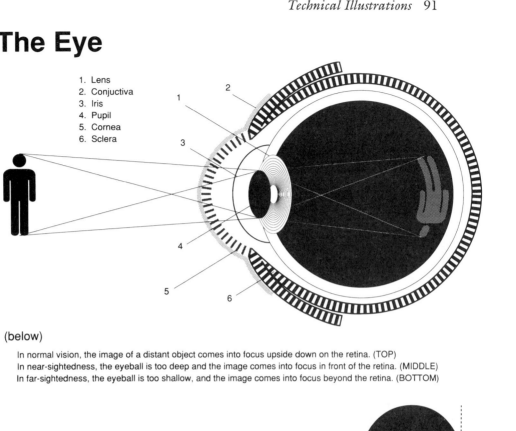

(below)

In normal vision, the image of a distant object comes into focus upside down on the retina. (TOP)
In near-sightedness, the eyeball is too deep and the image comes into focus in front of the retina. (MIDDLE)
In far-sightedness, the eyeball is too shallow, and the image comes into focus beyond the retina. (BOTTOM)

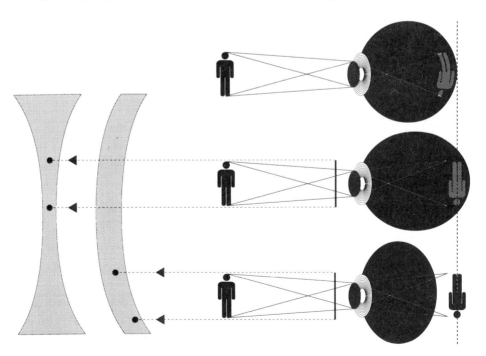

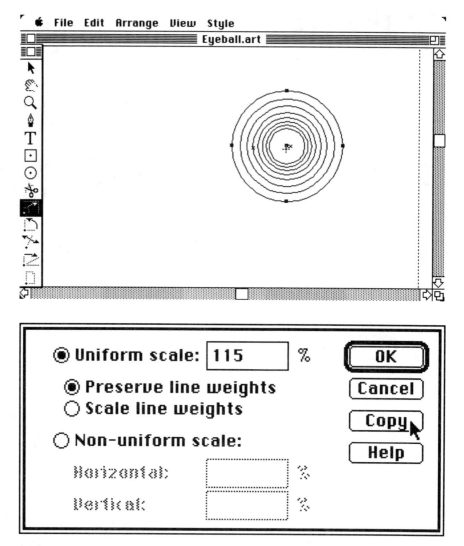

Figure 4-1.
Clicking the origin point for the scale, while at the same time holding down the Option key to get the Scaling dialog box.

which the image is scaled in uneven proportion for deliberate distortion.

Dean Dapkus started "Eyeball" by drawing concentric circles, and repeating a tranformation that used a precise scale percentage. First he used the circle drawing tool to draw a circle, then he selected that circle, clicked the scale tool, and held down Option while clicking the origin point (Figure 4-1) to get the Scaling dialog box.

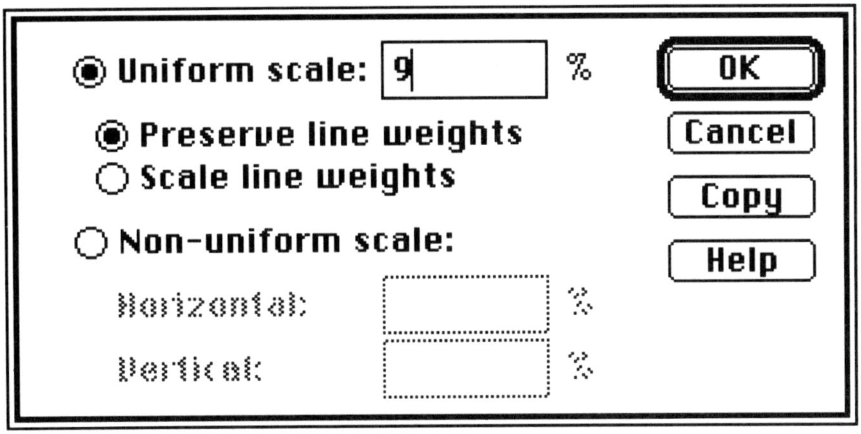

Figure 4-2.
Scaling precisely, with the option to scale or preserve line weights.

He typed a percentage under 100% for a uniform reduction (Figure 4-2), and clicked the option to preserve the line weights. He then clicked Copy to produce a reduced copy and preserve the first circle. The reduction percentage was consistent for the remaining circles, so Dean could use Command-D to repeat the transformation to make each subsequent circle.

Dean used the same technique to draw the lens of the eye: first he drew an ellipse for the outer edge of the lens, then he reduced a copy of the ellipse and repeatedly pressed Command-D to draw the concentric ellipses (Figure 4-3).

Multiple Rotations

To draw the many lines that look like spokes of a wheel that make up the outside edge, Dean drew the first line (Figure 4-4), then selected it for rotation. He clicked the rotation tool and held down the Option key while clicking the point of rotation at the center of the concentric circles.

In the Rotation dialog box (Figure 4-5), he specified a fractional percentage based on the number of lines divided into 360 degrees total. He clicked the Copy button to produce a duplicate while rotating and preserve the first line. The result was a duplicate line rotated slightly to the left (counterclockwise) of the first line. Positive-degree rotations are counterclockwise; to specify a clockwise rotation, subtract the degree of rotation from 360 degrees and

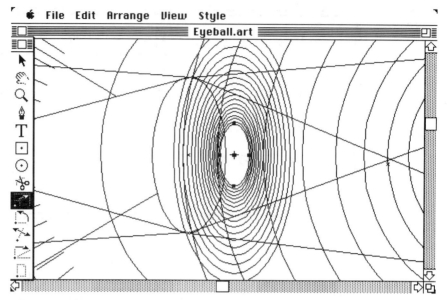

Figure 4-3.
The lens of the eye is made up of many concentric ellipses drawn using the same technique: Transform Again (Command-D) command after a scale transformation.

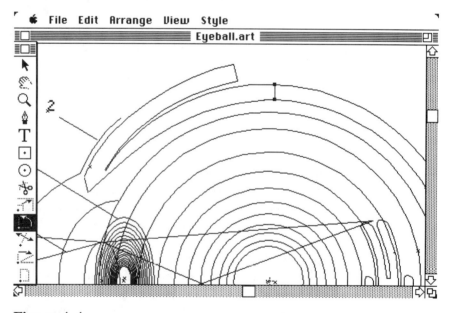

Figure 4-4.
The first line to duplicate and rotate to make the outer edge of the eyeball.

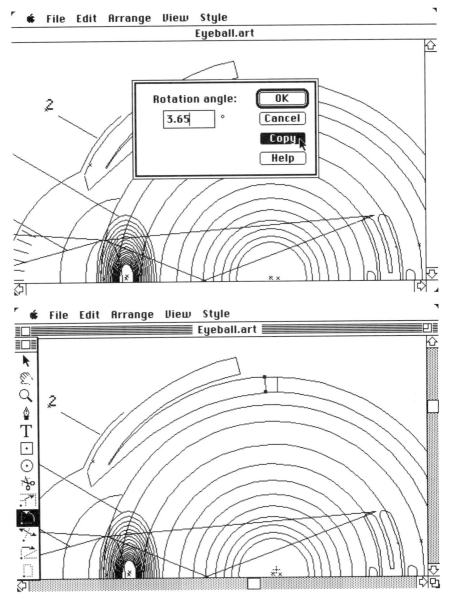

Figure 4-5.
The Rotation dialog box for precise angles, and a Copy button to make a duplicate when rotating.

use this figure as the degree of rotation.

After clicking the Copy button, the program remembered the transformation so that Dean could repeat it quickly by pressing

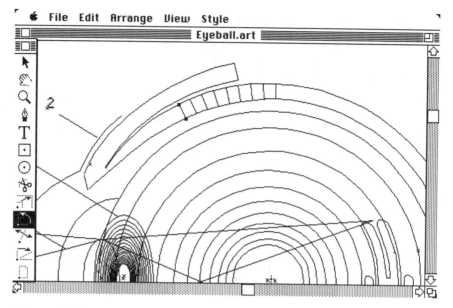

Figure 4-6.
Repeating the rotation transformation many times by pressing Command-D (or using Transform Again in the Arrange menu).

Command-D (Figure 4-6). After pressing Command-D about one hundred times, Dean had completed the ring of lines.

Reflecting Upside Down

Dean drew the human icon based on the American Institute of Graphic Arts (AIGA) symbol used by the Department of Transportation for men's bathrooms. (Page 22 shows other AIGA symbols Dean traced with Illustrator.) He then reflected the icon with a horizontal axis, so the mirror icon was turned upside down on the horizontal axis.

With the reflection tool, you can click to establish a point on the axis of reflection, or drag in a circular motion around the first fixed point you selected, establishing an area in which the program can calculate the axes by bisecting the angle between the starting position of the drag and the ending position. By holding down the Option key while dragging, you create a duplicate that is a mirror image of the original, reflected along the axis.

You can also reflect an image quickly over a horizontal or vertical axis, or an axis defined as a degree relative to the current x-y axes.

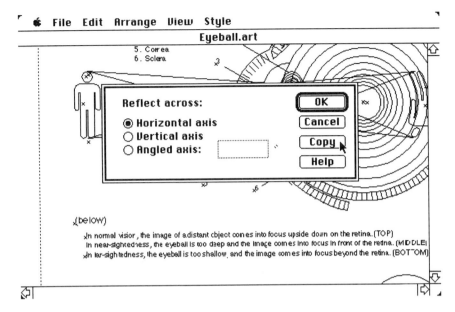

Figure 4-7.
The reflection dialog box, which appears if you hold down the Option key when clicking the first fixed point of the reflection axis.

After selecting the image to reflect, click the reflection tool, and hold down the Option key while clicking the fixed point on the imaginary reflection axis. The Reflect dialog box then appears (Figure 4-7), and you can select a horizontal, vertical, or angled axis, and click the Copy button to make a copy of the reflected image.

Editing Shapes

The reflection does not change the image. To bend the human shape to the curves of the concentric circles, Dean had to replace line segments with curved segments.

Fortunately his method of drawing the man made this editing change very easy. "I tried to use as few points as possible to draw the human icon. With the exception of the head, hands and balls of his feet, and his shoulders, he was made of straight lines, and each of these lines had two definition points. I made the straight reflected image, then selected the straight lines, and redrew them as curves."

Figure 4-8 shows the reflected human shape placed in the inner eye image. Dean first selected the line segment, then deleted it and redrew the segment as a curve. Figure 4-9 shows how he fine-tuned

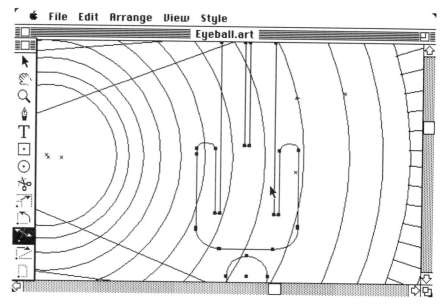

Figure 4-8.
The human shape, copied and reflected for placement in the inner eye image.

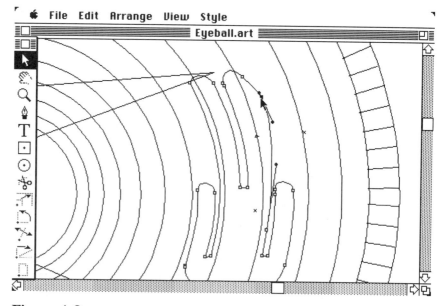

Figure 4-9.
Replacing a straight line with a curve, and adjusting the curve's direction points to bend the human shape in the direction of the concentric circles.

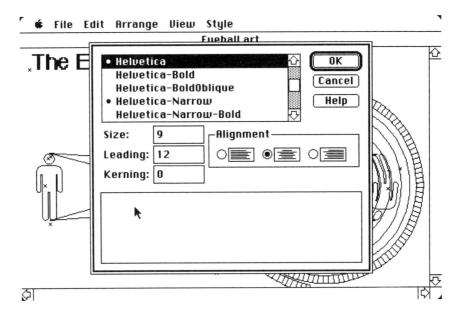

Figure 4-10.
The Text dialog box for adding and editing text, as it looks after selecting the text tool and clicking a starting point.

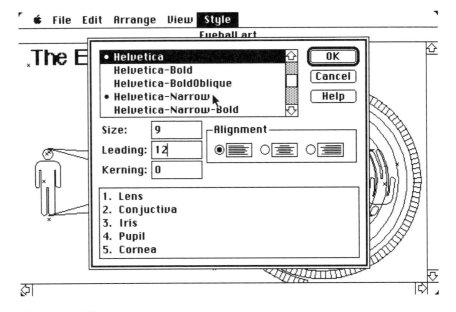

Figure 4-11.
The Type dialog box for editing text or changing type settings and margin justification.

the curves to match the curves of the concentric circles — by dragging the direction points.

Editing Type

To add text, Dean selected the text (T) tool, and clicked the text-editing (I-beam) pointer on the spot where he wanted the type to begin. The program displays a Text dialog box (Figure 4-10). He typed several lines of text by pressing Return to end each line, and selected the Helvetica 9-point font, with 12 points of leading and a ragged right margin.

To edit the text, or change the type settings and alignment, select the text and use the Type command in the Style menu (Figure 4-11). You can change the words and any of the settings.

Drawing With Constraints

Normally when you draw shapes such as rectangles and circles, you are drawing along standard *x-y* axes parallel to the sides of your display. You can rotate the axes, however, so that when you draw

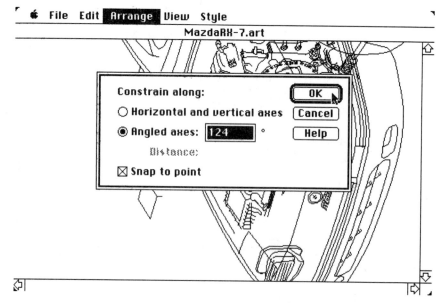

Figure 4-12.
Changing the axes counterclockwise from the standard x and y axes.

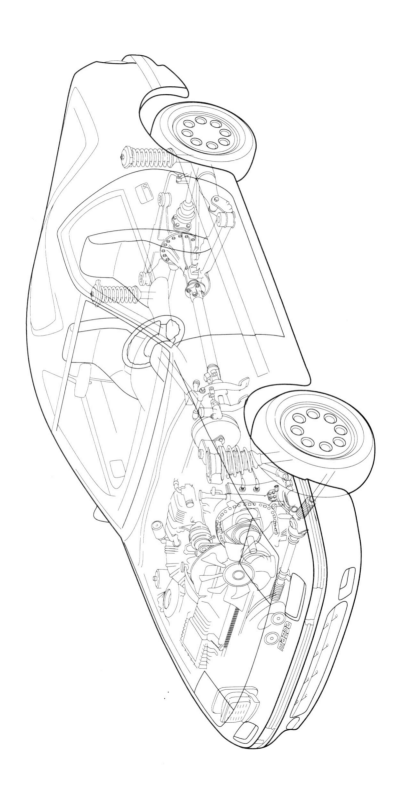

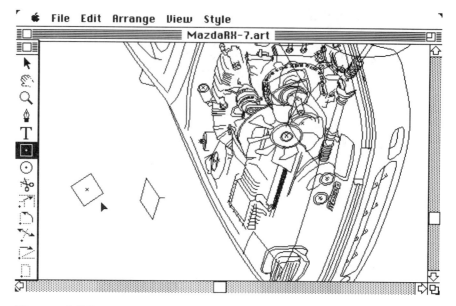

Figure 4-13.
Drawing a rectangle along the new axes.

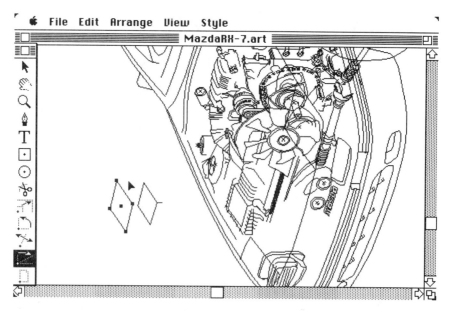

Figure 4-14.
Shearing the rectangle with the new axes in effect for constraining.

rectangles and circles, and when you constrain movements or transformations, the result is angled according to the new axes.

To add to the "Mazda" artwork, Keith Ohlfs could change the constraining axes with the Constrain (Command-K) command in the Arrange menu, which displays a dialog box in which he can specify an angle that is counterclockwise from the standard x and y axes (Figure 4-12). He can then draw a rectangular shape constrained along the new axes (Figure 4-13), and shear it to match the shape already used in the drawing (Figure 4-14).

By using slanted constraining axes you can draw a complex image to perspective and keep your geometric shapes accurate. You can also use the shear tool to slant the image along different axes.

Drawing a Complex Graphic

When an illustration has a lot of detail and cut-away views of interior construction, as with Keith Ohlfs' "Mazda," you have to dissect the image into layered objects. "You begin to think of things as all being layered on top of each other," says Keith about starting a complex illustration, "so you draw the background first, then draw the layers you want to be on top."

Technical illustrators usually have to choose a line weight that will be scaled when the entire image is scaled, but Keith discovered that he could draw the entire "Mazda" artwork using one line weight (and no fill). He then fine-tuned the image and changed some of the lines, such as the outer edges of the car body, to a thicker line weight. "It was really simple [to change line weights], and it's a great example of how a technical illustration can be done without worrying about line weights."

Keith found it easier to work on "Mazda" in sections, then join the sections as the last step. He started with the background detail, and the last object he drew was the outline. To work out the detail, Keith used the zoom tool to magnify the drawing. "You can zoom in [to the artwork] to make a little, very complicated part of a drawing almost a drawing by itself."

The "Mazda" artwork took about 12 to 16 hours to finish. Although this may seem a long time, it would take a lot longer using conventional methods (or a drawing system that would be a lot more expensive than a personal computer). It may take a while to learn all the tricks and techniques of using Adobe Illustrator, but these techniques can be utilized over and over, and pieces of the artwork can be reused, without worrying about scaling line weights. As Keith described his efforts, "I would never try to do these illustrations with a pen and ink. Only Illustrator makes it possible to do them."

Summary

Technical publications departments like Illustrator's feature of tracing over scanned images, as you can draw without using a template simply by measuring points in the original image and using the ruler in Illustrator to precisely place those points. Technical artists and illustrators also like its flexiblity in incorporating pieces of, or entire drawings in other drawings, and the ability to keep secure disk archives.

Another feature useful in technical illustrations is the ability to scale either one path, a group of paths forming an object, or an entire illustration, and have the choice of scaling or preserving the line weights. This choice comes only with the use of the dialog box for scaling — after selecting the scaling tool, hold down the Option key while clicking a scale origin point. If you drag to scale, the line weights are preserved (not scaled). The line weights are also preserved (not scaled) with non-uniform scaling. The Scaling dialog box lets you type a percentage for uniform scaling (scaling in proportion), and the choice of preserving or scaling line weights by the same percentage.

The "Eyeball" illustration demonstrated the use of multiple rotation transformations, the use of the reflection tool to create an upside-down image, and the techniques for editing lines into curves. The illustration was also a demonstration for creating and editing text with fonts.

Finally, "Mazda" showed how you can change the axes for constraining drawing and movement, and shear objects to match a design. The illustration is the most complex one supplied with the Gallery Disks, and has examples of a variety of Illustrator techniques that technical artists use, including rotations, reflected, sheared and scaled graphics.

CHAPTER 5

Illustrator Dissected

This chapter provides a complete description of each Illustrator tool, then each menu item, including dialog boxes.

The tools are discussed in sequence (from the top to the bottom of the tool palette); a copy of the tool palette in the margin of each page shows the selected tool. Each tool description is followed by a list of tool actions and keyboard commands.

The menus are then each discussed in sequence (from the top to the bottom, and from left to right). Dialog boxes are included in the descriptions of the menu items that invoke them, and keyboard command shortcuts are also given for the menu items that accept them.

Selection Tool

▸ — The arrow is the selection tool. The arrow is also referred to as the pointer by other Macintosh programs; however, in this book the term pointer is used more broadly to include other Illustrator tools that can also be used for pointing. The selection tool is used for selecting menu items, dialog box options, objects, line segments, and so on. It is also used for moving and re-sizing windows. Moving the mouse (or any other input device such as a trackball, graphics tablet stylus, etc.) moves the arrow around so that you can point to things on the screen for the purpose of selecting or manipulating them. The ratio between the amount the arrow moves and the amount the mouse moves can be adjusted in the Control Panel (see Figure 5-1).

To select an item from a menu, you point to the menu's title in the menu bar at the top of the screen and hold down the mouse button and the menu appears. Then, while continuing to hold down the mouse, you drag the arrow down the list of items in the menu until

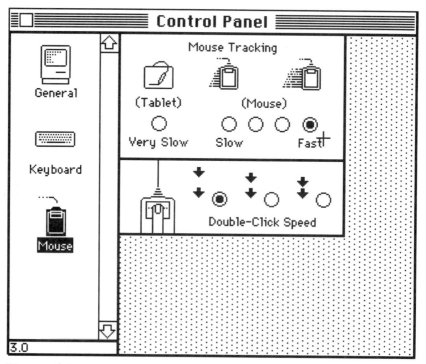

Figure 5-1.
Adjusting the mouse tracking option will alter the ratio between the amount the arrow moves and the amount the mouse moves.

you have selected (highlighted) the command you wish; releasing the mouse button chooses that command (see page 181 for a complete description of all Illustrator menus).

To select most dialog box options, Illustrator objects, and tools, you simply point the arrow and click the mouse to select the item you want. Sometimes you can point to an item and click twice in rapid succession; this is known as double-clicking. In other cases you can point to items and drag with the mouse instead of, or in addition to, clicking the mouse button.

Whenever any pointer is moved outside the active window, it changes into the arrow in order to let you select tools, issue commands, or move windows. To get the selection tool you can either click on the selection tool in the tool palette or use the tool temporarily by holding down the Command key while using another tool.

Selecting, Resizing, and Moving Windows

You can move and manipulate Illustrator windows using a variety of techniques. To change the size of a window, point to the window's size box (see Figure 5-2), hold down the mouse button, and drag with the mouse until the window is the size and shape you want it to be. When you release the mouse button, the window will change size and be redrawn by the program.

A shortcut for enlarging the window is to point to the zoom box in the window's title bar (in Figure 5-3 the zoom box is located in the upper right-hand corner of the window) and click the mouse; the window will enlarge until it fills up most of the Macintosh's standard 9-inch screen. If your Macintosh has a larger screen, hold down the

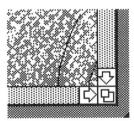

Figure 5-2.
In the lower right-hand corner of the active window is the size box that allows you to change the window's size and shape.

Option key while clicking in the zoom box; this will increase the window size until it almost fills the entire larger screen. If you hold down the Option key while clicking in the zoom box again, the window will return to its normal (9-inch) full screen size.

If you want to move the window, point to any place on the window's title bar (except the close box at the left end of the bar and the zoom box at the right end of the bar), hold down the mouse button, and drag the window to a new location on the Macintosh's screen (or onto an additional monitor if you are using two monitors that work together, such as on the Macintosh II, or the Radius display on other Macintoshes). If you move a window with this technique, it will become active if it was previously inactive.

If you want to move an inactive window and have the window remain inactive after it is moved, use the previous technique except hold down the Command key while dragging the window to its new location.

On the other hand, to make an active window inactive, point to the title bar of the window, hold down the Command key, and click the mouse button; this will deactivate the window and send it to the back, behind any other windows that are displayed. Similarly, you can point to the title bar of an active window and drag it to a new location while holding down the Command key in order to move it and deactivate it at the same time.

Selecting and Moving Illustrator Objects

Once you have drawn a path with Illustrator, you can use the selection tool to move the path to a new location, or to manipulate the path to change its shape. To move an object without changing it, the entire object (and all its connecting lines and points) must be selected; otherwise you may accidentally alter the artwork, since moving any anchor points, direction points, lines, or curves without moving all of them can change the shape of paths. To prevent objects from being changed when you move them, use the Group command on the Arrange menu to group the points, lines, and curves in the object into a single unified object. The grouped object is not only

Figure 5-3.
The title bar contains the name of the document (and template, if any). At the left end is the close box and at the right end is the zoom box.

resistant to accidental changes, it is also easier to select, because pointing and clicking anywhere on the object selects the entire object. To select an ungrouped object to move, you select all the items that comprise the object. You can select all the items by dragging a selection marquee (see Figure 5-4) completely around an object, being careful not to include any other objects. To select an entire path, point to any location on the path and click the mouse button while holding down the Option key.

Alternatively you can select one component of an object by pointing to it and clicking the mouse button (or by using the selection marquee), and then select another component by pointing and clicking while holding down the Shift key. If you hold down the Shift key before you click on or drag over an item, the item is added to the group of selected objects. If you hold down the Shift key after you start dragging, Illustrator interprets this as the Constrain function and will constrain movement of the arrow to increments of 45 degrees(°). Constraining movement with the Shift key makes it easier to move objects vertically, horizontally, or diagonally at a 45° angle.

If there are several objects on top of each other, you can select the top object by pointing to it, holding down the Option key, and clicking the mouse. You can then move it by releasing the Option key and dragging the object to a new location. If you hold down the

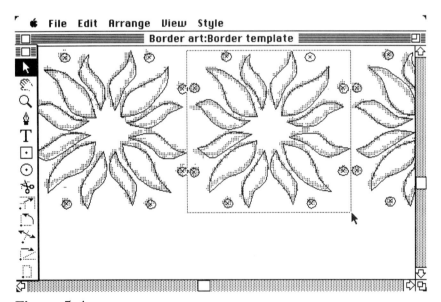

Figure 5-4.
You can drag the selection marquee around an object or group of objects to select everything inside the marquee.

Option key while you drag an object, it will create a duplicate of the object for moving, and the original will be left in its place. This duplication technique is extremely useful for duplicating items to reuse in your artwork.

Another way to move objects without changing them is to use the Move dialog box to specify precise amounts of movement. To move an object with the Move dialog box, you should first select the object, and then point to the selection tool in the tool palette and hold the Option key down while clicking the mouse button to request the dialog box (see Figure 5-5). After you release the mouse button, the Move dialog box will appear (Figure 5-6). The dialog box contains the values of the last move that took place, if any, during the current program session; if no move has yet taken place, the values will be set to a move distance of zero and horizontally.

To specify the distance to move the selected object(s), click in the box after the words "Move distance:" and type in the number of points (one point = 1/72 of an inch) that you want to move the object(s). Next specify the direction that you want the object(s) to be moved by clicking on either "Horizontal move," "Vertical move," or "Angled move." If you choose the Angled move option, you also need to specify the angle in degrees you want the move to

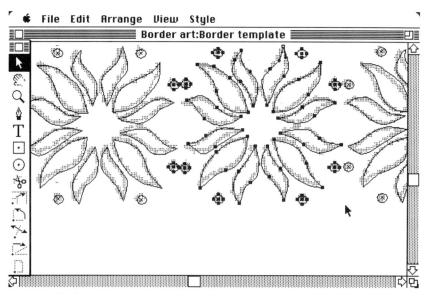

Figure 5-5.
You can request the Move dialog box by holding down the Option key while clicking on the Selection Tool.

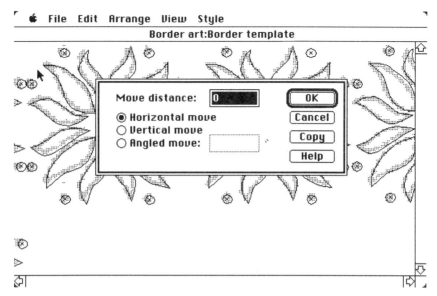

Figure 5-6.
The Move dialog box appears when you release the mouse button.

be made in. The angle is calculated from the horizontal axis (zero degrees) and the number of degrees is added counterclockwise from the horizontal origin. Specifying a positive number for a horizontal move will move selected items to the right, and a negative number moves them to the left. Likewise, specifying a positive number for a vertical move will move the selected items up, and a negative number will move the items down. Negative numbers specified for an angled move will move the items clockwise from the horizontal origin, rather that counterclockwise. After you have specified the amount and direction of the move, you can either click the OK button to initiate the move (the double line around this button indicates that it will be selected if you press the Return key); press the Cancel button to abandon the move and return to the active window; press the Copy button to create and move a duplicate while leaving the original in its place; or click the Help button to request the online help facility.

If you have altered the x and y axes using the Constrain command on the Arrange menu, then movement of the object(s) will be relative to the altered x and y axes; this may give the text a different appearance. In other words, if you have rotated the x and y axes by 20° using the Constrain command, any objects that you move will be moved at an additional 20° angle: specifying a horizontal move would result in a 20° move and specifying a 30° move would result in a 50° move. If you are moving objects and they seem to be moving in a tilted or exaggerated direction, check the alignment of the *x* and *y* axes by looking at the dialog box that appears after you select the Constrain command on the Arrange menu (or type Command-K). To restore the original orientation of the drawing, set the *x* and *y* axes back to their origins before moving the object(s).

If you want to move objects in front of or behind other objects, refer to the Paste In Front and Paste In Back commands on the Edit menu that are described later in this chapter. To move an object into the center of the active window, use the Paste command.

Selecting and Manipulating Illustrator Objects

In addition to using the selection tool for moving an entire object without changing it, you can use the tool to change or modify an object by moving one or more of its component parts (i.e., anchor points, direction points, lines and curves). Illustrator gives you a great deal of flexibility to change objects; this is a very powerful feature since it means that you can draw things very roughly and come back later and fine-tune the drawing.

Illustrator displays the same object a variety of different ways depending on how the object is selected. For example, Figures 5-7 through 5-12 show the same path selected in a variety of ways.

Selecting objects in Illustrator is important to master since an object must be selected before it can be manipulated or modified. Only objects in Illustrator artwork can be selected; the template or preview cannot be selected. If you point within two pixels (dots on the screen) of an object (or of several objects), the topmost object will be selected and all other objects will be deselected. If you point to a location more than two pixels away from any object and click the mouse, all objects will be deselected. If you want the feature that selects anything within two pixels of the arrow to be turned off, select the Snap to Point feature in the Constrain dialog box (see the Constrain command description later in this chapter for a complete description).

The main techniques used for manipulating objects with the selection tool are moving: anchor points, direction points, and line and curve segments. For making adjustments, the Join and Average commands on the Arrange menu useful in addition to the selection tool, since these two commands allow you to move anchor points or

Figure 5-7.
A path consisting of three segments with none of its curves or points selected.

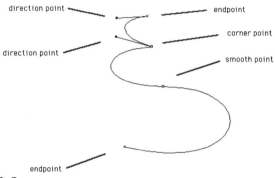

Figure 5-8.
How the path in Figure 5-7 looks with the topmost curve selected. The direction points and various types of anchor points (smooth points, corner points, endpoints) are labeled for identification.

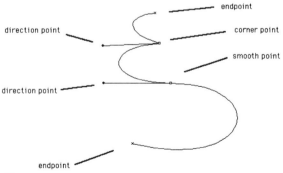

Figure 5-9
How the path in Figure 5-7 looks with the middle curve selected.

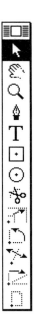
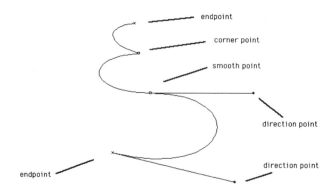

Figure 5-10
How the path in Figure 5-7 looks with the bottom curve selected.

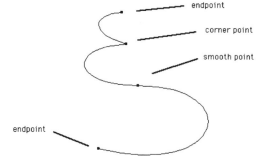

Figure 5-11.
How the path in Figure 5-7 looks with the entire path selected.

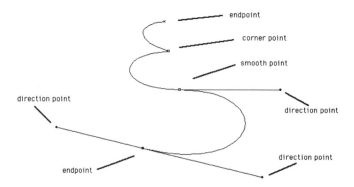

Figure 5-12.
How the path in Figure 5-7 looked right after the bottom curve was drawn. Notice the two direction points extending from the endpoint.

endpoints together and join any two of them into a single point. For additional information about the Join and Average commands, see the descriptions of these commands later in this chapter.

The scissors tool is helpful to use in addition to the selection tool since the scissors tool allows you to cut segments in two, and lets you add anchor points to a segment without cutting it. A detailed description of the scissors tool starts on page 149. Any segment, or group of segments, can be modified with the scale, rotate, reflect and shear tools. The combination of these tools, commands, and techniques allows excellent control over very precise modifications of the artwork — a luxury not provided with traditional pen and ink.

To move anchor points (or endpoints, which are also anchor points) with the selection tool, first select the point or points you want to move, then position the arrow on one of the selected anchor points and drag the point to a new location. As you drag the mouse you will notice that any lines or curves attached to any points moved will change as you move them. The curves will change in a way that will keep the curve directions constant at the anchor points that are being moved (see Figure 5-13).

The previous location and shape of the curve is displayed as well as the new location and shape. To move direction points with the selection tool, first select an anchor point (or an adjacent segment) whose direction point you want to move. Next, point to the direction point that you want to adjust and drag the direction point with the

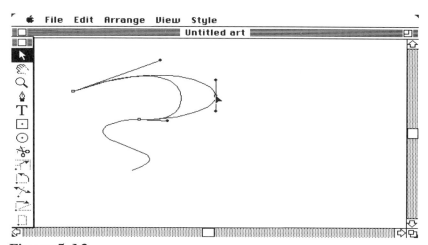

Figure 5-13.
Moving an anchor point with the selection tool.

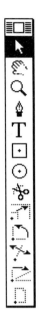
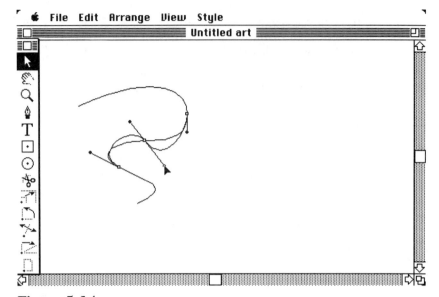

Figure 5-14.
Moving a direction point with the selection tool. The old position and shape of both curves affected by the direction point is displayed as well as the new position and shape of the curves.

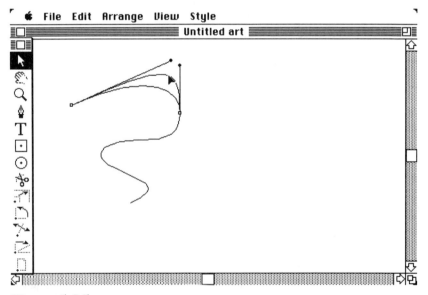

Figure 5-15.
Moving a segment with the selection tool. The old position and shape of the segment is displayed as well as the new position and shape of the segment.

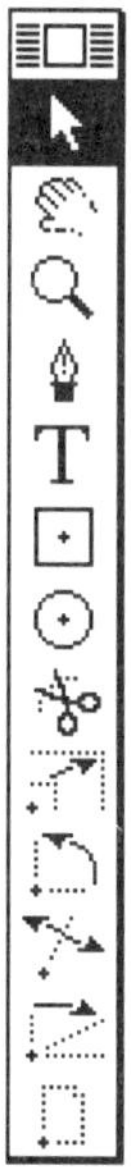

mouse to change the curve of the segment or segments that are connected to the anchor point whose direction point you are moving (see Figure 5-14).

To move the line or curve segment itself, select the segment(s) you want to modify, point to an area on the selected segment that is between its anchor points, and drag the segment. As you drag the segment(s), you will notice that all the selected segments change shape; their associated direction points move in accordance with the drag, but the selected segments' anchor points remain fixed (see Figure 5-15).

If you select an anchor point by clicking on it, you will also select any segments that are connected to it. If two anchor points are on top of each other, only the topmost anchor point will be selected by clicking on it. To select an anchor point and all the points underneath it, drag the selection marquee around the points. When an anchor point (or endpoint) is selected, it appears as a solid black square, and all the other anchor points in the object are also displayed; unselected anchor points appear as hollow squares, except for endpoints, which appear as x's. If you select a curved segment, no anchor points will be selected, but the direction points associated with the curved segment will appear as solid black circles (see Figure 5-8, a selected curve). If you select a straight line segment, the direction points will not be displayed since they would be on top of the segment's anchor points. When you select an entire path by either dragging the selection marquee around it or by pointing to it, holding down the Option key, and clicking the mouse, all the anchor points will be selected, and no direction points will be displayed (see Figure 5-11, a selected path). To select type, point to the baseline of the text and click the mouse button (see Figure 5-16). If several blocks of type are on top of each other, the topmost block of type will be selected. If you use the selection marquee to select type, all the type blocks whose baselines fall even partially within the marquee will be selected.

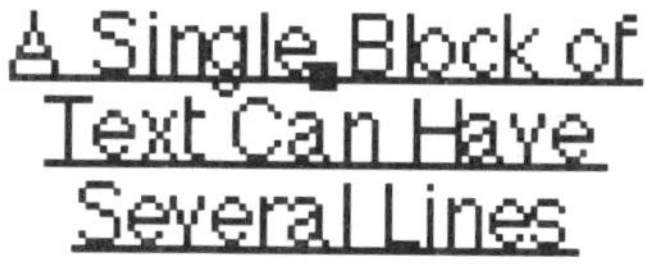

<u>A Single Block of
Text Can Have
Several Lines</u>

Figure 5-16.
How a block of centered text looks on the screen when it is selected. The small black square in the center of the first baseline is the alignment point of the type block.

Tool Use Summary

▸ +Click mouse — Selects the item you are pointing at.

▸ +Shift key+Click mouse — If you hold down the Shift key while you are clicking the mouse or before you start to drag with the mouse, it will extend (or reduce) your selection.

▸ +Option key+POINT TO PATH+Click mouse — If, while holding down the Option key, you point to a path and click the mouse button, the entire path will be selected.

Option key+POINT TO SELECTION TOOL+Click mouse — Gets MOVE dialog box for specifying precise movement.

▸+Shift key+Drag mouse — If you hold down the Shift key after you have started to drag something with the mouse, it will constrain the motion of the object or objects being dragged to horizontal movement (movement along the x axis), vertical movement (along the y axis), or movement in 45° increments (relative to the x and y axes).

▸+Option key+Drag mouse — Duplicates selected objects.

▸+Option key +POINT TO ZOOM BOX — Zooms window for a large-screen display.

▸ + ⌘+POINT TO WINDOW'S TITLE BAR+**Drag mouse** — Moves window without activating it.

▸ + ⌘+POINT TO WINDOW'S TITLE BAR+**Click mouse** —Deactivates window and sends it to the back of the group of windows displayed on the screen.

▸ + ⌘+POINT TO THE TITLE BAR OF A NON-ACTIVE WINDOW+**Drag mouse** — Moves the non-active window without activating it.

⌘— Temporarily converts the tool you are using into the selection tool.

The Hand Tool

— The hand tool is primarily for scrolling an image within an active window. Although you can also scroll the document with the scroll bars at the lower right of the window, the hand tool gives you more precise control over scrolling. To use the hand tool, point to ite in the tool palette and then click the mouse button. The arrow turns into a hand whenever you move it into the active window (Figure 5-17). Next, position the hand over the image, hold down the mouse button, and drag the image within the window. When you release the button, the image remains in its new position.

Another way to access the hand tool is to press the space bar while using any other tool. Whatever tool you are using changes into a hand while you hold down the space bar, but changes back into the original tool as soon as you release the space bar. This shortcut is handy for moving the image you are working on, since you don't have to go back to the tool palette to switch tools.

Tool Use Summary

+**Drag mouse** — Moves the document around under the active window.

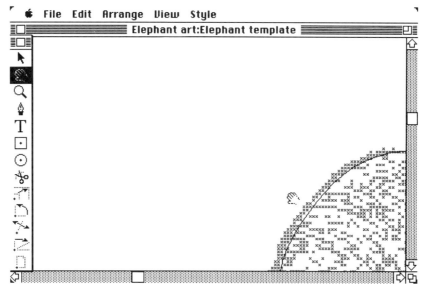

Figure 5-17.
You can move an image around in the window with the hand tool.

Space bar+Drag mouse — Temporarily converts the current tool into the hand and moves the document around under the active window.

Double-click mouse+ POINT TO 👆 — Fits the entire Illustrator document into the active window regardless of window size. This is the same as issuing the Fit In Window command.

Option key+Double-click mouse+POINT TO 👆 — Shows Illustrator at actual size (i.e., the size at which it will print).

The Zoom Tool

🔍 — The zoom tool is for zooming in on or zooming out from your view of the active window. Zooming in lets you inspect and work on your artwork in a great degree of detail. Zooming out lets you step back to get the big picture and work on large curves, lines, and objects. To zoom in on an object, point to the zoom tool on the tool palette and then click the mouse button. The arrow turns into the image of a small magnifying glass with a plus sign (+) in its center whenever you move it into the active window; this signifies that the zoom tool will enlarge your view if you click the mouse button. Position the zoom tool over the area you want to inspect before you click the mouse, and then click to zoom in on the artwork. Each click enlarges the view by a factor of two until you reach the largest magnification (1600% of the actual size), at which point the plus sign disappears from the center of the magnifying glass, indicating that no further enlargement is possible. An Illustrator document can be viewed in nine different magnifications (see Figures 5-18 through 5-26).

To zoom out, hold down the Option key after selecting the zoom tool; the plus sign in the center of the small magnifying glass will change to a minus sign (-), indicating that the tool will reduce your document rather than magnify it if you click the mouse. As long as you hold down the Option key, you will reduce your view by a factor of two each time you click the mouse button, until you reach the smallest reduction (6.75%). At the smallest reduction, the minus sign disappears from the center of the magnifying glass, indicating that no further reduction is possible (see Figure 5-18).

If you want to view the artwork at its actual size (100%), you can

Illustrator Dissected 121

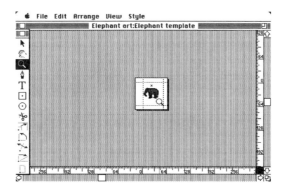

Figure 5-18.
An Illustrator document viewed at its smallest reduction, 6.75 percent of its actual size.

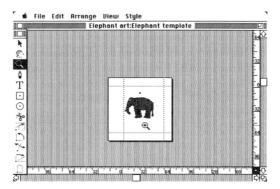

Figure 5-19.
The Illustrator document in Figure 5-18 viewed at 12.5 percent of its actual size.

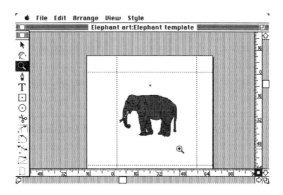

Figure 5-20.
The Illustrator document in Figure 5-18 viewed at 25 percent of its actual size.

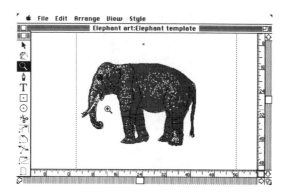

Figure 5-21.
The Illustrator document in Figure 5-18 viewed at 50 percent of its actual size.

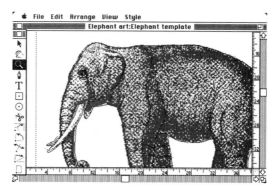

Figure 5-22.
The Illustrator document in Figure 5-18 viewed at its actual size.

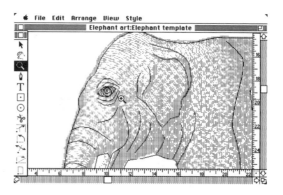

Figure 5-23.
The Illustrator document in Figure 5-18 viewed at 200 percent of its actual size.

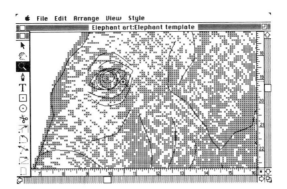

Figure 5-24.
The Illustrator document in Figure 5-18 viewed at 400 percent of its actual size. The view is zooming-in on the elephant's eye.

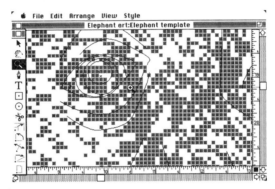

Figure 5-25.
The Illustrator document in Figure 5-18 viewed at 800 percent of its actual size.

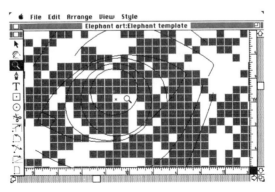

Figure 5-26.
The Illustrator document in Figure 5-18 viewed at 1600 percent of its actual size. The elephant's eye is larger than the entire window. Each square is equal to one pixel of a MacPaint document.

either select Actual Size from the View menu, press Command-H, or double-click on the hand tool in the tool palette while holding down the Option key. To fit the entire document (the entire 14-inch-by-14-inch document work space) into the window, you can select Fit In Window from the View menu, press Command-M, or double-click on the hand tool. Any of these commands also centers the document in the window; remember that although the Illustrator document may be centered in the window, your artwork may not be centered, depending on how Illustrator has interpreted the original PICT file or MacPaint file you used as a template. If you are opening your template for the first time and you don't see the template image in the active window, you should use one of the Fit In Window commands to view the entire document and then use the zoom tool to zoom in on the center of your template image.

Illustrator offers four levels of enlargement (200%, 400%, 800%, and 1600%, shown in Figures 5-23 through 5-28) and four levels of reduction (6.75%, 12.5%, 25%, and 50%, shown in figures 5-18 through 5-21), which, along with the 100% size (Figure 5-22), add up to nine different sizes at which you can view a document. Notice in the above percentages that each level is twice the magnification of the previous level and that the smallest view (a 6.75% reduction) is 512 times smaller than the largest view (a 1600% enlargement). Keep in mind that zooming in and zooming out enlarges or reduces only your view of the artwork; the actual size of the artwork itself does not change. Use the scale tool to enlarge or reduce the actual artwork.

The zoom tool also affects the optional rulers that can be displayed in an Illustrator window. To display the rulers, select Show Rulers from the View menu or press Command-R. Two rulers will appear, one along the bottom of the active window and the other down the right side of the window. If you want to remove the rulers from view, you can choose Hide Rulers from the View menu or type Command-R. The rulers use two different units of measurement, points (one point = 1/72 inch) and picas (one pica = 1/6 inch), depending on the magnification or reduction of the document. Illustrator displays picas as large numbers on the ruler and points as small numbers. When you view artwork at its actual size (100%), you get tick marks at 3-point (1/24-inch) intervals (see Figure 5-22), and the ruler has numbered subdivisions at 4-pica (2/3-inch) intervals. As the magnification or reduction of the view changes, the numbering system on the ruler also changes. For example, the smallest reduction (6.75% of the actual size) has tick marks at 4-pica intervals and numbered subdivisions at 64-pica intervals (see Figure 5-18); at the largest magnification (1600%), there are tick marks every 1/4 point and numbered subdivisions at each 3 point interval (see Figure 5-28). Here's a tip for people who want to work with inches: you can pretend that a pica (1/6th of an inch) is really an inch and then enlarge the final artwork by 600% using the scale tool.

A small size-indicator box in the lower right corner of the window (where the horizontal and vertical rulers intersect) gives you further visual feedback about magnification or reduction size. If you are looking at the document at its actual size (100%) or larger, the current size of a one-point-by-one-point square appears as a black square inside a white square; if you are looking at the document at a reduced size (smaller than 100%), the current size of a two-pica square appears as a white square inside a black box. See Figures 5-18 through 5-26 for examples of how the size-indicator box looks at different magnifications or reductions.

Here are some other tips for using the zoom tool. Illustrator offers a quick way to zoom in or zoom out while you are using another tool without having to go to the toolbox palette. If you are using another tool and you want to zoom in on your artwork, just hold down the Command key and the space bar simultaneously; whatever tool you are using will change into the zoom tool. Then click the mouse button to zoom in on the document. As soon as you release the Command key and the space bar, the zoom tool will revert to the original tool you were working with.

Similarly, if you are using another tool and you want to zoom out on your artwork, you can hold down the Command key, the space bar, and the Option key while simultaneously clicking the mouse button. As soon as you release the Command key, space bar, and Option key, your original tool will return.

If you want to quickly zoom in on the center of the window, simply point at the zoom tool in the tool palette and double-click the mouse button. Similarly, to quickly zoom out from the center of the window, double-click on the zoom tool while holding down the Option key. If you need to scroll and zoom at the same time, you can drag the zoom tool by holding down the mouse button continuously while moving the zoom tool in the window. These shortcuts are quite handy for experienced Illustrator users. Learning to use the shortcuts will make you an experienced Illustrator user, and you will save time if you don't have to select tools from the palette each time you want to use them.

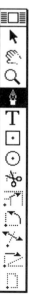

Tool Use Summary

🔍 +**Click mouse** — enlarges view (zooms in on the document).

🔍 +**Option key+Click mouse** — reduces view (zooms out from the document).

🔍 +**Drag mouse** — zooms then scrolls.

Double-click mouse+POINT AT 🔍 — zooms in on the center of the window.

Option key+Double-click mouse+POINT AT 🔍 — zooms out from the center of the window.

⌘+**Space bar+Click mouse** — temporarily converts the tool you are using into the zoom tool and zooms in.

⌘+**Option key+Space bar+Click mouse** — temporarily converts the tool you are using into the zoom tool and zooms out.

⌘ +**Space bar+Click mouse** — zooms in.

⌘ +**Space bar+Option key+ Click mouse** — zooms out.

⌘ +**Space bar+Drag mouse** — zooms then scrolls.

The Pen Tool

✒ — The pen tool is used to create points and lines. Since the main purpose of Illustrator is to create line drawings, the pen tool is the most important tool to understand. One of the main stumbling blocks in getting started with Illustrator is learning to use the pen tool. In most Macintosh graphics programs, drawing tools such as the paintbrush and pen tools, draw images in a direct correlation between the mouse movement and the drawing tool; i.e., as the mouse (or other input device) is moved, the drawing tool is moved, and the resultant drawing is a representation of the mouse movements. For example, to draw a flower in a typical Macintosh drawing program you would manipulate the mouse as if it were a pen or pencil (an activity likened by some artists to trying to draw with a bar of soap). In Illustrator, however, the pen tool is used much differently and there is not a literal translation between mouse movements and images drawn on the screen. Instead, the pen tool is used to manipulate points, lines, and curves in order to trace over existing images (the template) or to create new artwork without the use of a template.

Points

Another way to look at the pen tool is that it is used for placing and connecting dots, and for adjusting the curves and lines that connect those dots. To fully understand the use of the pen tool, it is important to first understand the terminology used by Illustrator for describing the different types of dots (or points) and lines that can be created and manipulated by the pen tool.

The main type of points used in Illustrator are anchor points; these are the dots that you create with the pen tool and connect with lines. (To present a complete discussion of the various types of points that you may encounter in Illustrator, this discussion also includes descriptions of points that are created with other tools.)

In addition to anchor points, other types of points used in Illustrator are: endpoints, direction points, smooth points, corner points, center points, and alignment points. Endpoints are the anchor points found at the beginning or end of a line or group of contiguous line segments. Illustrator displays an endpoint as an (x), unless it is selected. When selected, an endpoint is displayed as a small black square. See Figures 5-7 through 5-12 for examples of how various types of points look depending on how they are selected.

Direction points determine the direction that a curved or straight line is going from the point at which it is attached to its anchor points. Each line segment has two direction points associated with it; one connected to the anchor point at each end. The position of the two direction points relative to their respective anchor points determines the shape of the line.

Not only does each line segment have two direction points associated with it, but each anchor point also has two direction points associated with it for each of the two line segments that are connected by the anchor point.

A smooth point is a special type of anchor point that connects two line segments that have direction points that are on the same straight line as the anchor point (see Figures 5-7 through 5-12). It is called a smooth point because the line flows through the anchor point smoothly without making a sharp turn.

A corner point is another special type of anchor point that connects two line segments that make a sharp turn at the anchor point. The lines connected to the anchor point in a corner point have direction points that are not positioned on the same straight line as the anchor point. Corner points are used to connect line segments that are headed in different directions.

Other types of points found in Illustrator are created with tools other than the pen tool. A center point is the point found at the center of a rectangle, square, ellipse, or circle that has been created with the square tool or circle tool. (see Figure 5-27).

Although type characters can be drawn with the pen tool, you will probably use the type tool to create blocks of type. Alignment points (created with the type tool) are used to align a block of type. Alignment points are found on the baseline of the first line of a block of type (see Figure 5-28). If the text is aligned left (also known as, flush left, ragged right), then the alignment point appears at the left end of the baseline under the type. If the text is aligned right (flush right, ragged left), then the alignment point appears at the right end of the baseline. If the text is aligned at the center (each line centered in the column), then the alignment point appears at the center of the baseline under the type (Figure 5-16). The text block's alignment point is used to grab the type, in order to move it or select the type for modification, manipulation, or special effects. See the type tool, section starting on page 138 for more details.

Figure 5-27.
Center points are found in squares (and rectangles) created with the square tool and circles (and ellipses) created with the circle tool. The four anchor points at the corners of the square are corner points and the four points on the perimeter of the circle are smooth anchor points. The five points are grouped together into a single object.

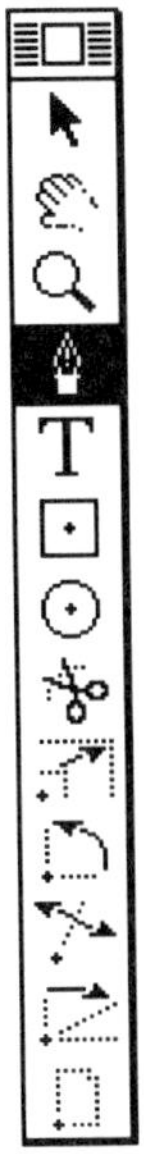

Lines, Curves, and Paths

Only two types of lines are used in Illustrator: straight lines and curves. All the artwork that you create in Illustrator is fashioned from a combination of straight lines and/or curves. Illustrator defines a segment as the single line (either curved or straight) that runs between two anchor points. The shape of the segment is determined by the position of the segment's two direction points, and the direction points are connected to the anchor point at each end of the segment. If both of the direction points are on the same line as their corresponding anchor points, then the line is a straight line; on the other hand, if one or both of the direction points are not on the same line as their corresponding anchor points, then the line is a curve.

A path is either a solitary anchor point, solitary segment, or a group of connected segments. A path is referred to as an open path if it starts at a distinct endpoint and can be followed continuously to another endpoint (see Figure 5-11, an open path). A path is referred to as a closed path if the group of lines are connected in a continuous loop with no endpoints (in Figure 5-27, both the circle and the square are closed paths). The difference between these two types of paths is important to keep in mind when you are manipulating paths, and when you fill in or paint paths. When Illustrator tries to paint an open path it first closes the path by drawing an imaginary line between the open path's two end points, and then it proceeds to paint the path as if it were closed by the imaginary line.

Drawing with the Pen Tool

To begin drawing a line segment, point to the pen tool in the tool palette and click the mouse button. The pointer will change into an (x) when you move it into the active window, to signify that you are about to place an endpoint and begin drawing a new path (see Figure 5-29).

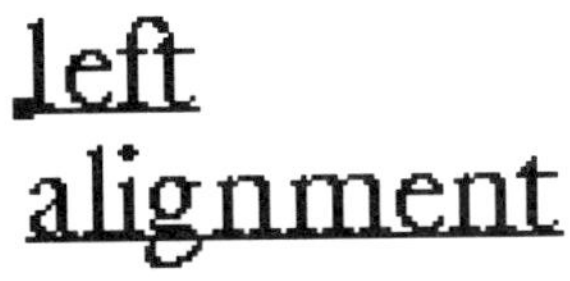

left alignment

Figure 5-28
Alignment points are found on the baseline of the first line of a block of type that has been created with the type tool.

To draw a straight line, point to where you want one end of the line to be, and click the mouse button. The pointer changes to a plus sign (+) to signify that a path is still under construction and that the next click of the mouse will draw a line from the most recently placed anchor point to the next point that you place. Then point to the location that you want to be the end of the straight line and click the mouse; a line will be drawn between the anchor point and the point where you just clicked. To continue drawing another straight line, simply point to the next point you want the line connected to and click the mouse. If you accidentally move the mouse while you are clicking (i.e., you accidentally drag with the mouse), the line will be curved, not straight. If you want to close off the path you are drawing into a solid object, connect the last point you drew to the first point by pointing to the first point and clicking the mouse; the pointer will turn into an x to indicate that you are ready to start drawing another path. If you are drawing a path you want to remain open, be sure to click on the pen tool in the toolbox palette when you are done drawing to indicate you are finished with that path; when you move the pointer back into the active window it will appear as an x to indicate that you are ready to start drawing a new path.

Drawing curves is similar to drawing straight lines except that you

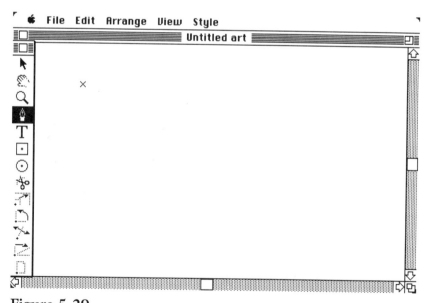

Figure 5-29.
The pen tool's pointer is shaped like an "x" to indicate that you are ready to begin drawing a new path.

click and then drag the mouse instead of just clicking it when you connect two points. As you begin dragging the mouse, an anchor point is created where you first started dragging (Figure 5-30), the pointer is changed into an arrowhead, and you drag the direction point of the curve that you are drawing as you move the mouse (Figure 5-31).

The direction point allows you to change the shape of the curve (Figures 5-32 and 5-33) by varying the distance and placement of the direction point relative to the anchor point that was created when you began to draw. You can continue adding curved segments to the path by pointing to a new location and dragging the mouse; each time you drag a new anchor point is established, a new curve is drawn, and you will be dragging the direction point of that newly drawn curve (Figures 5-34 through 5-39).

When you first begin using Illustrator, getting the hang of drawing curves can be tough. The best way to learn is to just experiment for a while; after a bit of practice you will find the process of drawing curves will come more naturally. In some ways it's like learning to ride a bicycle; what seemed hard to control at first soon becomes second-nature. Read chapters 1 through 4 to get some real-life examples of how various artists use Illustrator. For further practice, complete the tutorial provided in the Illustrator manual.

One of the special drawing techniques that is important to master is creating corners. You will need to create corners when you want a line to make an angled or sharp turn at the anchor point rather than flowing smoothly through the anchor point. To create a corner point to change the direction of a curve, first position the pointer over the anchor point that you wish to become a corner point, hold down the Option key and drag with the mouse; as you drag, the direction point of the next curve that you draw will be moved to the position that you drag it to. Then finish drawing the curve by releasing the Option key, moving the mouse to the location of the next anchor point, and dragging the mouse to create the new curve. As with the previous procedure, this takes a bit of practice. Just remember to hold down the Option key before you start to drag.

To append an existing open path, first select the pen tool from the tool palette. Then, draw a straight line by first clicking on the endpoint of the path that you wish to append and then clicking on the point that you want to become the next endpoint. The points will be connected with a straight line. To append a curved line onto an existing path, get the pen tool and first drag on the endpoint of the path to establish the direction points for a smooth point (or hold

132   ADOBE ILLUSTRATOR: THE OFFICIAL HANDBOOK FOR DESIGNERS

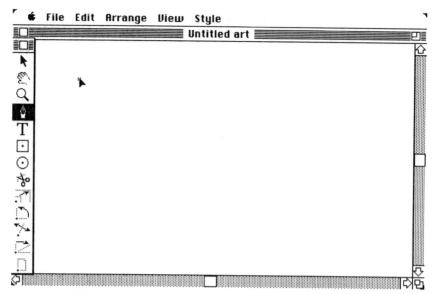

Figure 5-30.
Creating an anchor point by pressing the mouse button.

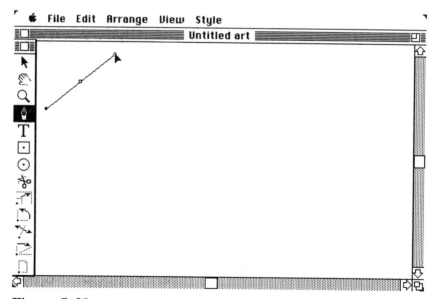

Figure 5-31.
Dragging a direction point to establish the direction in which the curve will leave the anchor point.

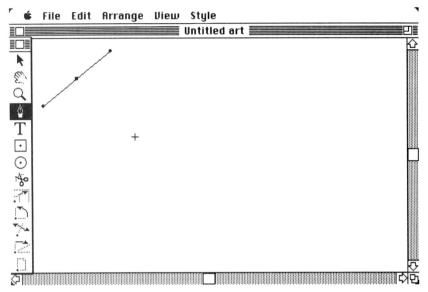

Figure 5-32.
Position the pen tool pointer where you want to create the second anchor point that will define the endpoint of the curve.

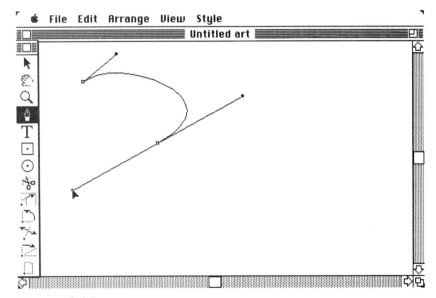

Figure 5-33.
Drag the direction point away from the second anchor point to define the shape of the curve.

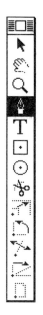

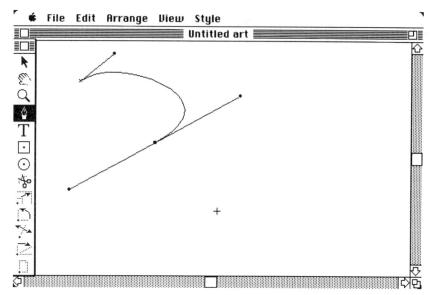

Figure 5-34.
Position the pen tool pointer where you want to create the third anchor point that will define the endpoint of the second curve.

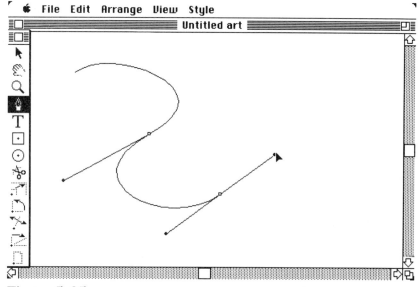

Figure 5-35.
Drag the newly created direction point away from the third anchor point to define the shape of the second curve.

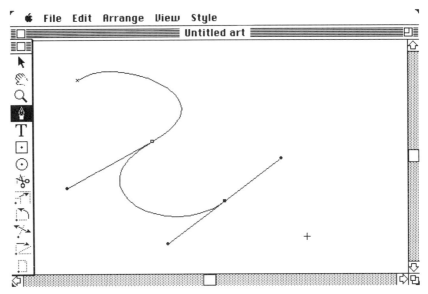

Figure 5-36.
Position the pen tool pointer where you want to create the fourth anchor point that will define the endpoint for the third curve.

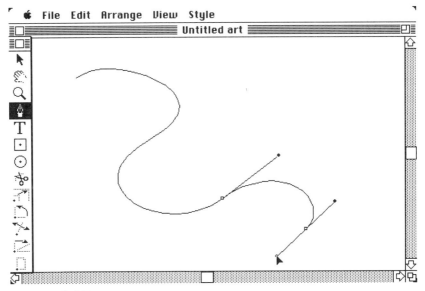

Figure 5-37.
Drag the newly created direction point away from the fourth anchor point to define the shape of the third curve. Note that all of the anchor points connecting curves are smooth points.

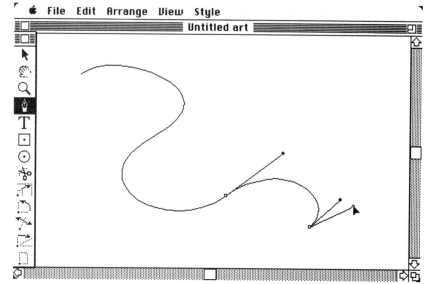

Figure 5-38.
Hold down the Option key while pointing at the endpoint and dragging to create a corner point, then drag the direction point of the next curve. If you drag the direction point at a sharp angle to the other direction point connected to the same endpoint, the endpoint becomes a corner point.

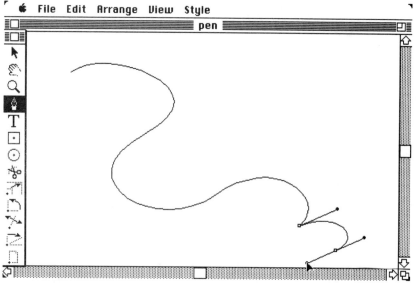

Figure 5-39.
Point to the next endpoint and drag the mouse to create the fourth curve, attached to the third curve by a sharp angle because a corner point was created (see Figure 5-38).

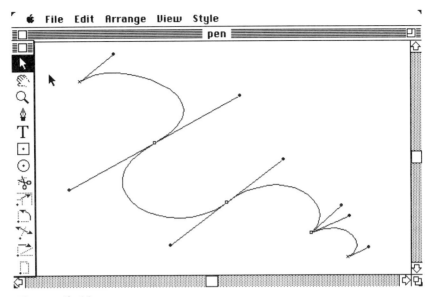

Figure 5-40.
Here is how the path looks with all its direction points selected but none of its anchor points or endpoints selected.

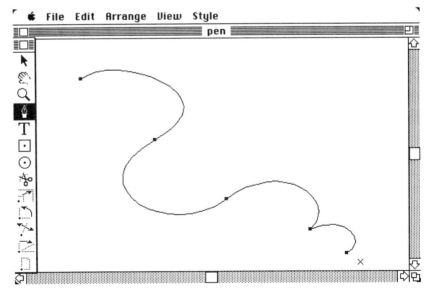

Figure 5-41.
Here is how the path looks with all its anchor points and endpoints selected but none of its direction points selected.

the Option key down and drag to create a corner point), then point to the location that represents the next anchor point and drag the mouse to establish the anchor point and connect the points with a curved segment; as you drag, you will be dragging the direction point of the newly formed curve.

Tool Use Summary

♦ +**Click mouse** — 1) creates the first anchor point if starting a new path; or 2) creates a second anchor point and a straight line if you are either creating the second anchor point or appending an existing path.

♦ +**Drag mouse** — creates a second anchor and a curved line if you are either creating the second anchor point or are appending an existing path.

♦ +**Shift key+Drag mouse** — If you hold down the Shift key while drawing with the pen, it will constrain the line being drawn horizontally (i.e., along the x axis), vertically (along the y axis), or in increments of 45° (relative to the x and y axes).

♦ +**Option key+Drag mouse** — creates a corner point and establishes a new direction for the next segment, thereby changing the direction of the path you are drawing.

The Type Tool

T— The type tool allows you to incorporate text and typography in your artwork. Any PostScript typeface that is installed on your PostScript printer or typesetting machine will work with the type tool. You can use the type tool to add new type, edit type, or to set type specifications and attributes. Illustrator treats a block of type as a single object that can be manipulated in the same way as any other artwork. Manipulating type that you create with the type tool is useful for creating such things as typographic design elements, logos, and special headlines. Special text effects can be achieved by rotating, reflecting, scaling, shearing, or painting type (see Figure 5-43 and the "Jar of Preserves" in Chapter 3 for examples of special text effects).

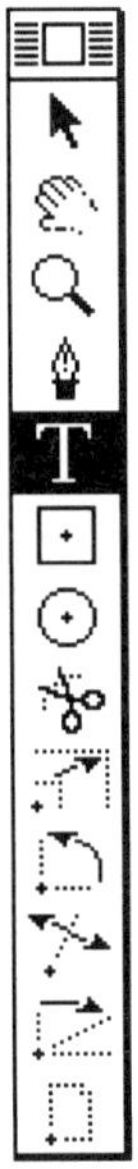

Creating Type

To create a block of type, first select the type tool by pointing to it in the tool palette and then clicking the mouse. When you move it into the active window, the pointer changes to the text placement cursor, shaped like an I-beam with a small horizontal line slightly above the bottom to represent the baseline of the first line of type that you will create (see Figure 5-42). Next, place the text placement cursor at the position where you want the first line of type to begin and click the mouse button. This places the text alignment point in the Illustrator document and brings up the Type dialog box (Figure 5-44). Enter the text you want placed in your Illustrator document into the text entry window in the Type dialog box (see Figure 5-45).

Two important things to keep in mind about entering text in the Type dialog box: you must put Returns at the end of lines, and you are limited to 254 characters of text. Long sections of text must be broken down into smaller sections of 254 characters or less, and then you can reassemble the smaller sections into the original longer section of text. Text can be edited in the Type dialog box using the standard Cut (Command-X), Copy (Command-C), Paste (Command-V), or Select All (Command-A) commands in the Edit menu. You can also use the Macintosh's Clipboard feature to transfer text into Illustrator from other programs such as word processors. If text pasted in from the Clipboard does not have line breaks, insert Returns manually into the text in the Type dialog box. If you don't, the text may run off the edge of Illustrator's 14-by-14-inch working area and be hidden from view. Text cannot be edited directly on the Illustrator document, it can only be edited in the Type dialog box. If you want to change type that is already on the Illustrator artwork,

Figure 5-42.
The text placement (I-beam) cursor with baseline guide.

Figure 5-43.
Type created normally (not italic), then sheared with the Shear Tool.

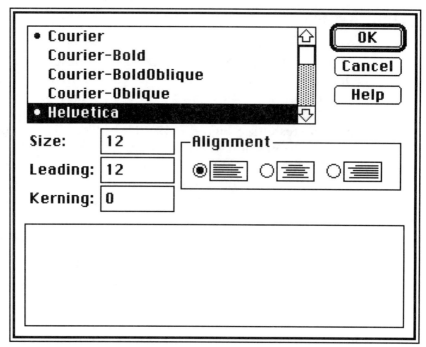

Figure 5-44.
The Type dialog box.

select the type block to edit with the selection tool and then choose Type from the Style menu (Command-T) to bring up the Type dialog box so that you can edit the text in the box.

You also use the Type dialog box to set the attributes of the type such as typeface, type size, leading, kerning, and alignment. Set the attributes either when you create new type or when you modify existing type. Illustrator's default type attribute settings are Helvetica typeface, 12-point type size, 12-point leading, 0 kerning, and left alignment. To set the typeface of selected text, choose from among the typefaces listed in the scroll box located in the upper left-hand region of the Type dialog box. The scroll bar on the right side of the scroll box lets you scroll through the available typefaces if there are more than will fit into the scroll box. The typefaces listed may have no prefix, or they may have a prefix of either a dot (•) or a question mark (?). If there is no prefix, the typeface is available in your Macintosh's system file but there is no proper screen font for displaying the typeface on your Mac's screen; Illustrator uses an alternate

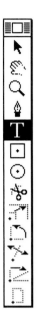
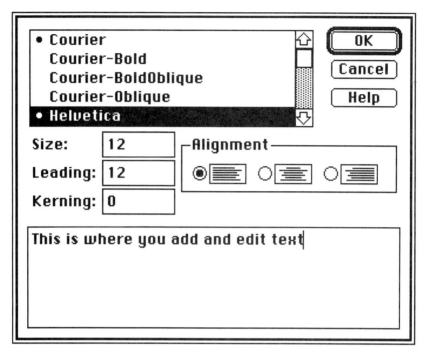

Figure 5-45.
Typing text into the Type dialog box.

screen font and loads the proper font to the printer if it is available. If the correct font is not available, then the PostScript interpreter in the printer substitutes an available printer font (usually Courier). If the typeface is prefixed by a dot (•), it is in your Macintosh's system file and there is also at least one proper screen font for displaying the typeface on your Mac's screen. Illustrator loads the proper font to the printer if it is available; if not, then Illustrator substitutes an available printer font (again, usually Courier). If the typeface is prefixed by a question mark (?) it means that you have opened an Illustrator document that uses typefaces not available in your Macintosh's system file, and that the document was created using a different system file. Illustrator will display the type on the screen using a Macintosh system screen font (usually Chicago) but no font will be downloaded to the printer for printing.

To set the type size, point to the small box after the word "Size:", click the mouse, and type the point size that you want the type to be. Type size is measured in points (one point = 1/72 inch). To set the leading, first point to the small box after the word "Leading:", click the mouse, and then type the leading that you want for the type. Leading is the amount of space between the lines of type, measured from baseline to baseline. For example, 12-point type on 12-point leading is the default setting, but if you increase the leading to 14 points, the lines will be spaced 2 points (1/36 inch) further apart.

Likewise, to set the kerning, first click the small box after the word "Kerning:", and then type the amount of kerning (in points)that you want to control the spacing of the type. Kerning is the measure of space between characters; typing a positive number adds space between characters, and typing a negative number brings characters closer together.

To set the alignment of type, point to one of the small circles in the Alignment area of the dialog box and click the mouse; a small black dot appears in the center of the circle. Clicking in the first circle (and its accompanying image of a paragraph) selects left alignment (flush left, ragged right); clicking in the second circle selects center alignment (each line centered under the next); and clicking on the third circle selects right alignment (flush right, ragged left).

To modify the attributes of existing type, select one or more blocks of type with the selection tool and then choose Type from the Style menu (Command-T); this will bring up the Type dialog box.

Square Tool

— The square tool is used to create rectangles and squares. Although it is certainly possible to construct rectangles and squares by using the pen tool to draw a path consisting of four straight lines, the square tool is much faster and easier to use for this task. To begin drawing a rectangle, point to the square tool in the tool palette and click the mouse. The pointer will change into a plus sign (+) when you move it into the active window, signifying that you are about to begin drawing an entire path rather than starting an endpoint (see Figure 5-46).

Place the (+) pointer at a point that represents one of the corners of the rectangle you want to create. Hold down the mouse button and drag the pointer until the rectangle is the size and shape you desire. When you first start the dragging process and press the mouse button down, Illustrator changes the cursor into an arrowhead; the point on the document where you first pressed the mouse button becomes the upper left-hand corner of the rectangle (see Figure 5-47).

While you are dragging the mouse, a rectangle forms starting at the point where you clicked the mouse, with the current pointer position representing the corner diagonally opposite from the original corner (see Figure 5-48).

Although the way that Illustrator usually creates a rectangle is from corner to corner, you can also draw a rectangle from the center point to the corner. The procedure for drawing a rectangle from center to corner is the same as drawing one from corner to corner, except that you hold down the Option key while dragging with the mouse. The point at which you start dragging will be the center point and the point at which you release the mouse button will be a corner point.

Rectangles created with the square tool are actually two grouped paths. One path consists of the four straight lines that are connected by the four corner points (this is a closed path), and the other path is the center point. The center point is created by Illustrator as a reference point for aligning or manipulating a rectangle. The center point looks like an "x" when it is not selected, and like a regular small square anchor point when it is selected (see Figure 5-49).

Since the center point and the four lines are a group, selecting the center point will also select the lines and vice versa. You can ungroup

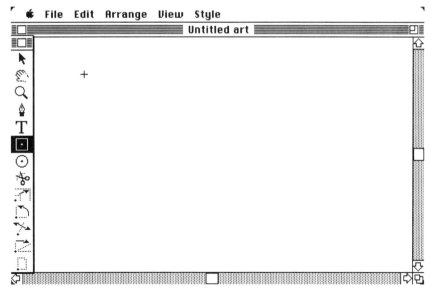

Figure 5-46.
The square tool pointer.

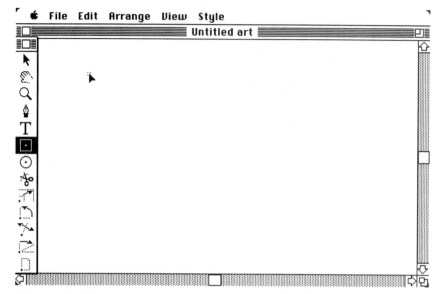

Figure 5-47.
The square tool, as you start drawing a rectangle (or square).

the two paths if you want to remove the center point; to do this, select both paths and choose Ungroup from the Arrange menu (or press Command-U).

You create a square the same way that you create a rectangle except

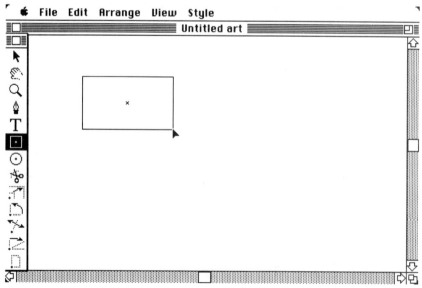

Figure 5-48.
How the square tool looks as you draw a rectangle.

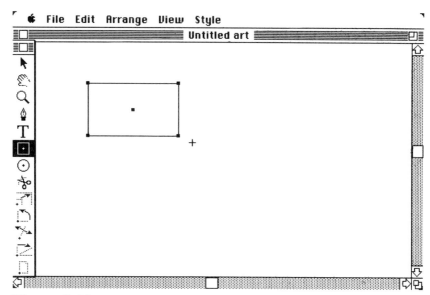

Figure 5-49.
How a rectangle looks after you finish drawing it with the square tool.

that you hold down the Shift key (to constrain the rectangle into a square) while dragging diagonally with the mouse. The four sides of any rectangle or square that you draw are aligned with the coordinates of Illustrator's current x and y axes, so if you have altered the x and y axes using the Constrain command on the Arrange menu, the diagonal dragging of the mouse (and therefore the construction of the square) is relative to the *new x* and *y* axes. For example, if you have rotated the x and y axes by 30° using the Constrain command, any rectangles and squares you create with the square tool will be drawn at a 30° angle. If you are drawing squares that don't look square, check the alignment of the x and y axes by looking at the dialog box that appears after you select the Constrain command on the Arrange menu (Command-K).

Tool Use Summary

⊡ **+Drag mouse** — draws a rectangle from corner to corner as you drag the mouse.

⊡ **+Shift key+Drag mouse** — draws a square by constraining a rectangle.

⊡ **+Option key+Drag mouse** — draws the rectangle from its

center to its edge as you drag instead of drawing the rectangle from corner to corner.

⊡+**Option key+Shift key+Drag mouse** — draws a square from center to corner as you drag instead of drawing the square from corner to corner.

Circle Tool

⊙ —The circle tool is used to create ellipses and circles. Although you can construct ellipses and circles by using the pen tool to create a series of connected curves, the circle tool is much faster and easier to use. To draw a circle, first point to the circle tool in the tool palette and then click the mouse. The pointer will change into a plus sign (+) when you move it into the active window, signifying that you are about to begin drawing an entire path rather than starting an endpoint (see Figure 5-50).

Place the (+) pointer at a point that represents a point on the perimeter of the ellipse that you want to create. Hold down the mouse button and drag the pointer until the ellipse is the size and shape you desire. When you first start the dragging process and press the mouse button down, Illustrator changes the cursor into an arrowhead; the point on the document where you first pressed the

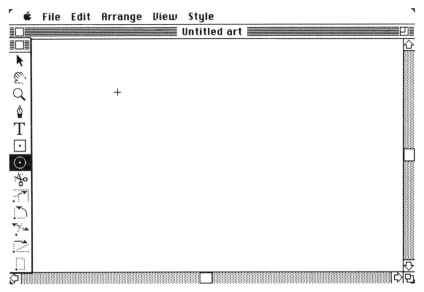

Figure 5-50.
How the circle tool looks before you start drawing an ellipse (or circle).

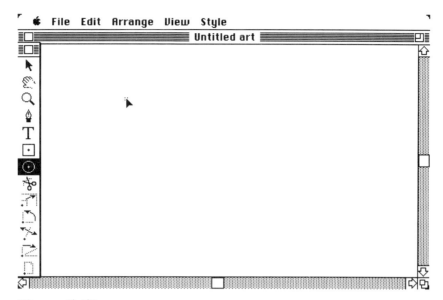

Figure 5-51.
How the circle tool looks just as you start drawing an ellipse (or circle).

mouse button becomes the upper left-most point on the perimeter of the ellipse (see Figure 5-51).

While you are dragging the mouse, an ellipse forms starting at the point where you clicked the mouse, with the current pointer position

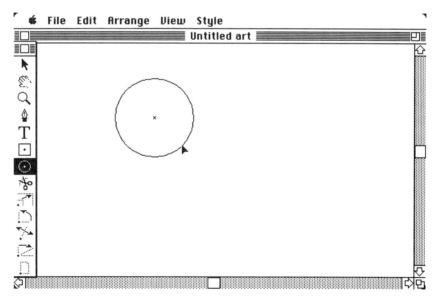

Figure 5-52.
How the circle tool looks as you draw a circle.

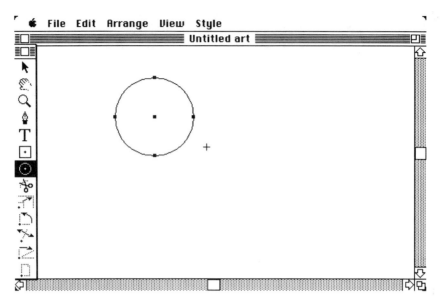

Figure 5-53.
A circle, after drawing it with the circle tool.

representing the edge opposite from the edge you started at (see Figure 5-52).

Although the way that Illustrator usually creates an ellipse is from the edge to edge of the perimeter, you can also draw an ellipse from the center point to the perimeter's edge. The procedure for drawing an ellipse from center to edge is the same as drawing one from edge to edge except that you hold down the Option key while dragging with the mouse. The point at which you start dragging will be the center point and the point at which you release the mouse button will be an anchor point at the edge of the ellipse.

Ellipses created with the circle tool are technically two grouped paths. One path consists of the four curved lines connected by four anchor points (this is a closed path), and the other path is the center point. The center point is created by Illustrator as a reference point for aligning or manipulating an ellipse (Figure 5-53).

Since the center point and the four lines are a group, selecting the center point will also select the lines and vice versa. You can ungroup the paths if you want to cut the ellipse with the scissors; to do this, select the ellipse and either choose Ungroup from the Arrange menu or press Command-U.

You can create a circle in much the same way as you create an ellipse except that you hold down the Shift key while dragging diagonally with the mouse. Holding down the Shift key constrains the ellipse into a circle. It's important to remember that if you have altered the *x* and *y* axes by using the Constrain command on the Arrange menu, the diagonal dragging of the mouse is relative to the *x* and *y* axes. Also, the horizontal and vertical axes of the circle or ellipse that you draw are aligned with the coordinates of Illustrator's current *x* and *y* axes. This means that if you have rotated the *x* and *y* axes by 30° using the Constrain command, any ellipses and circles you create with the circle tool will be drawn at a 30° angle. If you are drawing circles that don't look like perfect circles, check the alignment of the *x* and *y* axes by looking at the dialog box that appears after you select the Constrain command on the Arrange menu (or type Command-K as a shortcut).

Tool Use Summary

⊙ + **Drag mouse** — draws an ellipse from edge to edge as you drag the mouse.

⊙ + **Shift key + Drag mouse** — draws a circle by constraining an ellipse.

⊙ + **Option key + Drag mouse** — draws an ellipse from its center to its edge as you drag instead of drawing it from edge to edge.

⊙ + **Shift key + Option key + Drag mouse** — draws a circle from its center to its edge as you drag instead of drawing it from edge to edge.

Scissors Tool

— The scissors tool is used to cut a segment into two segments, cut an open path into two open paths, break a closed path into one open path, split an anchor point into two endpoints, and add anchor points to a segment. The scissors tool cannot be used to split endpoints of an open path, nor will it work on any grouped objects. If you want to use the scissors tool on a grouped object you must first select the object and ungroup it by selecting Ungroup from the Arrange menu (or by typing Command-U as a shortcut).

To use the Scissors Tool, first select the tool by pointing to it on the tool palette and clicking the mouse button. The pointer will turn into a plus sign (+) when you move it into the active window (see Figure 5-54).

To cut a segment into two segments, place the pointer over the point in the segment where you wish to cut and then click the mouse button. The segment will be split into two segments where you made the cut and two new endpoints will appear. If it at first appears that there is only one anchor point, it is because the two new endpoints will be directly on top of each other, and they will both be selected. Since you can't tell from looking at the screen that there are actually two endpoints on top of each other, it's a good idea to move the endpoints apart right after you make the cut. To move the two new endpoints apart, get the selection tool (arrow) by clicking on it in the tool palette (or by holding down the Command key). Then point to the endpoints with the arrow, hold down the Shift key, and click the mouse. This action will deselect the endpoint on top while leaving the one beneath it selected. You can then move the bottom endpoint by pointing to it with the arrow and holding down the mouse button and dragging the endpoint to a new location.

The procedure for cutting an open path into two new open paths is quite similar. The only difference is that you can either cut a path in the middle of a segment to create two new endpoints, or you can cut a path on an anchor point to turn the existing anchor point into

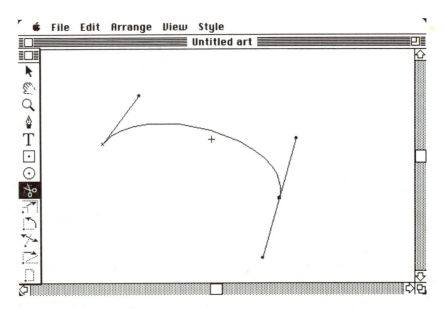

Figure 5-54.
A single segment that will be cut into two segments using the scissors tool.

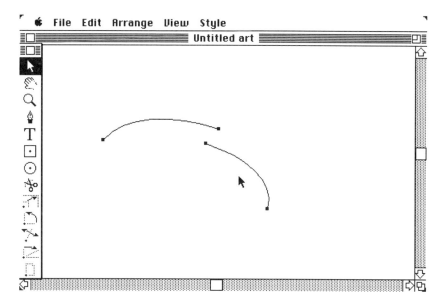

Figure 5-55.
The two segments were created by cutting the segment in Figure 5-54.

an endpoint and create a new endpoint on top of it. Since you'll be faced with the same problem of having two endpoints on top of each other, you'll either want to move the endpoints as described above,

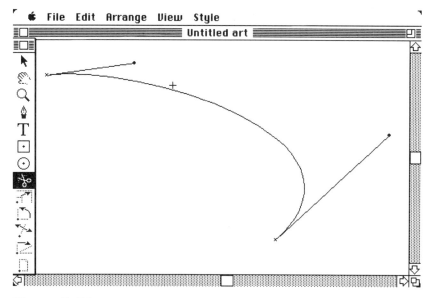

Figure 5-56.
A single segment with both endpoints not selected.

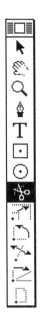
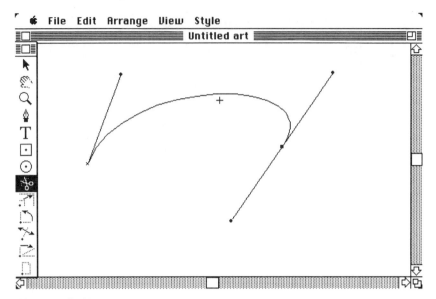

Figure 5-57.
A single segment that will have an anchor point added to it.

or you may want to move one of the new paths. In order to move a path, first get the selection tool from the tool palette (or hold down the Command key). Then point somewhere in the active window

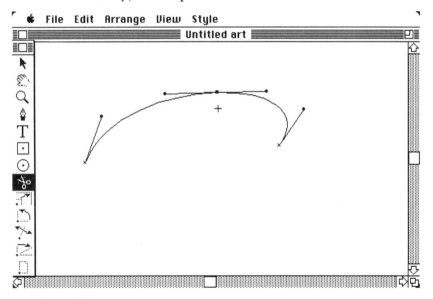

Figure 5-58.
An anchor point has been added to the segment in Figure 5-57, and it is the only point that is selected.

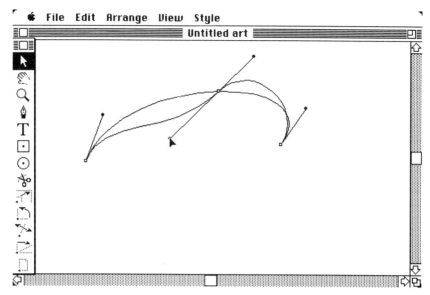

Figure 5-59.
The direction points of the new anchor point can be manipulated with the selection tool to change the shape of the path.

(away from any artwork) and click the mouse button; this will insure that all the objects in the artwork are deselected. Next point to the path that you want to move, hold down the Option key, and click the mouse; this will select the path. Then move the path to the new location by pointing to it, holding down the mouse button, and using the mouse to drag the path to a new location.

Breaking a closed path into an open path is much like the previous procedure except that you wind up with only one path instead of two. Whether you cut the closed point in the middle of a segment or at an anchor point, it's a good idea to move the two endpoints away from each other right after you cut them, since it is impossible to see from the screen that there are two, not just one, endpoints at that location.

You can also use the scissors tool for creating new anchor points at any place along any line segment in a path without cutting or breaking the path. Since adding anchor points does not add any new endpoints or break any paths, a single open path remains a single path, and a closed path stays closed. Adding new anchor points gives you a greater degree of control over the shape of a path or object since you can change the shape of the line segments where the new anchor points are added. This technique is very useful for fine-tuning small details in a complex piece of artwork. To add new anchor points to an existing line segment, first get the scissors tool by clicking on it in the tool palette.

Next, position the (+) pointer on the point in the line segment where you want the new anchor point to be located. Then, while holding down the Option key, click the mouse button. A new anchor point will appear, and it will be the only selected point in the document (see Figures 5-57 through 5-59).

Tool Use Summary

+Click mouse — cuts a segment into two segments, cuts an open path into two open paths, breaks a closed path into one open path, splits an anchor point into two endpoints.

+Option key+Click mouse — adds a new anchor point to a line segment, creating two segments but not cutting or breaking the original segment.

The Scale Tool

— The scale tool is used for stretching or shrinking paths or other objects. You can manipulate items horizontally (i.e., along their x axis), vertically (along their y axis), or a varying amount of both. The scale tool can also be used as a built-in "stat camera" that allows you to enlarge or reduce your artwork to fit into an allotted space in a page layout or to fit in with some other graphic design element. Using Illustrator as a stat camera involves stretching or shrinking items in equal amounts both vertically and horizontally; this is best accomplished through use of the Scale dialog box described in Figure 5-64.

Items are scaled relative to a fixed point of origin that you specify, which gives you more flexibility in performing various types of scaling operations for special effects. Scaling a path or other object is the only way to alter its size; zooming in, zooming out, or setting the enlargement or reduction options in the Page Setup dialog box do not affect the actual size of paths or objects. Since Illustrator is limited to a 14-by-14-inch work area, the scale tool can also be handy

Illustrator Dissected 155

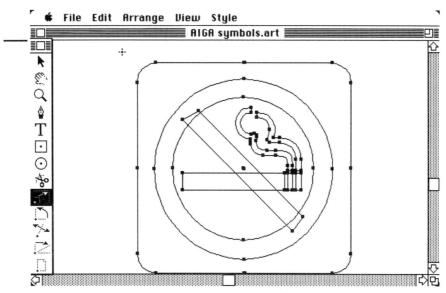

Figure 5-60.
The cursor is shaped like a plus sign (+) indicating that the fixed point of reference for the scale operation has not yet been specified.

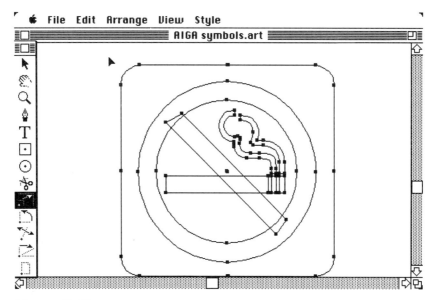

Figure 5-61.
The cursor is shaped like an arrowhead indicating that the fixed point of reference for the scale operation has now been established.

for shrinking the size of your artwork to fit in the work area or to fit on a single page.

Before using the scale tool you must first select the path(s) or object(s) you want to scale. To select an object to scale, simply point at the object and click the mouse; alternatively, you can drag a selection marquee around the object you wish to select using the selection tool and the mouse. To select an entire path for scaling, first position the pointer anywhere on the path, hold down the Option key, and press the mouse button. To select more than one object to scale, either drag a selection marquee around the objects, or select one object first, then hold down the Shift key and continue to select the remaining objects. To select the entire piece of artwork for scaling, either choose Select All from the Edit menu or press Command-A . Once you have selected the item that you wish to scale, you can proceed one of two ways: you can either use the mouse to scale the selected item(s) by hand, or you can request the Scale dialog box and specify precise amounts of enlargement or reduction, whether to scale or preserve line weights, and other scaling options.

If you want to use the mouse to stretch or shrink the selected item(s) by hand, first select the scale tool by pointing to it on the tool palette and clicking the mouse button. The pointer will turn into a plus sign (+) whenever you move it into the active window (Figure 5-60).

Point to the spot that you want to become the fixed point of reference for the origin of the scaling operation, and then click the mouse button to establish the point of origin. The pointer changes to an arrowhead to indicate that the point of origin has been established (Figure 5-61).

Now, point to another spot that indicates the relative direction in which you want to stretch or shrink the selected item(s). The closer your second spot is to the point of origin, the less mouse movement is required to alter the size and shape of the selected item(s). To get better control of the scaling process, it's a good idea to select a second spot that is as far away from the point of origin as practical; you can select a second spot at the edge of the active window if you are shrinking the selected item(s), but you do need to allow some elbow room if you are stretching the item(s).

Then, while holding down the mouse button, drag the mouse in the direction that you want the selected item(s) to be scaled. If you want to stretch the item(s), move the mouse away from the point of origin; if you want to shrink the item(s), move the mouse towards the

Illustrator Dissected 157

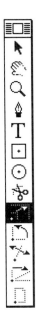
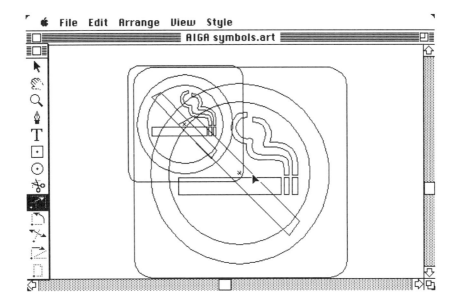

Figure 5-62.
The selected items are being shrunk with the scale tool.

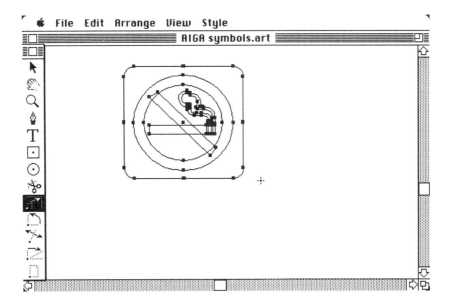

Figure 5-63.
The scaled down version of the original artwork. All the items originally selected are still selected after the scale operation has been performed.

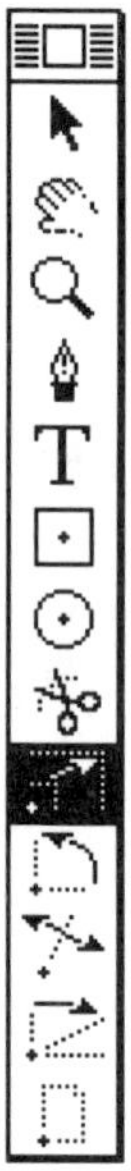

point of origin. The direction in which you drag the mouse also affects the way in which the selected item(s) are scaled; if you move the mouse horizontally, the item(s) will be stretched (or reduced) horizontally; if you move the mouse vertically, the item(s) will be stretched (or reduced) vertically; and if you move the mouse diagonally, the item(s) will be stretched (or reduced) both vertically and horizontally.

While you are dragging the mouse you will see both the original item(s) you selected and their scaled counterpart(s) (Figure 5-62).

When you have finished stretching or shrinking the selected item(s), release the mouse button and the original item(s) will be erased, leaving only the scaled item(s) (see Figure 5-63).

If you hold down the Option key while dragging the mouse, a scaled duplicate will be created and the original will be left in place. Scaling objects by hand is good for quick stretching or shrinking, but it can be hard to control.

To get better control over scaling, hold down the Shift key while dragging the mouse; this constrains the direction in which the selected item(s) are scaled. If the Shift key is held down while you stretch or shrink something, dragging the mouse horizontally will only scale the item(s) along the *x* axis; dragging the mouse vertically will only scale the item(s) along the *y* axis; and dragging the mouse diagonally will scale the selected item(s) equally along both axes.

For more precise control over scaling, use the Scale dialog box

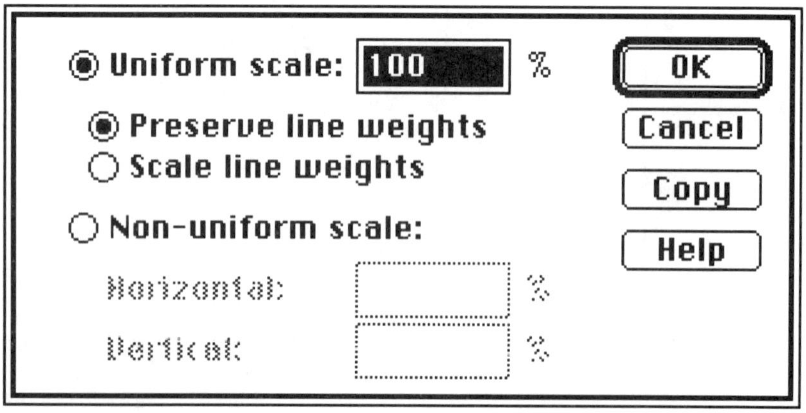

Figure 5-64.
The Scale dialog box with the Uniform scale option selected.

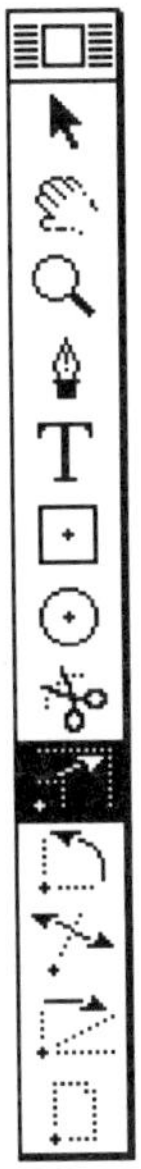

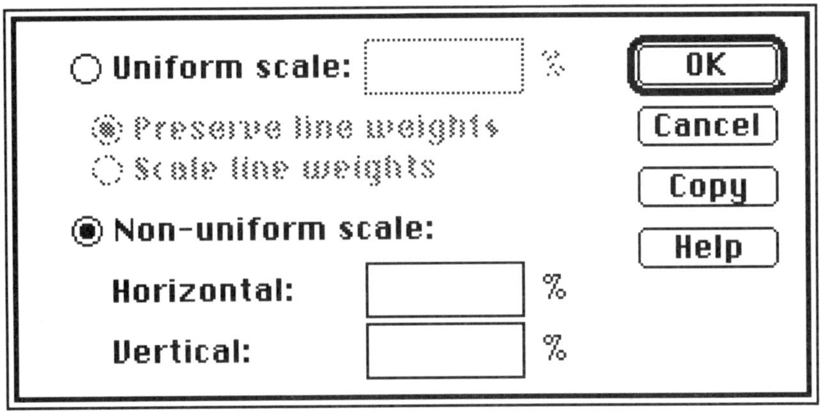

Figure 5-65.
The Scale dialog box with the Non-uniform scale option selected.

(Figure 5-64). Line weights cannot be scaled by hand; you must use the Scale dialog box for this task.

Use the Scale dialog box for precise enlargement or reduction, or to scale the line weights of the items being stretched or shrunk. First select the scale tool by pointing to it on the tool palette and clicking the mouse button. The pointer will turn into a plus sign (+) when you move it into the active window. Then point to the spot that you want to become the fixed point of reference for the origin of the scaling operation and click the mouse button to establish the point of origin. Now, instead of pointing to a second spot as you would if you were scaling by hand, simply hold down the Option key while clicking the mouse button. As soon as you hold down the Option key, the (+) pointer changes into a (+-) pointer, indicating that the Scale dialog box is ready to be requested; as soon as you click the mouse, the Scale dialog box will appear.

The Scale dialog box allows you to choose between uniform scaling and non-uniform scaling, and between preserving the line weights or scaling the line weights. When the dialog box appears, it contains the settings from the previous scaling operation; if this is the first use of the scale tool since you started up the program, the values will be set to "Uniform Scale" at 100% and "Preserve line weights." If you want uniform scaling; i.e., scaling performed equally along the *x* and *y* axes, make sure that the small circle in front of "Uniform scale:" is checked (it should have a small black spot inside the circle).

Then point to the small box after the "Uniform Scale:" heading, click the mouse, and enter the scaling factor number as a percentage. Numbers greater than 100 will enlarge the item(s) and numbers smaller than 100 will reduce the item(s).

If uniform scaling is selected, you can also specify whether or not you would like the lines weights of the selected item(s) scaled or preserved (when scaling by hand, line weights are always preserved). Simply click the mouse inside the circle preceding the line weight scaling option you desire.

One of the features of Illustrator that makes it especially valuable to graphic artists is the ability to preserve line weights while scaling, which is why that is the default setting. Preserving the line weights of a drawing while enlarging or reducing it is useful when you want consistent line weights throughout the drawing. Normal enlargement or reduction methods, such as using a stat camera, always scale line weights. When you want line weights scaled, use the "Scale line weights" option in the Scale dialog box.

If you choose the "Non-uniform scale:" option by clicking in the circle preceding it, you will not be able to scale line weights but you will be able to type in different scaling factors for the horizontal and vertical axes. To enter the horizontal scale factor, point to the box after the word "Horizontal:", click the mouse button, and type the scaling factor number.

Likewise, to enter the vertical scale factor, point to the box after the word "Vertical:", click the mouse button, and type the scaling factor number. You enter the scale factor as percentages of either enlargement (numbers over 100) or reduction (numbers between 0 and 100). You can also type in negative numbers, which is equivalent to dragging the mouse to the left (or above) the point of origin when scaling by hand. As with scaling by hand, you can use the scaling function to create a reflection of the selected item(s) along an imaginary line that passes through the point of origin you established for the scaling operation.

For an example of reflecting, try specifying 100% horizontal scaling and 100% vertical scaling; the result will be a reflection of the image across a vertical line that passes through the point of origin. By using percentages other than 100%, scaling and reflecting can be accomplished simultaneously. For better control over reflecting we suggest, however, that you use the reflect tool.

When you are finished specifying the scaling options, click the OK button in the dialog box to perform the scaling operation; click the

Cancel button to abandon your specifications and return to the unaltered active window; or click Copy to create a scaled copy while leaving the original in its place. The double line surrounding the OK button indicates that pressing the Return key can be used as a shortcut for selecting the OK option. After you have finished scaling, you can repeat the procedure as often as you want by selecting Transform Again from the Arrange menu or by pressing Command-D as a shortcut.

Again, it is important to remember that if you have altered the *x* and *y* axes by using the Constrain command on the Arrange menu, the scaling of the selected item(s) is relative to the *x* and *y* axes. This means that if you have rotated the *x* and *y* axes by 30° using the Constrain command, any items you scale with the scale tool will be drawn at a 30° angle.

If you are unsure about the alignment of the *x* and *y* axes, you can check their settings by looking at the dialog box that appears after you select the Constrain command on the Arrange menu (or type Command-K as a shortcut for requesting the dialog box).

Tool Use Summary

+Drag mouse — stretches or shrinks any selected objects relative to a point of origin that you specify.

+Shift key+Drag mouse — constrains the object(s) being scaled along the *x* axis, the *y* axis, or both axes.

+Option key+Click mouse — displays the Scale dialog box for specifying precise scaling amounts.

+Option key+Drag mouse — creates a scaled duplicate while leaving the original object in its place; useful for creating different sized copies of an object.

The Rotate Tool

— The rotate tool is used for rotating objects around a reference point that you specify. The rotate tool is useful for rotating items around a common point such as spokes on a wheel or petals of a flower, for rotating items for positioning, or for creating special effects.

Before you use the rotate tool you must first select the path(s) or other object(s) you want to rotate. To select a path to rotate, first position the pointer anywhere on the path, hold down the Option key and click the mouse. To select a grouped object to rotate, simply point at the object and click the mouse; alternatively, you can drag a selection marquee around the object you wish to select by using the selection tool and the mouse. To select more than one object to rotate, either drag a selection marquee around the objects, or select one object first by pointing to it and clicking the mouse, then hold down the Shift key and select the remaining objects by pointing to them and clicking the mouse. To select the entire piece of artwork for rotating, either choose Select All from the Edit menu or press Command-A as a shortcut. Once you have selected the item(s) that you wish to rotate, you can proceed one of two ways: you can either use the mouse to rotate the selected item(s) by hand, or you can request the Rotate dialog box for specifying precise amounts of rotation.

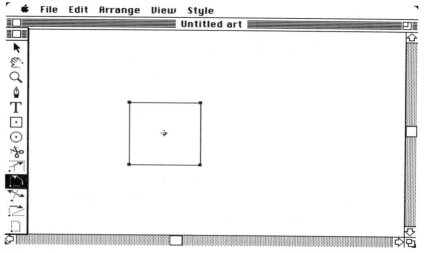

Figure 5-66.
To rotate the square, position the pointer over the desired axis of rotation and then click the mouse to establish the axis point.

If you want to use the mouse to rotate the selected item(s) by hand, first select the rotate tool by pointing to it on the toolbox palette and clicking the mouse button. The pointer will turn into a plus sign (+) whenever you move it into the active window. Next, point to the spot that you want to become the axis around which the selected item(s) will be rotated, and click the mouse button to establish the center of rotation (see Figure 5-66).

The pointer will change to an arrowhead to indicate that the center point has been established. Then, hold down the mouse button and drag the mouse in a circular motion around the center point; the selected items will rotate around the center point (see Figure 5-67).

While you are dragging the mouse, you will see both the original item(s) you selected and the rotating counterpart(s). When you have finished rotating the selected item(s), release the mouse button and the original item(s) will be erased, leaving only the rotated item(s) (see Figure 5-68).

If you hold down the Option key while dragging the mouse, a rotated duplicate will be created and the original will remain in its place (see figure 5-69).

Rotating objects by hand looks easy, but it can be hard when you are trying to control precise amounts of rotation. In order to get

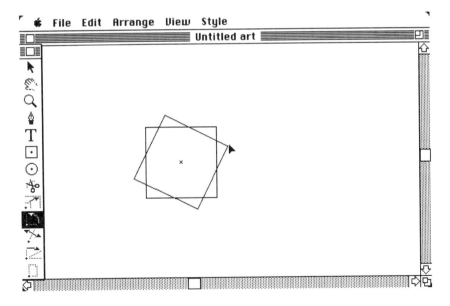

Figure 5-67.
As you drag the mouse the square will rotate around the axis point that you specified when you first clicked the mouse.

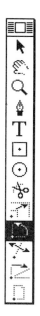
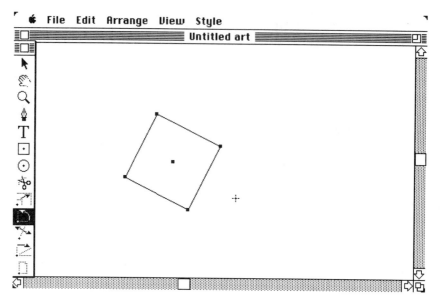

Figure 5-68.
After you finish rotating the square the image of the original disappears.

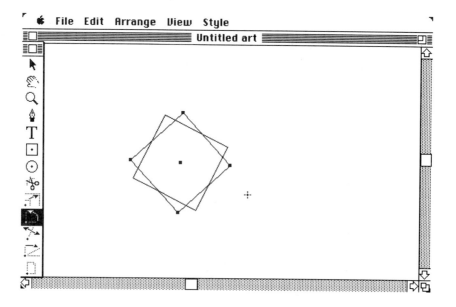

Figure 5-69.
Holding down the Option key while you rotate something with the rotate tool leaves the original in its place while creating a rotated duplicate.

Illustrator Dissected 165

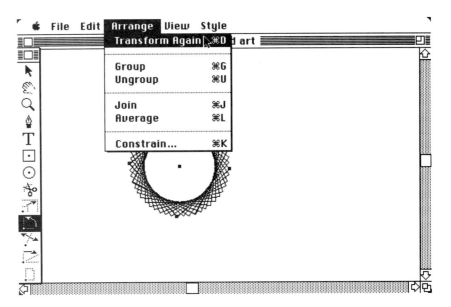

Figure 5-70.
Special effects can be created by rotating and copying objects a number of times in a row using the Transform Again command found on the Arrange menu.

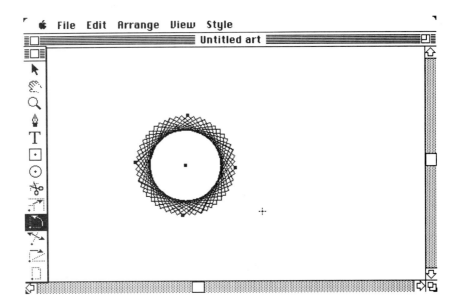

Figure 5-71.
Here is the square rotated and copied many times in a row.

better control over rotation, you can hold the Shift key down while dragging the mouse; this constrains the rotation to multiples of 45°. For even more precise control over rotation, use the Rotate dialog box. You will notice that while rotating you can also create a reflection of the item(s); however, it is easier to use the reflect tool to create reflections.

If you want to use the Rotate dialog box for rotating items by a precise amount, first select the rotate tool by pointing to it on the tool palette and clicking the mouse button. The pointer will turn into a plus sign (+) when you move it into the active window. Next, point to the spot that you want to become the axis around which the selected item(s) will be rotated, hold down the Option key, and click to establish the center of rotation. As soon as you hold down the Option key, the (+) pointer changes into a (+-) pointer, indicating that the Rotate dialog box is ready to be requested; as soon as you click the mouse, the Rotate dialog box appears (see Figure 5-72)).

The dialog box contains the settings from the previous rotation; if this is the first use of the rotate tool since you started up the program, the rotation angle will be set to zero. Specify the desired angle of rotation in degrees. The angle of rotation that you specify is applied relative to the x axis, and items are rotated around the center point (which is the intersection of the x and y axes). You can specify angles from 360 to -360 degrees. Positive numbers will rotate the selected item(s) counterclockwise and negative numbers will rotate the item(s) clockwise. By specifying a 180° rotation, the item will be reflected across the x axis; however, for better control over reflecting, we suggest that you use the reflect tool.

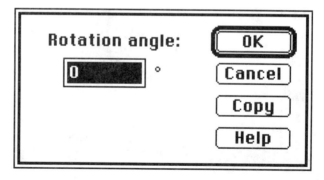

Figure 5-72.
The Rotate dialog box.

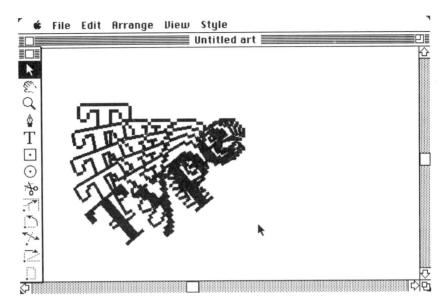

Figure 5-73.
You can rotate Type with the rotate tool and repeat the rotation with the Transform Again command to create special effects.

When you are finished specifying the angle of rotation, you can either click the OK button in the dialog box to perform the rotation; click the Cancel button to abandon your specifications and return to the unaltered active window; or click Copy to create a rotated copy while leaving the original in its place. The double line surrounding the OK button indicates that pressing the Return key can be used as a shortcut for selecting the OK option. After you have finished rotating, you can repeat the procedure as often as you want by selecting Transform Again from the Arrange menu or by pressing Command-D.

It's important to remember that if you have altered the x and y axes by using the Constrain command on the Arrange menu, the rotation of the selected item(s) is relative to the x and y axes. This means that if you have rotated the x and y axes by 30° using the Constrain command, any items you rotate with the rotate tool will be rotated at an additional 30° angle. If you are unsure about the alignment of the x and y axes, you can check their settings by looking at the dialog box that appears after you select the Constrain command on the Arrange menu (or type Command-K as a shortcut for requesting the dialog box).

Tool Use Summary

+Click mouse ON AXIS+Drag mouse — rotates any selected objects around a reference point that you specify.

+ Click mouse ON AXIS +Shift key+Drag mouse — constrains the rotation of the selected object(s) to increments of 45° (relative to the *x* and *y* axes).

+Click mouse ON AXIS+Option key+Click mouse — displays the Rotate dialog box for specifying precise amounts of rotation.

+Click mouse ON AXIS+Option key+Drag mouse — creates a rotated duplicate while leaving the original object in place.

The Reflect Tool

— The reflect tool is used to create mirror images of objects. Before you use the reflect tool, you must first select the path(s) or other object(s) that you want reflected. To select a path to reflect, first position the pointer anywhere on the path, hold down the Option key, and click the mouse. To select a grouped object to reflect, simply point at the object and click the mouse; alternatively, you can drag a selection marquee around the object(s) you wish to select using the selection tool and the mouse. To select more than one object to reflect, either drag a selection marquee around the objects, or select one object first by pointing to it and clicking the mouse and then hold down the Shift key and select the remaining objects by pointing to them and clicking the mouse button. To select the entire piece of artwork for reflecting, either choose Select All from the Edit menu or press Command-A. Once you have selected the item that you wish to reflect, you can proceed one of two ways: you can either use the mouse to reflect the selected item(s) by hand, or you can request the Reflect dialog box for specifying precise amounts of reflection.

If you want to use the mouse to reflect the selected item(s) by

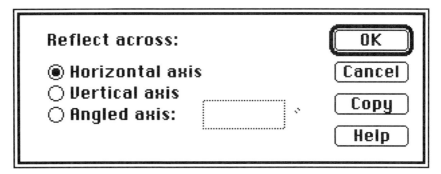

Figure 5-74.
The Reflect dialog box with a reflection across the horizontal axis specified.

hand, first select the reflect tool by pointing to it on the tool palette and clicking the mouse. The pointer will turn into a plus sign (+) whenever you move it into the active window. Point to the spot that you want to become the first point of the axis around which the selected item(s) will be reflected and click the mouse button. The pointer will change to an arrowhead to indicate that the first axis point has been established. Then, select a second point that along with the first point will define the imaginary line that Illustrator will use for the axis of reflection.

On the other hand, if you want to adjust the axis of reflection, hold the mouse button down while dragging the arrowhead pointer around the original reference point; the axis of reflection will change as you drag the mouse.

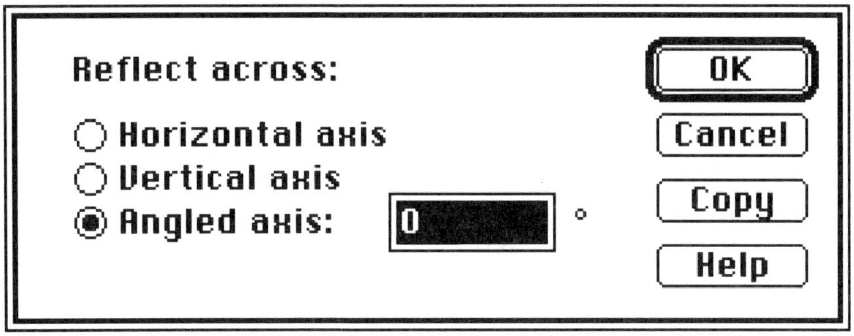

Figure 5-75.
The Reflect dialog box with a reflection across an angled axis selected, but the actual angle of the axis is not yet specified and is set to zero.

While dragging the mouse you will see both the original item(s) you selected and the reflected counterpart(s). When you have finished reflecting the selected item(s), release the mouse button to erase the original item(s), leaving only the reflected item(s). If you hold down the Option key while dragging the mouse, a reflected duplicate will be created while the original remains in its place.

To get better control over reflection, you can hold the Shift key down while dragging the mouse; this constrains the reflection axis to multiples of 45°. For more precise control over rotation, use the Reflect dialog box (Figure 5-74).

If you want to use the Reflect dialog box for rotating items by a precise amount, first select the reflect tool by pointing to it on the toolbox palette and clicking the mouse button. The pointer will turn into a plus sign (+) whenever you move it into the active window. Next, point to any spot along an imaginary line that you want to become the fixed point that will define the axis around which the selected item(s) will be reflected, hold down the Option key, and click the mouse button. As soon as you hold down the Option key, the (+) pointer changes into a (+-) pointer, indicating that the reflect dialog box is ready to be requested; as soon as the mouse button is clicked, the Reflect dialog box appears.

The dialog box contains the settings from the previous reflection; if this is the first use of the reflect tool since you started up the program, the reflection option will be set to reflect items across the horizontal axis. Next, specify whether you want the selected item(s) reflected across a horizontal axis running through the fixed point, a vertical axis through the point, or across an angled axis by clicking in the circle preceding the desired option. If you select the option for reflecting items across an angled axis (Figure 5-75), you must then enter a number in the box that represents the angle of rotation (in degrees) of the reflection axis about the fixed point relative to the x and y axes. When you are finished specifying the reflection options, you can either click the OK button in the dialog box to perform the reflection; click the Cancel button to abandon your specifications and return to the unaltered active window; or click Copy to create a reflected copy while leaving the original in its place. The double line surrounding the OK button indicates that pressing the Return key can be used as a shortcut for selecting the OK option. After you have finished reflecting, you can repeat the procedure as often as you want by selecting Transform Again from the Arrange menu or by pressing Command-D as a shortcut.

It's also important to remember that if you have altered the *x* and *y* axes by using the Constrain command on the Arrange menu, the reflection of the selected item(s) is relative to the *x* and *y* axes. This means that if you have rotated the *x* and *y* axes by 30° using the Constrain command, any items you reflect with the reflect tool will be rotated at an additional 30° angle. If you are unsure about the alignment of the *x* and *y* axes, you can check their settings by looking at the dialog box that appears after you select the Constrain command on the Arrange menu (or type Command-K as a shortcut for requesting the dialog box).

Tool Use Summary

+Click mouse ON FIRST POINT OF REFLECTION.

AXIS+Drag mouse — reflects a mirror-image of any selected object(s) across a reflection line that you specify (an imaginary line through the point where you click and the point where you start dragging defines the reflection axis).

+Click mouse+Shift key+Drag mouse — constrains the reflection of the selected object(s) to horizontal (reflected across the *x* axis), vertical (reflected across the *y* axis), and increments of 45° (relative to the *x* and *y* axes).

+Option key+Click mouse — displays the Reflect dialog box for specifying precise amounts of reflection.

+Click mouse ON FIRST POINT OF REFLECTION.

AXIS+Option key+Drag mouse — creates a reflected duplicate while leaving the original object in its place.

The Shear Tool

— The shear tool is used to put a slant on an object.

Before you use the shear tool, you must first select the path(s) or other object(s) that you want to shear. To select a path to shear, first position the pointer anywhere on the path, hold down the Option key, and press the mouse button. To select a grouped object to shear, simply point at the object and click the mouse; alternatively, you can drag a selection marquee around the object you wish to select using the selection tool and the mouse. To select more than one object to shear, either drag a selection marquee around the objects or select one object first by pointing to it and clicking the mouse, and then hold down the Shift key and select the remaining objects by pointing to them and clicking the mouse button. To select the entire piece of artwork for shearing, either choose Select All from the Edit menu or press Command-A as a shortcut. Once you have selected the item that you wish to shear, you can proceed one of two ways: you can either use the mouse to shear the selected item(s) by hand, or you can request the Shear dialog box for specifying precise amounts of shearing.

If you want to use the mouse to shear the selected item(s) by hand, first select the shear tool by pointing to it on the tool palette and

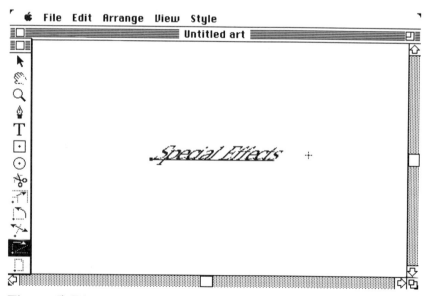

Figure 5-76.
You can use the shear tool for creating text that is much more slanted than italics.

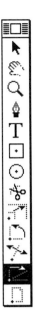
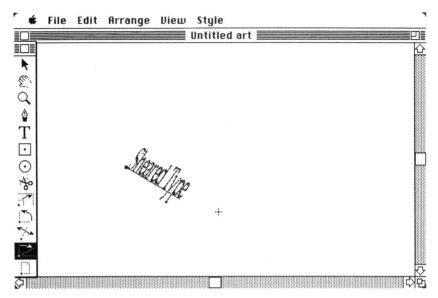

Figure 5-77.
The shear tool can also be used for skewing the text along both the x and y axes.

clicking the mouse button. The pointer will turn into a plus sign (+) whenever you move it into the active window. Point to the spot that you want to become one of the points that will define the axis along which the selected item(s) will be sheared, click the mouse button to establish the first point of the shear axis, and all the points along the shear axis will remain fixed. The pointer will change to an arrowhead to indicate that the shear axis has been established. Next, move the pointer away from the original point you clicked on; the further away from the first point that you position the pointer, the greater control you will have over the amount the selected item(s) are sheared. Then, hold down the mouse button to establish the second point that will define the axis. Drag the mouse horizontally to shear the selected item(s) along the *x* axis, drag the mouse vertically to shear along the *y* axis, or drag the mouse diagonally to shear along both the *x* and *y* axes.

While you are dragging the mouse you will see both the original item(s) you selected and the sheared counterpart(s). When you have finished shearing the selected item(s), release the mouse button and the original item(s) will be erased, leaving only the sheared item(s). If you hold down the Option key while dragging the mouse, a sheared duplicate will be created while leaving the original in its place. To get better control over shearing, you can hold the Shift key down while dragging the mouse; this constrains shearing to an angle that is a multiple of 45° (relative to the *x* and *y* axes). For more precise control over shearing, use the Shear dialog box (Figure 5-79).

If you want to use the Shear dialog box for shearing items by a precise amount, first select the shear tool by pointing to it on the tool palette and clicking the mouse button. The pointer will turn into a plus sign (+) when you move it into the active window. Next, point to the spot that you want to become the fixed point on the axis along which the selected item(s) will be sheared, hold down the Option key, and click the mouse button. As soon as you hold down the Option key, the (+) pointer changes into a (+-) pointer, indicating that the Shear dialog box is ready to be requested; as soon as you click the mouse button, the Shear dialog box appears.

The dialog box contains the settings from the previous shearing; if this is the first use of the Shear Tool since you started up the program, the shear angle will be set to zero and horizontal shearing will be selected. Specify the desired angle of shearing in degrees by clicking the mouse in the box located after the words "Shear Angle:".

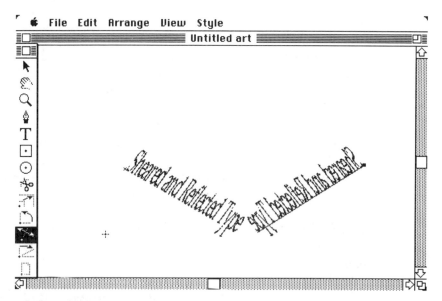

Figure 5-78.
You can create very exotic effects using combinations of tools. In this example the shear tool, reflect tool, and copy command were used on a block of type to create a reflected mirror image of the sheared type.

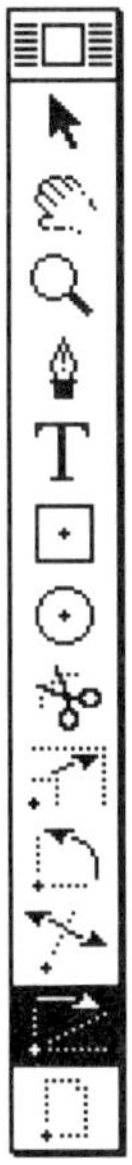

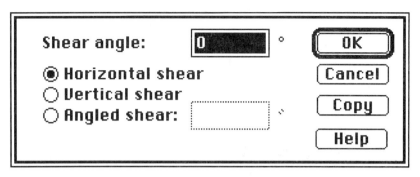

Figure 5-79.
The Shear dialog box with the default settings.

The angle of shearing that you specify corresponds to the amount of slant you want to put on the selected item(s) relative to a line that is perpendicular to the shear axis point that was established when you requested the dialog box. A positive angle performs a clockwise shear and a negative angle performs a counterclockwise shear (this is in contrast to rotation angles, where a positive angle performs a counterclockwise rotation and a negative angle performs a clockwise rotation). Next specify whether you want a horizontal shear, vertical shear, or angled shear by clicking in the circle preceding the desired option. If you select an angled shear you must also click the mouse in the box after the words "Angled Shear:" and then specify the angle (in degrees) of the shear axis around the fixed point that you established, relative to the *x* and *y* axes.

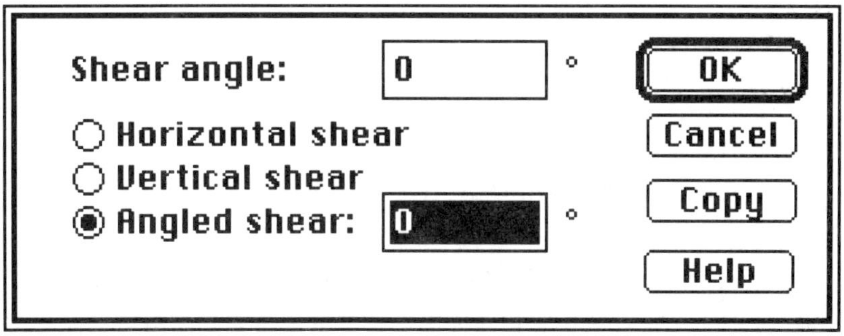

Figure 5-80.
The Shear dialog box with an angled shear selected, but the actual angle of the shear not yet specified.

When you are finished specifying the shear options, you can click the OK button in the dialog box to perform the shear; click the Cancel button to abandon your specifications and return to the unaltered active window; or click Copy to create a sheared copy while leaving the original in its place. The double line surrounding the OK button indicates that pressing the Return key can be used as a shortcut for selecting the OK option. After you have finished shearing, you can repeat the procedure as often as you want by selecting Transform Again from the Arrange menu or by pressing Command-D as a shortcut.

Remember that if you have altered the x and y axes by using the Constrain command on the Arrange menu, the shearing of the selected item(s) is relative to the x and y axes. This means that if you have rotated both axes by 30° using the Constrain command, any items you shear with the shear tool will be sheared at an additional 30° angle. If you are unsure about the alignment of the x and y axes, you can check their settings by looking at the dialog box that appears after you select the Constrain command on the Arrange menu (or type Command-K as a shortcut for requesting the dialog box).

Tool Use Summary

+Click mouse ON FIRST POINT OF SHEAR AXIS **+Drag mouse** — slants any selected object(s) uniformly along an axis that you specify (an imaginary line that runs through the point where you click and the point where you start dragging defines the shear axis).

+Click mouse+Shift key+Drag mouse — constrains the shearing of the selected object(s) to horizontal (sheared along the x axis), vertical (sheared along the y axis), and shearing in increments of 45° (relative to the x and y axes).

+Option key+Click mouse — displays the Shear dialog box for specifying precise amounts of shearing.

+Click mouse ON FIRST POINT OF SHEAR

AXIS+Option key+Drag mouse — creates a sheared duplicate while leaving the original object in its place.

The Page Tool

— The page tool is used to control how Illustrator breaks up its 14-by-14-inch work area into pages for printing. Since very few PostScript printers are capable of printing the entire 14-by-14-inch work area on a single piece of paper, Illustrator needs to split the work area up into smaller sections for printing. When you start up Illustrator, the program divides the work area into regions, with only one full-sized page region that is located in the center of the work area. These regions are related to the printable area of the page size specified in the Page Setup dialog box . The printable area is the region within the page that your PostScript printer is capable of actually printing; in the case of Apple's LaserWriter Plus, the printable area on an 8 1/2-by-11-inch piece of paper is 8.0 inches by 10.9 inches centered on the 8 1/2-by 11-inch page.

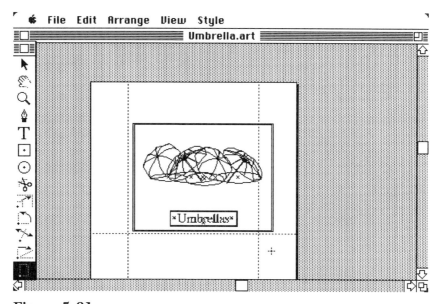

Figure 5-81.
The page grid in this example would print the artwork onto two pages however, the current page breaks would break off the right edge of the umbrellas onto the second page

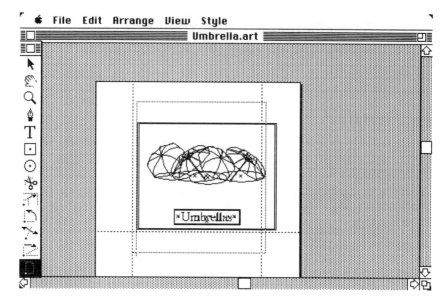

Figure 5-82.
When you hold down the mouse button while using the page tool, Illustrator displays a dotted rectangle that corresponds to the printable area on a single page.

In order to let you know where the page breaks will occur, Illustrator marks the 14-by-14-inch work area with a page grid made of dotted lines that represents the printable area of a page. The dotted lines of the page grid are visible in all views of the active document (e.g. if you have another view of the same piece of artwork in another window, the page grid will be transferred to that view as well). Illustrator measures the height and width of your artwork to create an imaginary rectangle of page boundaries around your artwork. Illustrator then numbers the actual pages it will print from left to right and top to bottom, starting in the upper left-hand corner of the imaginary rectangle of page boundaries.

Depending on the shape of your artwork and how Illustrator interprets the page boundaries, the program may print one or more blank pages; this is not a bug in the program but merely a result of the method that the program uses to divvy up the work area for printing. This system for numbering the pages is only used internally by Illustrator and the numbers are not printed on the pages, although they are displayed in the Print dialog box as you are printing the document as a way to gauge the process of the print job.

The size and shape of the printable page region is automatically changed if you change the page size specifications by choosing Page

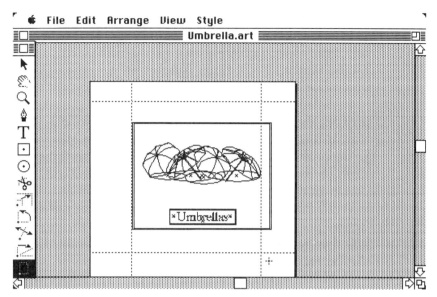

Figure 5-83.
The new Page grid keeps the umbrellas entirely on the first page.

Setup from the File menu and altering the specifications in the Page Setup dialog box. It's important to remember that the Page Setup dialog box is not always the same; since the page setup capabilities are different from printer to printer, the information displayed in the Page Setup dialog box is supplied by the printer icon in the system file for the printer that is actively in use (the Chooser in the Desk Accessory menu allows you to inspect and/or change the active printer). However, the way that Illustrator automatically breaks up the work area into regions may not be well suited to your particular piece of artwork. In order to correct this, you can use the page tool to control how Illustrator splits up the 14-by-14-inch work area into printable page areas.

If your artwork is large enough to fit on a single page but Illustrator's preset page breaks cause your artwork to be split into two or more pages, the page tool can be used to position the artwork entirely within one page region. If your artwork is too large to fit on a single page, the page tool can be used to place the page breaks on the best places to divide your artwork. Placing the page breaks creatively can make it easier to reassemble large pieces of artwork from their component printouts.

Before you use the page tool you will probably want to use either the zoom tool to zoom out to a view that will allow you to see the entire 14-by-14-inch work area within the active window or choose

Fit In Window from the View menu (or press Command-M or double-click on the hand tool as shortcuts). To use the page tool, first select the tool by pointing to it on the tool palette and clicking the mouse button. The pointer will turn into a plus sign (+) whenever you move it into the active window.

In order to move the page grid, first place the pointer over your artwork and hold down the mouse button; as soon as you hold down the button, Illustrator displays a dotted rectangle that corresponds to the printable area of a page (as currently defined in the Page Setup dialog box). The pointer (+) will be positioned at the lower left-hand corner of the dotted rectangle (see Figure 5-82).

While holding down the mouse button, drag the rectangle to the desired position over your artwork and release the button; Illustrator will then redraw the page grid according to your placement of the dotted rectangle.

If the artwork doesn't quite fit onto a single page you can experiment with reducing the image that will be printed on the page by choosing Page Setup from the File menu and altering the reduction specifications in the Page Setup dialog box. This will squeeze more artwork on the page and will also enlarge the size of the printable page area on the page grid of the active document.

If your artwork is short and wide rather than tall and narrow, you can also use the Page Setup dialog box to change the orientation of the page from normal (the image in the dialog box is vertical) to landscape (the image in the dialog box is on its side).

For more detailed information on the Page Setup dialog box see the section about the Print command on the File menu. Keep in mind that reducing or enlarging the image using the Reduce or Enlarge options in the Page Setup dialog box only affects printing and has no effect on the size of the artwork in your Illustrator document; the only way to alter the size of your artwork is with the scale tool.

The Apple Menu

The Apple menu is located to the far left of the menu bars and appears as a small Apple Computer logo. It contains the About Illustrator command, the Help command, and the Macintosh's desk accessories that are always available to you while you are using most Macintosh applications. The exact number and type of desk accessories that appear on this menu depends on what desk accessories have been installed in your Macintosh startup disk's system file with the Font/Desk Accessory Mover or other program. See your Macintosh owner's manual for more information about the Font/Desk Accessory Mover and the Macintosh's desk accessories.

About Illustrator

The About Illustrator command brings up the About Illustrator dialog box shown in Figure 5-86. Useful information found in the About Illustrator dialog box includes the version number of the

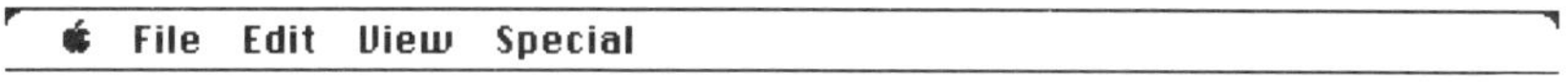

Figure 5-84.
The Macintosh Finder's menu bar.

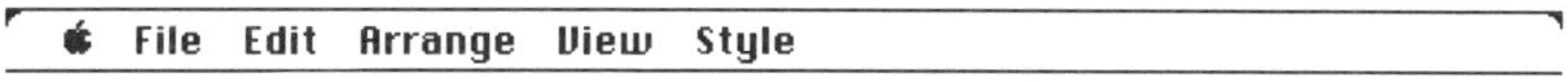

Figure 5-85.
Adobe Illustrator's menu bar.

Figure 5-86.
The Adobe Illustrator information box.

program and the amount of free memory available when you started the program without any open documents (expressed both in terms of bytes and as a percentage of free memory).

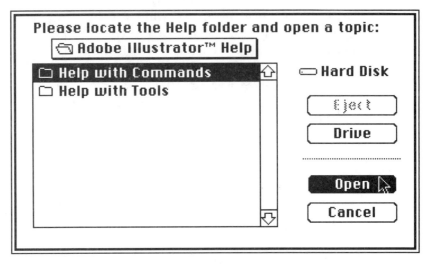

Figure 5-87.
Opening the Help with Commands folder from the Help dialog box.

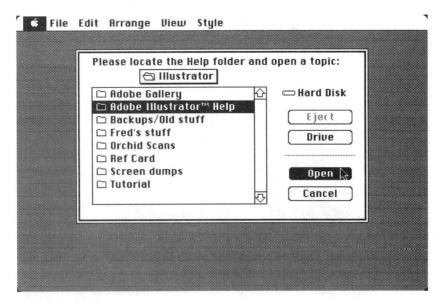

Figure 5-88.
Opening the Help folder.

Help

The Help command is used for accessing help screens that explain how commands and tools work. Selecting Help from the Apple menu brings up the Help dialog box shown in Figures 5-87 and 5-88. Tto use Illustrator's Help facility you must have the help folder on the same disk as the Illustrator program.

The Alarm Clock

Selecting the Alarm Clock desk accessory from the Apple menu brings up a box containing the date and time (Figure 5-89). When first displayed, the clock only displays the time; clicking on the small lever at the right-hand side of the desk accessory expands the clock to allow you to see or set the date and alarm or set the time. Set the time by clicking on the image of the clock face (bottom left). Change the date by clicking on the calendar (bottom center). Set the alarm by clicking on the alarm clock (bottom right). When the clock is displayed, you can use the Copy and Paste commands to copy the displayed time and paste it into any Macintosh document.

Calculator

Selecting the Calculator desk accessory from the Apple menu brings up the image of a small calculator (see Figure 5-91). This can be useful for calculations such as the amount of reduction or enlargement needed to scale your artwork to fit into a particular page layout.

Figure 5-89
The Clock accessory after it has been opened.

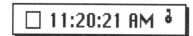

Figure 5-90
The Clock accessory.

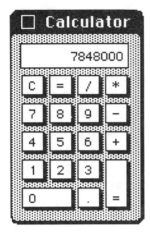

Figure 5-91
The Calculator accessory.

The calculator supports the standard Cut, Copy, and Paste commands so that you can copy a number from a document and paste it into the calculator for use in a calculation, or you can copy the result of the calculation and paste it into any Macintosh document.

To remove the Calculator desk accessory, click the small box in the upper left-hand corner of the desk accessory.

Chooser

Selecting the Chooser desk accessory from the Apple menu brings up the Chooser dialog box that is used for selecting printers, file servers, and other remote devices that can be attached to your Macintosh.

See your computer manual for more information about the version of the Chooser accessory for your computer.

Control Panel

Selecting the Control Panel desk accessory from the Apple menu brings up the Control Panel dialog box that is used for selecting options related to the mouse, keyboard, monitor or other system peripheral currently being used by your Macintosh.

See your computer manual for more information about the version of the Chooser accessory for your computer.

Key Caps

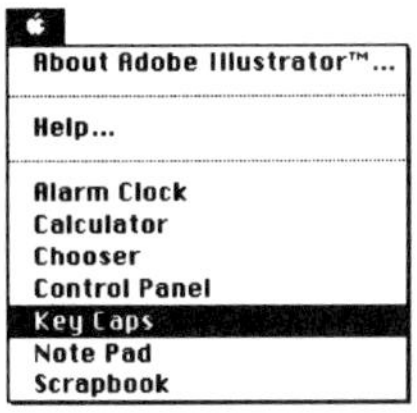

Selecting the Key Caps desk accessory from the Apple menu brings up an image of the keyboard that appears in the middle of the screen, and a special Key Caps menu that appears as the last item on the menu bar. The Key Caps menu (Figure 5-92) allows you to choose one of the typefaces (fonts) available in the system file of the startup disk for displaying on the Key Caps keyboard. The Key Caps keyboard (Figure 5-93) lets you see what the different typefaces installed in your Macintosh's system file look like. When you choose a typeface from the Key Caps menu, you will see its lowercase character set on the Key Caps keyboard. If you want to see the uppercase characters, simply press the Shift key. Likewise, pressing the Caps Lock, Shift, or Option keys, or any combination, will display the characters that will be generated if you were to type the same combination of keys in that particular typeface while using any Macintosh application. This provides a handy way to find out how to generate special characters and symbols in a particular typeface.

You can type on the actual keyboard by hand, or you can type on the Key Caps keyboard by pointing to a key and clicking the mouse. Anything you type while the Key Caps desk accessory is active will be

Figure 5-92.
The Key Caps menu.

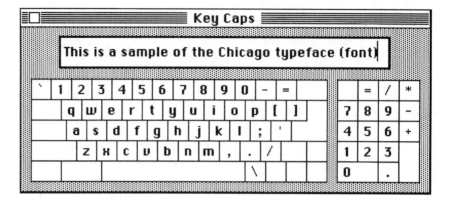

Figure 5-93
The Key Caps desk accessory displaying the Chicago typeface.

displayed in the text window at the top of the Key Caps keyboard; this text can be cut, copied, or pasted into any other desk accessory or Macintosh document. To remove the Key Caps desk accessory, click the small box in the upper left-hand corner of the desk accessory.

Note Pad

Selecting the Note Pad desk accessory from the Apple menu brings up an image of a small 8-page note pad (Figure 5-94) that can be used for storing text only. Text can be cut, copied, and pasted to and from a Macintosh document using the Edit menu. Text in the Note Pad can be cut and pasted into the Type dialog box in sections up to 254 characters in length. Text in the Note Pad is automatically saved when you close the Note Pad. To close the Note Pad, click the small box in the upper left-hand corner of the desk accessory.

Figure 5-94.
The Note Pad desk accessory.

Scrapbook

Selecting the Scrapbook desk accessory from the Apple menu brings up the Scrapbook. The Scrapbook can hold many items, either text or graphics. To place something in the Scrapbook, first select it, then move it to the Clipboard by cutting it or copying it. Next, open up the Scrapbook by selecting it from the Apple menu and paste it into the Scrapbook by using the Paste command on the Edit menu. To get something out of the Scrapbook, first select Scrapbook from the Apple menu and then issue the copy command by either selecting Copy from the Edit menu or by pressing Command-C.

The Scrapbook displays items in a window (Figure 5-95). This window often doesn't let you see the entire item, but it is good enough for most identification purposes. Below the window is a scroll bar that scrolls the various items that are stored in the Scrapbook past the window. You can move forward or backward through the items in the Scrapbook by clicking in front of or behind the box in the scroll bar; alternatively you can click the small arrow on the right end of the scroll bar to go forward or the small arrow on the left end to go backward. Beneath the left end of the scroll bar are a pair of numbers separated by a slash. In the above illustration the numbers are 39/41. These numbers indicate that the item that you can view in the window is the 39th item out of a total of 41 items. Beneath the right end of the scroll bar is a word, in this case the word "PICT," indicating that the item being viewed is stored in the Scrapbook in the PICT file format. It should be noted that items

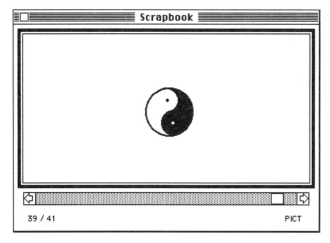

Figure 5-95.
The Scrapbook desk accessory.

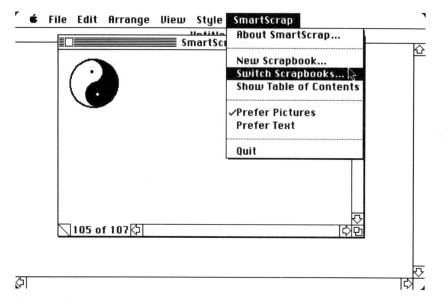

Figure 5-96.
The SmartScrap desk accessory from Solutions, Inc. is a more versatile version of Apple's standard scrapbook, offering the ability to work with multiple scrapbooks. SmartScrap also offers a scrolling selection marquee for selecting objects bigger than the scrapbook display window..

stored in the PICT and MacPaint formats in the Scrapbook cannot be pasted into template documents with Illustrator; you must paste them into template documents with the MacPaint program or another painting or drawing program that is compatible with MacPaint or PICT files. However, pieces of Illustrator artwork such as paths or other objects can be pasted into the Scrapbook as Illustrator objects and stored for later use.

To close the Scrapbook, point to the small box in the upper left-hand corner of the desk accessory and click the mouse button. You can save different scrapbooks by renaming the Scrapbook File icon in the system folder (usually named "System Folder") and saving it in a different folder. The Macintosh operating system will only use the Scrapbook named "Scrapbook File" that is located in the same folder as the System and Finder icons; renaming a Scrapbook or moving it to another folder or disk prevents it from being used. If the system does not find a Scrapbook named "Scrapbook File" in the same folder with the System and Finder icons, the system will automatically create a new empty Scrapbook in that same folder as soon as you select Scrapbook from the Apple menu.

File Menu

The File menu is used for working with Illustrator artwork and template documents. The commands on the File menu let you create new Illustrator documents, open existing Illustrator documents, open a template document while creating a new Illustrator document, close and save Illustrator documents, set up pages for printing, print Illustrator documents, and quit the Illustrator program to return to the Macintosh's Finder. The File menu gives you access to the Macintosh's operating system from within the Illustrator program.

New...

The New command creates a new Illustrator document. Select New from the File menu (or press Command-N as a shortcut) to bring up the New Document dialog box, which presents you with several options for creating a new Illustrator document (see Figure 5-96). You can then use the scroll box to select either a MacPaint file or PICT file to use as a template for tracing with Illustrator, or you can click on the button labeled "None" to create a new Illustrator

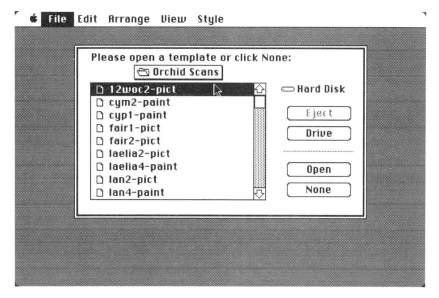

Figure 5-96.
Selecting a PICT file to use as a template.

document without a template. New documents are automatically given the name "Untitled art" followed by a colon (:) and the name of the template, if a template was used. To name a new Illustrator document, you must save the document using either the Save, Save As or Quit options from the File menu. The Illustrator program will not let you quit without first naming any unnamed documents.

Open...

The Open command opens an existing Illustrator document and an associated template (if any) or opens a template document with a new untitled Illustrator document. You can issue the Open command by either selecting Open from the File menu or by pressing Command-O as a shortcut. Use the Open command when you want to work on an existing Illustrator document, or as an alternative to the New command when you want to create a new Illustrator document from an existing template. After you select Open, the Get File dialog box appears and prompts you to select either an Illustrator document or a template (MacPaint or PICT file) from the scroll box. If you select an Illustrator document, the Illustrator program will attempt to locate the template that was used to create the Illustrator document (if there was a template). When the active window appears, it will have the name of the Illustrator document in the window's title bar; if there is a template associated with the Illustrator document, the name of the Illustrator document will be followed by a colon (:) and then the name of the template document. If you want to force the Illustrator program to prompt you to select a template when you open an existing Illustrator document (instead of automatically

Figure 5-97.
The title bar of a window after opening a template called "music stand template" with a new, untitled Illustrator document.

Figure 5-98.
The title bar of a window after opening an existing Illustrator document (called "music stand art"). The associated template, "music stand template," is automatically opened.

trying to retrieve a template), you can hold down the Option key while selecting Open from the File menu (or while pressing Command-O as a shortcut). Forcing Illustrator to prompt you for a template is useful when you are creating a piece of artwork that is based on more than one template.

If you select a template document from the scroll box, Illustrator will assume that you want to create a new Illustrator document based on that template. When the new active window appears, the name of the Illustrator document will appear as "Untitled Art" followed by a colon (:) and then the name of the template document (see Figure5-97).

After you open the template and/or Illustrator document, you may not be able to see all of (or any of) the image in the active window. To bring the image into view, you should first try scrolling the image using either the scroll bars or the hand tool (see page 119 for more information about the hand tool). If the image is too large to fit into the active window, you can use the zoom tool to zoom out from the image step by step until it fits in the window. Alternatively, you can select Fit In Window from the View menu or double-click on the hand tool to fit the entire 14-by-14-inch document in the window and then use the zoom tool to zoom in on the image.

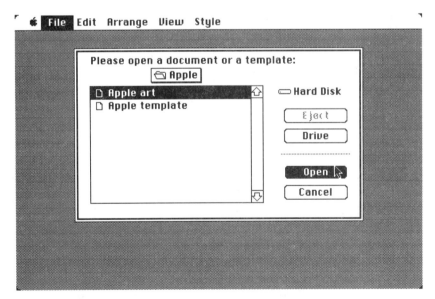

Figure 5-99.
Selecting the Illustrator document "Apple art" from the Get File dialog box.

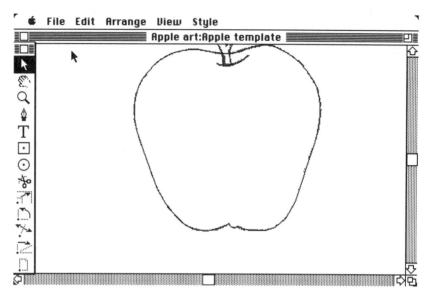

Figure 5-100.
How the screen looks after the illustrator document and its associated template are opened.

Close

The Close command is used to close the current Illustrator document and template (if any) without quitting the Illustrator program. Use the Close command when you have finished working with one document and want to work on another. Selecting Close from the File menu is equivalent to clicking the mouse button inside the small box located in the upper left-hand corner of the window's title bar. When you issue the Close command, the file is closed and removed from the Illustrator desktop if no changes have been made to the document since the last time it was saved. If changes have been made since the last save, a dialog box will ask if you want the changes to be saved. Press the Yes button by clicking on it with the mouse button if you want to save the changes; click No to close the document without saving the changes; or click Cancel to return to the Illustrator file and cancel the Close command. The bold double line surrounding the Yes button indicates that if you simply press the Return key, that button will be activated to save your changes.

If it is a new untitled document, the program will bring up the Save File dialog box and request that you give the document a name and save it.

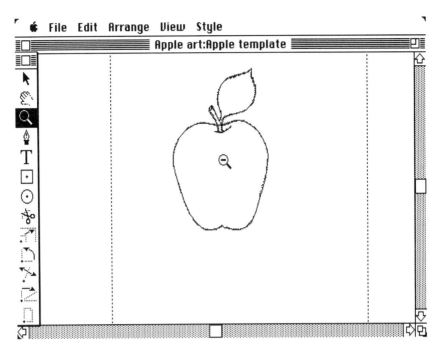

Figure 5-101.
Zooming out from the document allows you to view all of the artwork in the window.

Save

The Save command is used to save and name a new untitled Illustrator document or to periodically save an existing document. You should remember to save your documents frequently while you are working on them as a preventative measure against a problem with the document, a system crash, or a power failure. You can issue

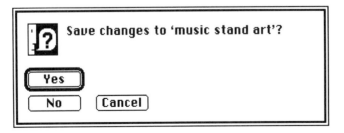

Figure 5-102.
The Save Changes dialog box will appear if you try to close a document without first saving your changes.

the Save command by either selecting Save from the File menu or by pressing Command-S (see Figure 5-103). The Save command does not affect the template document since the template cannot be altered by the Illustrator program. If you are saving a new untitled document for the first time, you will be presented with the Save As dialog box, which will prompt you for the name that you want to use for saving the document. For more information about the Save As dialog box see the section on the Save As command below.

If you have already saved the document (i.e., if it already has a name other than "Untitled Art"), then issuing the Save command will not bring up the Save As dialog box. Instead, the document will be saved under the current name, on the same volume (folder, disk drive, or other storage device) that it was opened from, and the saved document will replace the previous version of the document.

Save As...

The Save As command is used to either save the active Illustrator document under a different name, on a different volume (a volume can be a folder, disk drive, or other storage device), or in a different file format. To issue the Save As command, you must select Save As from the File menu; this command brings up the Save As dialog box

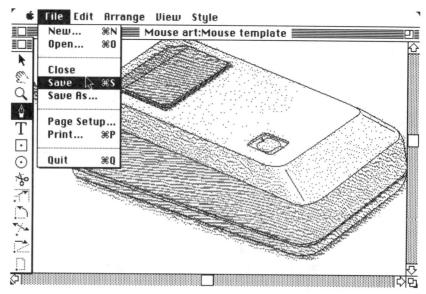

Figure 5-103.
Issuing the Save command from the File menu.

that lets you specify how you want the Illustrator document in the active window to be saved. If you want to save the document under a different name, you simply type in the new name in the box that appears below the words "Save document as:" in the dialog box. You can then either save the file in the current folder that is displayed at the top of the dialog box, or you can select a different file folder and/or disk drive. To select a different folder, point to the folder name and scroll down the list of folders (if any) that will appear under the current folder. If the file is stored on the disk without being placed in a folder, the icon and name of the disk will appear where the folder appears at the top of the dialog box.

If you want to save the file on a different disk drive, point to the Drive button and click the mouse button; each click will display a different disk drive until all the drives connected to the system (including AppleShare and other network drives) have been displayed. If only one drive is connected, the Drive button will be grayed-out and cannot be used. In figure 5-105, the Eject button is grayed-out, signifying that the hard disk cannot be ejected. If a drive with removable disks is selected, the Eject button appears normal and pressing it would eject the disk from its drive so that another disk could be inserted. Illustrator normally saves Illustrator documents as PostScript-only files.

You can use Illustrator-created artwork with page layout programs (such as PageMaker from Aldus, MacPublisher III from Boston Publishing Systems, XPress from Quark, ReadySetGo! 3 from Letraset, Scoop from Target Software, Ragtime from Orange Micro, FullWrite Professional from Ann Arbor Softworks, More from Living Videotext, and Microsoft's Word) and other programs on the Macintosh or on IBM computers if you save the files in the appropriate Encapsulated PostScript format (EPSF). However, some programs are not capable of reading Encapsulated PostScript files, and other programs do not save the required "well-behaved" EPSF file. Check your application program to verify that it will work with Encapsulated PostScript files before you decide to use that program with Illustrator-created artwork.

To select one of the two Encapsulated PostScript formats, point to the small circle preceding the format you want to select and click the mouse button. A small dot will appear inside the circle you choose to indicate that you have selected that format. Illustrator uses special icons to represent Encapsulated PostScript files which, unlike regular Illustrator files, cannot be viewed and edited with most word processing programs. Also, Macintosh Encapsulated PostScript files contain a QuickDraw PICT format image of the preview artwork for use as a guide in placing it in a page layout or other program.

It is sometimes possible to transfer Illustrator artwork to other Macintosh applications via the Clipboard, using Illustrator's option-copy feature (see Appendix A of the Illustrator User's Manual). This method is not recommended because it will not work with some applications (such as PageMaker 1.2) and because the Clipboard cannot handle very large/complex artwork. While not recommended, it does seem to work with current versions of ReadySetGo! 3 and Microsoft Word 3.0.

Another alternative is available if your application has a PostScript Place function (i.e., the ability to incorporate PostScript commands directly into a document). The disadvantages here are that the application will not be able to display a screen representation of the PostScript artwork and you may need to know where the importing application expects the origin (0,0 point) to be, and other details specific to PostScript. To use this method, you should save your Illustrator file as "PostScript only" (rather than Encapsulated PostScript). Since "PostScript only" is simply a text file of PostScript commands, it should be possible to incorporate these commands into any application that has a PostScript Place capability.

When you have finished selecting the Save As options you desire, point to the Save button and click the mouse button. If you want to return to the Illustrator program without saving your work, press the Cancel button to send the dialog box away and return to the program.

Illustrator document

Mac encaps. PostScript

PC encaps. PostScript

Figure 5-104.
The screen icons for the three different types of PostScript documents created by Illustrator.

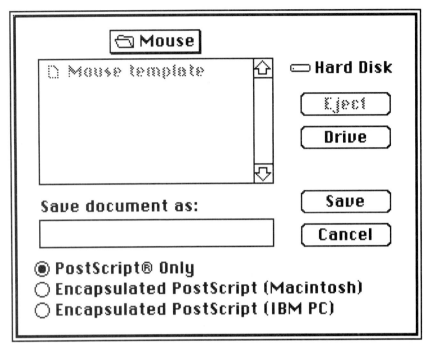

Figure 5-105.
The Save As dialog box.

Page Setup...

The Page Setup command is used to select the page-oriented (as opposed to printer-oriented) options that affect how the page will be printed. Selecting the Page Setup command from the File menu brings up the Page Setup dialog box, allowing you to specify the paper size, either vertical (portrait) or horizontal (landscape) page orientation, a percentage of reduction or enlargment, and other printer options available for the selected printer. Unlike most of the other dialog boxes in Illustrator, the Page Setup dialog box and the related Print dialog box are provided by the Macintosh's operating system, not the Illustrator program. Although the Page Setup dialog boxes for different printers appear similar, there are some important differences, described here in greater detail. For more information about printing, see the section on the Print command.

The options you specify in the Page Setup dialog box are only applied to the Illustrator document displayed in the window that was

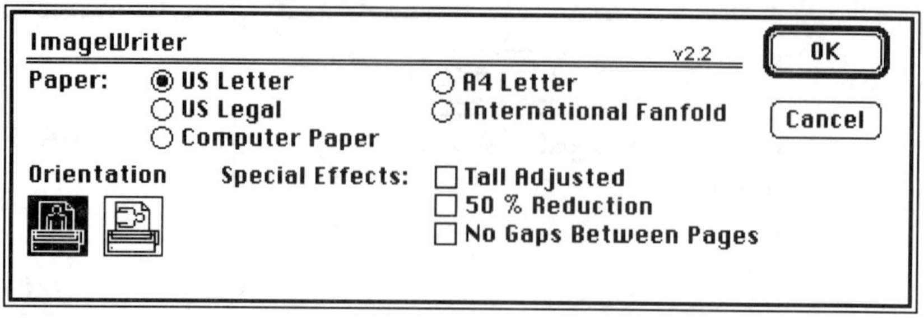

Figure 5-106.
The ImageWriter Page Setup dialog box.

active when you selected the Page Setup command. Any options you specify will be saved with the Illustrator document. Since the options you select only affect the document in the active window, you will need to select Page Setup and specify the options for other documents separately, after you have activated each of the windows that display those documents. Because the Page Setup options are saved with the document, and the options and dialog boxes vary for different printers, Illustrator will not automatically change all the Page Setup options if you change printers. If you use a different printer than the one you specified in the Page Setup dialog box, Illustrator will use the default options provided by the new printer's system resource file instead of the options that were saved with the document. Therefore, if you change printers, check the Page Setup dialog box to make sure that the options you desire are selected.

If you are using the ImageWriter for printing, the Page Setup dialog box will look similar to the one shown in Figure 5-106. The Page Setup dialog box is revised from time to time, and the current version number is displayed at the top of the dialog box near the OK button. In Figure 5-106, the version of the dialog box is v2.2. This version number should match the number displayed in the Print dialog box.

The first set of options, grouped together under the heading "Paper," allows you to specify the exact size of the paper you are using with the ImageWriter. US Letter means single sheets of standard 8 1/2-by-11-inch paper. US Legal refers to single sheets of 8 1/2-by-14-inch paper. A4 Letter describes international-sized sheets that are 210mm wide by 297mm tall. Select one of these three types of paper if your printer is equipped with an optional single-sheet feeder.

Computer Paper refers to 8 1/2-by-11-inch continuous fanfold paper used with the tractor-feed that is standard on the ImageWriter and most other dot-matrix printers. International fanfold is the A4-sized sheets in a continuous fanfold for use with tractor-feed equipped printers. Select a paper type by clicking the mouse button in the small circle preceding the desired option; a small dot appears inside the circle you select.

The next set of options (see Figure 5-106) lets you specify the orientation of the printout. The first icon represents a vertical (also known as portrait) orientation for printing; this is the standard way pages are printed. The second icon represents a horizontal (also known as landscape) orientation for printing. When horizontal orientation is selected, the artwork is printed sideways; an ideal choice for printing a short, wide image that would not fit on the page in the vertical orientation. If you want to control how the page orientation affects the Illustrator document, you can use the page tool to preview how the page will be set up and change the way Illustrator splits up the pages for printing. Changes made in the Page Setup dialog box will be reflected in the grid controlled by the page tool. (For more information about the page tool see page 177.) You can select either the vertical orientation icon or the horizontal orientation icon by simply pointing to it and clicking the mouse button. The selected icon will appear black.

The "Special Effects" options in the ImageWriter's Page Setup dialog box relate to special effects to select to modify the printing process. The first of these effects is called "Tall Adjusted"; it adjusts the ImageWriter's printing to compensate for the fact that, unlike the LaserWriter, there are a different number of dots per inch vertically than there are horizontally. Because Illustrator was designed for a PostScript printer with the same number of dots both horizontally and vertically, you should always select the Tall Adjusted option when printing Illustrator documents on the ImageWriter to prevent the artwork from being distorted. To select the Tall Adjusted option, point to the small box preceding the option and click the mouse button. A small "x" will appear inside the box to signify that the option has been selected. The next option is called "50% Reduction"; it allows you to specify whether or not you want your artwork reduced by 50% (i.e., shrunk down to half its size) before it is printed. You select this option by clicking in the box preceding it. The last option is "No Gaps Between Pages;" this option is not relevant to Illustrator and should not be selected.

LaserWriter Page Setup

If you are using the LaserWriter for printing, you will see a Page Setup dialog box that resembles the ImageWriter's dialog box. The LaserWriter's Page Setup dialog box is revised from time to time by Apple, and the current version number is displayed on the top right of the dialog box near the OK button. In the example shown in Figure 5-107, the version of the dialog box is indicated as v3.3. This version number should match the number displayed in the Print dialog box.

The first set of options are grouped together to the right of the word "Paper." These options allow you to specify the exact size of the paper that you are using with the printer. US Letter means sheets of the standard 8 1/2-by-11-inch paper. US Legal refers to sheets of 8 1/2-by-14-inch paper. Although the LaserWriter can handle legal-sized sheets of paper, it will only print on the top section of the paper in an area equivalent to that of a regular 8 1/2-by-11-inch page. However, there are other PostScript printers that can print on the entire legal-sized page or even larger pages. A4 Letter refers to international-sized sheets of paper that are 210mm wide by 297mm tall. B5 Letter refers to a smaller type of international-sized sheets of paper that are 176mm wide by 250mm tall. Select the type of paper you are using by clicking the mouse in the small circle preceding the desired option. A small dot appears inside the circle for your selection.

To the right of the "Paper" option is the "Reduce or Enlarge:" option that lets you specify a percentage to enlarge or reduce the Illustrator document for printing. After the words "Reduce or Enlarge:" is a small box followed by a percent sign(%). If you want to reduce or enlarge your document prior to printing, you can point to this box, click the mouse button to select it, and enter a percentage

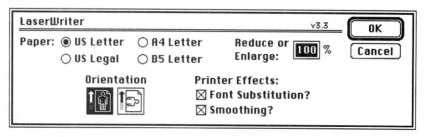

Figure 5-107.
The LaserWriter Page Setup dialog box.

that represents the final size you desire. Selecting a 70% reduction will print the page 30% smaller, and selecting 140% will print the page 40% larger. Each PostScript printer has a different range of enlargements or reductions that it can perform; the Apple LaserWriter Plus allows a maximum 400% enlargement (four times as large) and a minimum 25% reduction (four times as small). Therefore, with the LaserWriter Plus you can enter any percentage between 25% and 400%. Reducing the image can be handy for getting it to fit on a single page; enlarging is great for inspecting details. Keep in mind that reducing or enlarging documents with the Page Setup dialog box does not affect the size of the actual document or the artwork in the document. The only way to actually change the size of the artwork in a document is to use the scale tool (a description of the scale tool begins on page 154).

The Orientation options lets you specify the orientation of the printout. The first icon represents a vertical (portrait) orientation for printing; this is the standard way pages are printed. The second icon represents a horizontal (landscape) orientation for printing. When a horizontal orientation is selected, the artwork will be printed out sideways; this is good for printing a short, wide image that would not fit on the page in the vertical orientation. If you want to control how the page orientation affects the Illustrator document, you can use the page tool to preview how the page will be set up and change the way Illustrator splits up the pages for printing. Changes made in the Page Setup dialog box will be reflected in the page-division grid controlled by the page tool. (For more information about the page tool, see the description that begins on page 177.) You select either the vertical orientation icon or the horizontal orientation icon by simply pointing to it and clicking the mouse button. The icon that is selected will turn black.

The last of the LaserWriter's Page Setup options is titled "Printer Effects." This set of options is not relevant to the Illustrator program. Smoothing is used to smooth out the step-ladder effect of bit-mapped images such as a MacPaint document; since Illustrator stores artwork as vector graphics as opposed to bit-mapped graphics, the Smoothing option is ignored by Illustrator. Although the Font Substitution option also has no effect on the printout, turning it off wastes computer memory and can slow down printing. Therefore, you should be sure that the Font Substitution option is selected (i.e., be sure that there is a small "x" in the box preceding the words "Font Substitution?"). If the Font Substitution option is not selected, select it by pointing to the small box preceding the option and clicking the mouse button. A small "x" will appear inside the box to signify that the option has been selected.

Print...

The Print command is used to select the printer-oriented (as opposed to page-oriented) options that affect how the page will be printed. Before printing you should familiarize yourself with the Page Setup options described above and make sure that the proper options are selected in the Page Setup dialog box. Selecting the Print command from the File menu (or pressing Command-P as a shortcut) brings up the Print dialog box. If you want to print without bringing up the Print dialog box (because you have already set the printer options the way you want), hold down the Option key while issuing the Print command.

The Print dialog box allows you to specify the number of copies to be printed, the range of pages to be printed, how the paper is handled by the printer, and other options that may be available for a particular printer. Unlike most of the other dialog boxes in Illustrator, the Print dialog box and the related Page Setup dialog box are provided by the Macintosh's operating system, not the Illustrator program. Although the Print dialog boxes for different printers look similar, there are some important differences which are described below in greater detail. The exact dialog box that will be presented depends on what printer is currently installed in the system and selected for use. To select a printer (if there is more than one installed in your system and connected to your Macintosh), you use the Chooser desk accessory described on page 184. It's usually a good idea to check the Chooser before printing to make sure the correct printer has been chosen.

Keep in mind that Illustrator was designed to work with PostScript printers. If you are using an ImageWriter or other dot-matrix or laser printer that uses the Macintosh's native QuickDraw graphics language instead of PostScript, the results will not be as good as they would be with a PostScript printer. Be sure to check your printer's documentation to find out if it uses PostScript. Some printers provide for PostScript as an option; if so, check to find out if that option is installed in your printer. Although the ImageWriter and other QuickDraw printers do not produce the best results, they are still useful for getting a rough idea of how the final PostScript printout will look. If you don't own a PostScript printer, you can make drafts on your ImageWriter (or similar printer) and take your

Illustrator document to a service bureau or other location that has a PostScript printer connected to a Macintosh for getting the final printout. If the place where you take your document to be printed doesn't have the Illustrator program, take along your original Illustrator Program diskette or a copy of the SendPS program that is described in chapter 1.

ImageWriter Printing

If you are using the ImageWriter printer (and it is properly attached, chosen, and set up) issuing the Print command will bring up an ImageWriter Print dialog box similar to the one pictured in Figure 5-108. The Print dialog box is revised periodically, and the current version number is displayed at the top right of the dialog box near the OK button. In the example shown in Figure 5-108, the version of the dialog box is indicated as v2.2. This version number is also the version number of the printer resource file that is usually found in the system folder.

The first set of options is labeled "Quality:." The print quality options let you select from two different densities of dots, "Best" and "Faster," and a high-speed text-only printing mode called "Draft." Illustrator artwork can only be printed in the Best or Faster modes. Illustrator text files can be printed in any mode using a word-processing program. Since the Illustrator program only prints the artwork, choose either Best or Faster; as implied in the choice, the Best mode takes considerably longer to print. Because the ImageWriter is usually only used for printing rough drafts, we usually print documents in the Faster mode to save time and wear on the printer and ribbon.

Below the "Quality:" options are the "Page Range:" options. Usually you will want to select all pages to be printed. "All" is the default setting, so it will probably be selected already. You can tell if

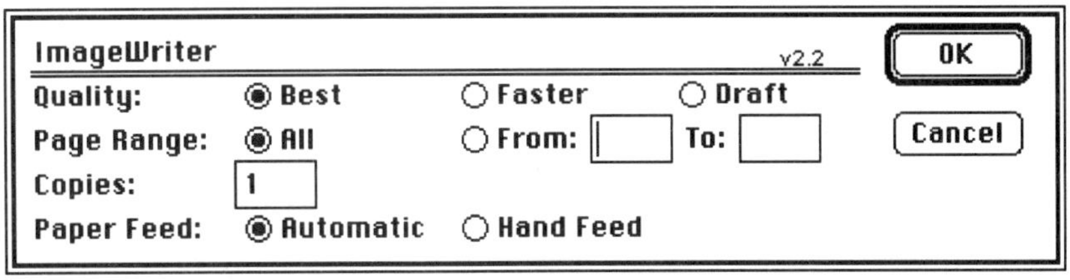

Figure 5-108.
The ImageWriter Print dialog box.

it is selected by the small spot inside the circle that precedes the word "All." If it is not selected, you can select it by pointing to the small circle in front of the word "All" and clicking the mouse button. You might have to print a specified range of pages if you are printing a piece of artwork that will not fit on one page and you do not want to print the entire 14-by-14-inch document. In order to determine (or control) how the Illustrator program divides the Illustrator document into pages for printing, you should familiarize yourself with the page tool that is described on page 177. If you know how Illustrator will number the pages (described in the section about the page tool), you can specify the range by clicking inside the circle preceding the word "From:" and then entering the two range numbers in their respective boxes. Before you can type a number in one of the range boxes, you must select the box by pointing to it and clicking the mouse.

Below the "Page Range:" option is the "Copies:" option that lets you specify how many copies of the document you would like to be printed. The default value is one copy. If you want to print two or more copies, point to the box after the word "Copies:," click the mouse button, and enter the number of copies you want printed.

At the bottom of the ImageWriter's Print dialog box are the "Paper Feed:" options. Select the "Automatic" option by clicking on it (if it's not already selected) if you are using a tractor-feed or automatic sheet-feeder on your ImageWriter. Select the "Hand Feed" option if you are going to hand feed each sheet into the printer.

When you have selected the Print options that you want, you can initiate the printing process by pointing to the OK button and clicking the mouse. If you don't want to print, click on the Cancel button to return to the Illustrator program. The double line around the OK button indicates that the button will be pushed if you press the Return key. After you press the OK button, a dialog box will be displayed, indicating that the connection to the printer is being established. Once the printing process has started, another dialog box is displayed, indicating which page is currently being sent to the printer.

If you want to stop the printing process while either of the two above dialog boxes are displayed, hold down the Command key while typing a period(.); this will cancel the printing. The printer may not stop right away due to the fact that the ImageWriter contains a small memory buffer that must be depleted before the Cancel command actually takes effect.

LaserWriter Printing

If you are using the LaserWriter printer (and it is properly attached, chosen, and set-up) issuing the Print command will bring up a LaserWriter Print dialog box similar to the one pictured in Figure 5-109. The Print dialog box is revised periodically by the printer manufacturer, and the current version number is displayed at the top right of the dialog box near the OK button. In Figure 5-109, the version of the dialog box is indicated as v2.2. This version number is also the version number of the printer resource file in the system folder.

The first of the LaserWriter print options is the "Copies:" option that lets you specify how many copies of the document you would like printed. The default value is one copy. If you want to print two or more copies, point to the box after the word "Copies:," click the mouse button, and enter the number of copies you want printed.

Next to the "Copies:" option is the "Pages:" option that lets you specify the range of pages you want printed. Usually you will want to select all pages to be printed, and "All" is the default setting that will probably be selected when the dialog box appears. You can tell if it is selected by a small spot inside the circle that precedes the word "All." If there is no spot inside the circle, it is not selected; you can select it by pointing to the circle (or anywhere on the word "All") and clicking the mouse. You will need to print only a specified range of pages if you are printing a piece of artwork that will not fit on one page and you do not want to print the entire piece of art. In order to determine (or control) how the Illustrator program divides the Illustrator document into pages for printing, you should familiarize yourself with the page tool.

If you know how Illustrator will number the pages (described in the section about the page tool), you can specify the range by clicking inside the circle preceding the word "From:" and then entering the

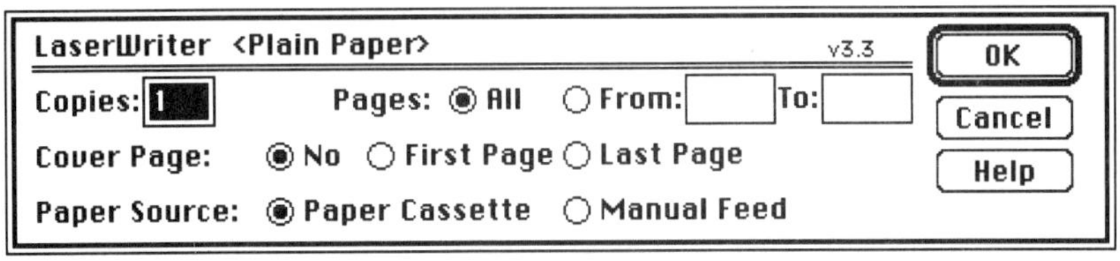

Figure 5-109.
The LaserWriter print dialog box. The words "<Plain Paper>" refer to the name of the printer; printers should be given unique names when there is more than one printer attached to the same network.

two range numbers in their respective boxes. Before you can type a number in one of the range boxes, you must select the box by pointing to it and clicking the mouse.

The next set of options is the "Cover Page:" options. Cover pages are not usually used, so the "No" selection is the default setting and will probably be selected when you bring up the dialog box. If you do want a cover page, select "First Page" by clicking on it to print the cover page before your artwork, or select "Last Page" by clicking on it to print the cover page after your artwork.

At the bottom of the LaserWriter's Print dialog box are the "Paper Source:" options. Select the "Paper Cassette" option by clicking on it (if it's not already selected) if you are using the normal paper tray in your LaserWriter. Select the "Manual Feed" option if you are going to hand feed each sheet into the printer.

When you have selected the Print options that you want, you can initiate the printing process by pointing to the OK button and clicking the mouse. If you don't want to print, click on the Cancel button to return to the Illustrator program. The double line around the OK button indicates that the button will be pushed if you press the Return key. After you press the OK button, a dialog box will be displayed, indicating that the connection to the printer is being established and, if necessary, that the Macintosh is initializing the printer. Once the printing process has started, another dialog box is displayed, indicating which page is currently being printed.

If you want to stop the printing process while either of the two above dialog boxes are displayed, hold down the Command key while typing a period(.); this will cancel the printing. The printer may not stop right away due to the fact that the LaserWriter contains a memory buffer that must be depleted before the Cancel command actually takes effect; using a print spooler can further prolong the time it takes to stop printing.

Quit

The Quit command ends your current session with Illustrator and returns you to the Macintosh desktop. You can issue the Quit command by either selecting Quit from the File menu or by pressing Command-Q as a shortcut. If you have not made any changes to the Illustrator document since the last time you saved it (changing the

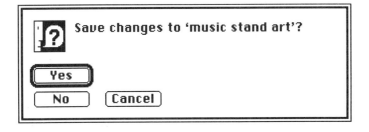

Figure 5-110.
The Save Changes dialog box

Page Setup options would count as a change), the program will end your session, close any documents, and automatically return you to the Macintosh desktop. However, if you have made any changes to the Illustrator document, the program will display the following dialog box to inquire whether or not you would like to save any changes you've made.

If you select the "Yes" button by pointing to it and clicking the mouse, Illustrator will save any open documents and then close them before returning to the Macintosh desktop. The double lines around the Yes button indicate that it will be selected if you press the Return key. If there are any new Illustrator documents (i.e. any that are named "Untitled Art"), the Save As dialog box will be displayed so that you can name the document(s) before quitting. If you select the "No" button by clicking on it, that document will be closed without any changes being saved. If you select the Cancel button, the Quit command will be canceled and you will return to the Illustrator program.

Edit Menu

The Edit menu is used for selecting various commands used to edit your Illustrator documents. The commands on the Edit menu allow you to undo the last action made by you or the computer; redo actions that were undone; cut, copy, and paste items to and from the clipboard; delete Illustrator artwork objects; select all the objects in a document, display the Clipboard, and hide the Clipboard once it is has been displayed.

Undo

The Undo command can be used to undo the last operation you or the computer performed. To issue the Undo command (see Figure 5-112), select Undo from the Edit menu or press Command-Z as a shortcut. The Undo command is not always available. If the Undo command is not available, it will appear grayed-out. If the Undo command is available, it will be listed in the menu followed by the action that will be undone if the command is issued. To undo the Undo command, see Redo below.

Redo

The Redo command can be used to undo the last Undo command that you issued. To issue the Redo command, select Redo from the Edit menu or press Command-Z as a shortcut. The Redo command is only available after the Undo command has been issued. If the Redo command is not available, it will appear grayed-out. If the Redo command is available, it will be listed in the menu followed by the action that will be redone if the command is issued. To undo the Redo command, see Undo above.

Cut

The Cut command removes all the selected items from the active window and places them in the Clipboard for temporary storage. You can issue the Cut command by either choosing Cut from the Edit menu or by pressing Command-X as a shortcut. Issuing the Cut command replaces whatever else was contained in the Clipboard with the selected items. After you issue the Cut command, you can check the contents of the Clipboard by issuing the Show Clipboard command. In the illustration of the Clipboard below, the words "28 artwork objects" means that there were 28 Illustrator objects se-

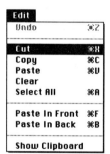

Figure 5-111.
The Clipboard.

Figure 5-112.
In these three examples the first image shows the Undo Pen selection, used for cancelling the Pen tool, the second image shows the option to Redo the Pen tool, and in the third image neither Undo or Redo is an available option

lected when the Cut command was issued, and these 28 objects are being temporarily stored in the Clipboard.

In order to permanently store items that are temporarily placed in the Clipboard, you must transfer them to the Scrapbook by selecting the Scrapbook command from the Apple menu and issuing the Paste command. If you want to undo a cut that you have made, select Undo Cut from the Edit menu or press Command-Z as a shortcut. In order to retrieve an item that was cut and placed in the Clipboard, click inside the window where you want the item to go and then issue one of the Paste commands (Paste, Paste In Front, or Paste In Back); the item will be pasted into the active window in accordance with the Paste command that you issued.

Copy

The Copy command is similar to the Cut command described above except that it places a copy of the selected items in the Clipboard without removing them. To issue the Copy command, either choose Copy from the Edit menu or press Command-C as a shortcut. Issuing the Copy command copies all the selected items in the active window and places them in the Clipboard for temporary storage (this replaces whatever else was contained in the Clipboard). To retrieve an item that was cut and placed in the Clipboard, click inside the window where you want the item to go and then issue one of the Paste commands described below (Paste, Paste In Front, or Paste In Back); the item will be pasted into the active window. The Copy command can also be used to generate a PICT-format image of the Preview view of the Illustrator artwork. To create a PICT preview of the artwork, hold down the Option key while issuing the Copy command.

Paste

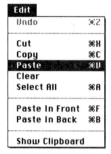

The Paste command retrieves items that are temporarily being stored in the Clipboard. You can issue the Paste command by either selecting Paste from the Edit menu or by pressing Command-V as a shortcut. Only Illustrator artwork objects that were cut or copied can be pasted directly into an Illustrator document with the exception of type into a typeblock. When you issue the Paste command, any Illustrator objects that are in the Clipboard will be pasted into the center of the active window and will be placed on top of all the other objects in the document. Even though pasting places all the objects in the Clipboard on top of everything else in the document, the relative painting order of the objects being pasted stays the same. If you want to place the pasted item in back of all or some of the objects, or if you want the objects pasted at the same locations they were cut or copied from, use one of the other Paste commands (either Paste In Front or Paste In Back). When you paste Illustrator objects from the Clipboard into an Illustrator document using the Paste command, the objects that are pasted will be selected and all the other objects will be deselected. Pasting does not remove the contents of the Clipboard.

Clear

The Clear command deletes any objects that are selected. You can issue the Clear command by selecting Clear from the Edit menu or by pressing either the Backspace key or the Clear key as shortcuts. For more information on how to select the object(s) that you want to delete, refer to the section about the selection tool. To delete all of the objects in an Illustrator document, first click in the document's window, then choose Select All from the Edit menu (or press Command-A as a shortcut), and then choose Clear from the Edit menu (or press the Backspace or Clear key as a shortcut). This action will delete everything in the active window, and all the objects in the window will disappear.

Select All

The Select All command selects all of the objects (points, lines, curves, etc.) that are contained in the document represented in the active window. You can issue the Select All command by either choosing Select All from the Edit menu or by pressing Command-A as a shortcut. If you want to deselect all the objects, simply point to any blank area in the document and click the mouse button. If you want to deselect one of the selected objects, point to the object you want to deselect and hold down the Shift key while clicking the mouse button; alternatively you can hold down the Shift key and drag the selection marquee around the object to deselect it (be careful not to accidently include another object in the marquee). If you want to deselect more than one of the selected objects, you can continue the deselection process just described by holding down the Shift key while pointing to the next object you want to deselect and either clicking on the object or dragging the selection marquee around it. Be sure that the objects you want deselected are actually selected in the first place; if you try deselecting an object that is not already selected, it will be added to the group of already selected objects instead. Also keep in mind that selecting or deselecting objects has no effect on the order in which they are painted by the program.

Paste In Front

The Paste In Front command is used for pasting items stored in the Clipboard in front of the items that are selected in an Illustrator document. You can issue the Paste In Front command by either selecting Paste In Front from the Edit menu or by pressing Command-F as a shortcut. Only Illustrator artwork objects that were cut or copied onto the Clipboard can be pasted directly into an Illustrator document. When you issue the Paste In Front command, any Illustrator objects that are in the Clipboard will be pasted in front of all the selected objects that are in the document represented by the active window, and behind the objects in the document that are not selected. Even though pasting the group of objects in the Clipboard changes the order in which that group is painted by the program, the relative painting order of the objects being pasted stays the same. If you want to place the pasted item in back of all or some of the objects, use the Paste In Back command described below.

When you paste Illustrator objects from the Clipboard into an Illustrator document using the Paste In Front command, the objects that are pasted will be selected and all the other objects will be deselected. It will also paste in front of everything if nothing is selected. Issuing the Paste In Front command does not remove the contents of the Clipboard. The Paste In Front command is handy for placing duplicates of objects on top of each other for special effects, such as placing an object that was outlined over an object that was filled with a shade of gray or color. Since pasting does not remove the contents of the Clipboard, all you need to do to create a duplicate of an object is to select it, copy it to the Clipboard, and issue the Paste In Front command.

Paste In Back

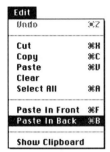

The Paste In Back command is used for pasting items stored in the Clipboard behind the items that are selected in an Illustrator document. You can issue the Paste In Back command by either selecting Paste In Back from the Edit menu or by pressing Command-B as a shortcut. Only Illustrator artwork objects that were cut or copied onto the Clipboard can be pasted directly into an Illustrator document. When you issue the Paste In Back command, any Illustrator objects that are in the Clipboard will be pasted in back of all the selected objects that are in the document that is in the active window, and in front of the objects in the document that are not selected. Even though pasting the group of objects in the Clipboard changes the order in which that group is painted by the program, the relative painting order of the objects being pasted stays the same. If you want to place the pasted item in front of all or some of the objects, use the Paste In Front command described above. When you paste Illustrator objects from the Clipboard into an Illustrator document using the Paste In Back command, the objects that are pasted will be selected and all the other objects will be deselected. It will also paste in back of everything if nothing is selected. Issuing the Paste In Back command does not remove the contents of the Clipboard.

Show Clipboard

The Show Clipboard command displays the current contents of the Clipboard each time you select Show Clipboard from the Edit menu. The Clipboard is a temporary storage area used by the Macintosh for storing items generated by the Cut and Copy commands. Items

Illustrator Dissected   213

stored in the Clipboard can be retrieved using the Paste commands. The Clipboard is common to virtually all Macintosh applications and can be used to easily move small amounts of data between applications.

Although many types of data can be stored in the Clipboard, only three types are relevant to Illustrator: Illustrator artwork objects, text, and PICT data. Only Illustrator artwork objects can be pasted directly into any window. Text can be cut or copied into the Clipboard from another program, from the Note Pad, or from the Scrapbook, but it can only be pasted into the Type dialog box, and it can only be 254 characters long. (For more information about the Type dialog box, refer to the type tool section.) PICT-formatted graphic images cannot be pasted into any Illustrator window (templates cannot be altered with Illustrator), but PICT images of the artwork's Preview view can be copied into the Clipboard by holding down the Option key while you issue the Copy command. Figures 5-113 through 5-115 show examples of how the three types of data stored in the Clipboard look when you issue the Show Clipboard command. The text and PICT images look like the actual data, whereas Illustrator artwork objects cannot be viewed and are represented by a statement of how many objects are currently in the Clipboard.

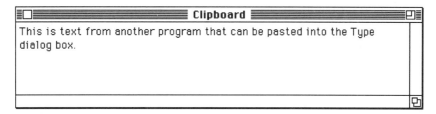

Figure 5-113.
Clipboard window showing text from a word processing program that can be pasted into the Type dialog box.

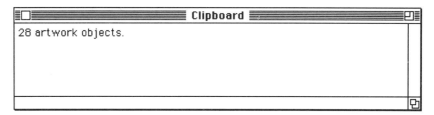

Figure 5-114.
Clipboard window showing Illustrator artwork pasted in the Clipboard.

Hide Clipboard

The Hide Clipboard command is used to hide the Clipboard after it has been displayed with the Show Clipboard command. To issue the Hide Clipboard command, either select Hide Clipboard from the Edit menu, select Close from the File menu, or click the mouse in the small close box located in the upper left-hand corner of the Clipboard window's title bar. The Clipboard can also be hidden by clicking in any other window besides the Clipboard window.

Arrange Menu

The Arrange menu is used for manipulating, modifying, and arranging Illustrator artwork objects. The commands on the Arrange menu allow you to repeat the transformation (scaling, rotating, reflecting, shearing, or moving) of an object or group of objects, combine objects into a unified group, join two endpoints, average two or more endpoints, and rotate the master *x* and *y* axes of a document.

Transform Again

The Transform Again command repeats the last transformation of an object or group of objects. You can issue the Transform Again command by either selecting Transform Again from the Arrange menu or by pressing Command-D as a shortcut. The word transformation refers to the actions of scaling, rotating, reflecting, shearing, and moving. If your last transformation created a transformed duplicate (because you held down the Option key while performing the transformation), the Transform Again command will both transform and duplicate the object again each time that you issue the command.

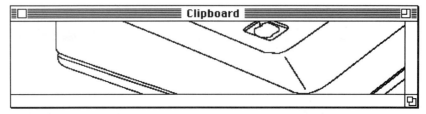

Figure 5-115.
Clipboard window showing a PICT Preview of the artwork pasted in the Clipboard.

Repeating transformations a number of times can be used to create special effects. For example, objects can be rotated around a central point (e.g. spokes on a wheel, petals on a daisy, etc.) by using the rotate tool and Rotate dialog box to specify a precise amount of rotation for an object, clicking on the Copy button in the dialog box, and issuing the Transform Again command to repeat the rotation and duplication. The Transform Again command can be issued repeatedly (to create any number of transformed duplicates) until you ultimately run out of memory in your computer. Although one megabyte of RAM memory is required as a minimum to run Illustrator, larger amounts of RAM may be required for extremely complex artwork.

Group

The Group command consolidates a number of Illustrator artwork objects into a single object. To issue the Group command, either select Group from the Arrange menu or press Command-G as a shortcut. Issuing the Group command converts all the objects that are selected in the active document into a single composite object. To select the objects that you want to group together you can either: 1) drag the selection marquee around the objects; 2) select the objects one-by-one by first pointing to and clicking on an object and then holding down the Shift key while you point to and click on the other objects you want included in the group; 3) select all the objects in the document for grouping by issuing the Select All command found in the Edit menu; or 4) issue the Select All command and then deselect the objects that you don't want in the group. Keep in mind that only complete paths can be grouped; therefore if any of the objects you have selected for grouping includes a partially selected path, the entire path will become part of the group. After you have selected the objects that you want grouped together you can issue the Group command to combine all the selected objects into a single grouped object.

Once a number of objects are grouped together with the Group command they can be selected, deleted, moved, scaled, rotated, reflected, sheared, cut, copied, pasted, or painted as a single unit. Combining objects into a group does not change the relative painting order of the objects in the group, but it does change the painting order of the group as a whole. When objects are grouped together Illustrator paints them starting with the top object in the group. If you want to change the order in which Illustrator objects and groups are painted, you must use the Paste In Front and Paste In Back commands in the Edit menu.

If you want to change the painting order of objects within a group, you must first ungroup the objects using the Ungroup command described below, and then use the Paste In Front and Paste In Back commands to change the order in which the component objects are painted by Illustrator. Grouped objects can be combined with other groups and/or objects to create a larger grouped object. Grouped objects cannot be changed with the pen tool unless they are ungrouped with the Ungroup command. Because grouped objects are more resistant to changes than ungrouped objects, grouping objects is a convenient way to "freeze" a path or object once you are finished drawing it to prevent accidental changes.

Ungroup

The Ungroup command breaks a grouped object down into its original component parts. You can issue the Ungroup command by either selecting Ungroup from the Arrange menu or by pressing Command-U. If any of the original components were also grouped objects, the Ungroup command will leave the component groups intact. If you want to break any of these component groups down into their original parts, you must repeat the Ungroup command after selecting the component group. Issuing the Ungroup command has no effect on which items are selected or on what order Illustrator paints the objects that were contained in the group.

Join

The Join command is used to connect two endpoints in order to either create a closed path from an open path or to combine two open paths into a single open path. The Join command either connects two endpoints that are apart from each other with a straight line or it combines two endpoints that are directly on top of one another into a single anchor point.

To issue the Join command, either select Join from the Arrange menu or press Command-J as a shortcut. You can only issue the Join command when two endpoints are selected. To select two endpoints that are on top of each other, drag the selection marquee over the points.

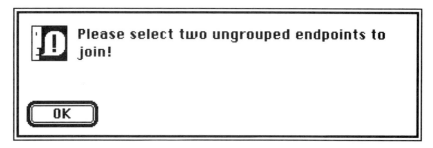

Figure 5-116.
If you attempt to issue the Join command when there are not exactly two endpoints connected, you will be presented with this error alert box.

Also, the two endpoints cannot belong to a grouped object; you must ungroup the object with the Ungroup command before joining the two desired endpoints. If you have issued the Join

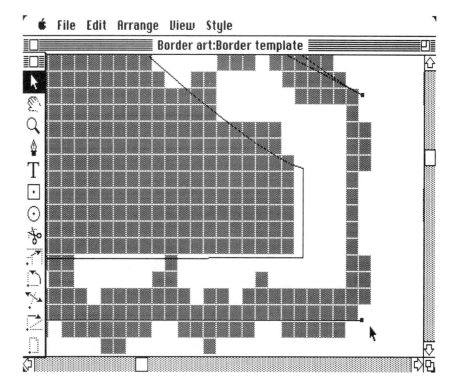

Figure 5-117.
This screen shows a piece of artwork that contains an open path with two endpoints that have been selected (the arrow is pointing to one of the endpoints).

command when exactly two endpoints are selected, Illustrator will either 1) draw a straight line segment between two endpoints that are apart from one another, leaving both the line and the two endpoints selected, or 2) combine two endpoints that are on top of each other into a single anchor point, leaving the new anchor point selected. If you selected the two endpoints of an open path when you issued the Join command, the path will be closed with a straight line. If you selected the endpoints of two different paths when you issued the Join command, the two paths will be connected (either with a straight line or by combining the two points) and will become one longer path. Joining points that are on top of each other is handy for connecting objects that were cut apart with the scissors tool. Figures 5-118 through 5-121 show the Join command in action.

Average

The Average command moves two or more anchor points to the average location of the points. You can issue the Average command by either selecting Average from the Arrange menu or by pressing Command-L as a shortcut. You can only issue the Average command if there are two or more anchor points selected (see Figure 5-122).

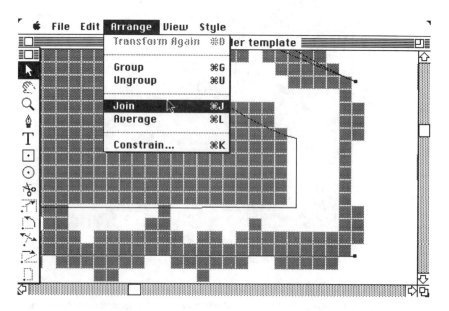

Figure 5-118.
Selecting the Join command from the Arrange menu.

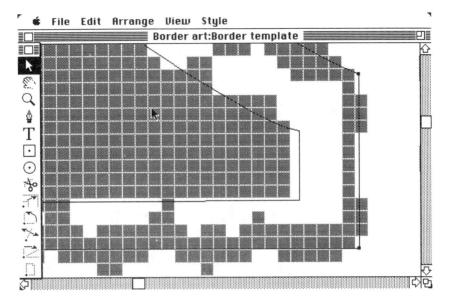

Figure 5-119.
The Join command instructs the computer to draw a straight line between the two endpoints, and leave the line and the endpoints selected.

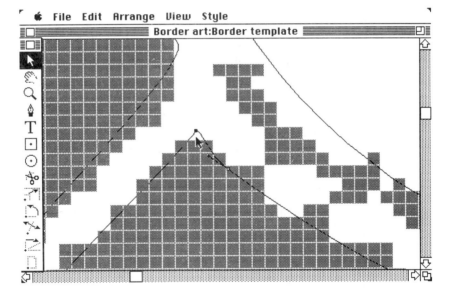

Figure 5-120.
Two endpoints are on top of each other, and they are both selected (the arrow is pointing to the two endpoints, although it looks like only a single anchor point). Use the selection marquee to select the two endpoints that are on top of one another.

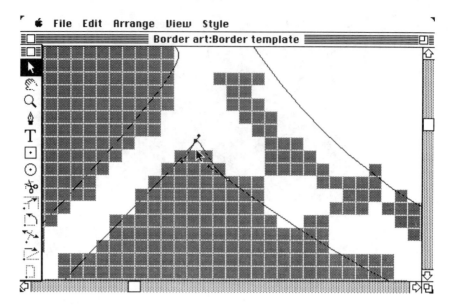

Figure 5-121.
This time the Join command was issued directly from the keyboard as a shortcut (Command-J). The screen shows the single anchor point that was created when the two endpoints were merged.

If you have issued the Average command with two or more anchor points selected, all the selected anchor points will move to their average location, and the paths and shapes connected to the points will change shape as they always do when any of their anchor points are moved. The Average command only moves anchor points on top of each other; it does not connect them, merge them, or join them. If you want to connect anchor points, you have to use the Join

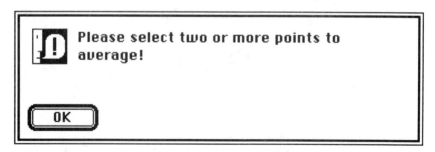

Figure 5-122.
If you attempt to issue the Average command when there are no points, or only one point selected, you will be presented with this error alert box.

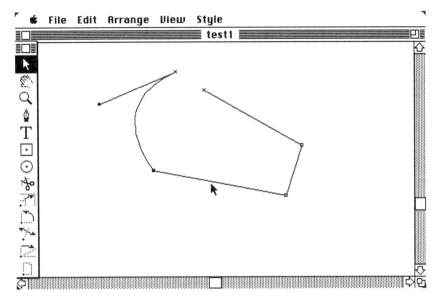

Figure 5-123.
This screen shows an open path; the two endpoints are not selected and therefore appear as small x's.

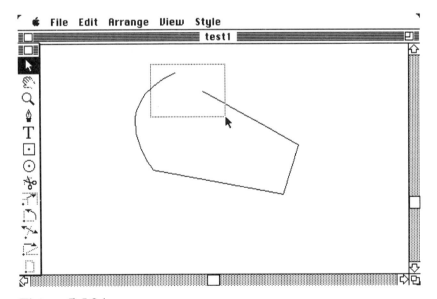

Figure 5-124.
The next step is to select the two endpoints that you want to move together. In this example we are using the selection marquee to select the open path's two endpoints.

command described above to connect them two at a time. Averaging anchor points is used mainly for moving points, paths, or other objects next to each other.

Figures 5-123 to 5-127 show how to close an open path with the Average command used in conjunction with the Join command.

Constrain

The Constrain command allows you to rotate the x and y axes of the active document and to set the "Snap to Point" option. Each time you start the Illustrator program, the *x* and *y* axes are set parallel to the sides of any document. You can use the Constrain command to alter the angle of the *x* and *y* axes relative to the sides of a document, but the new axes will affect any other documents you open or create during that Illustrator session. If you want to reset the axes, you must either use the Constrain command to reset them or quit and restart the program. Also, changes made to the *x* and *y* axes are not saved with a document; the next time you open the document (during another program session) the axes will be reset to their original position parallel to the sides of the document.

To issue the Constrain command select Constrain from the Arrange menu or press Command-K. Use the Constrain command to

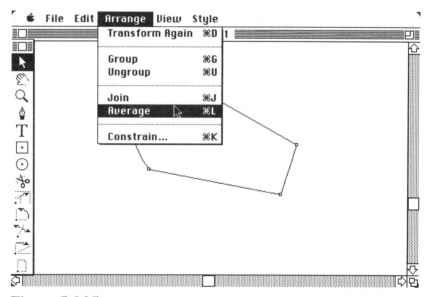

Figure 5-125.
The next step is to issue the Average command.

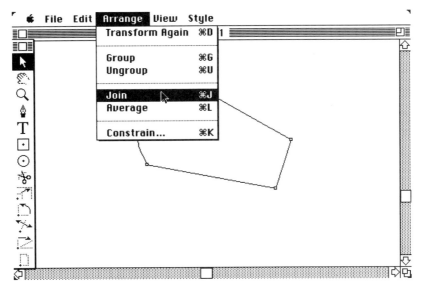

Figure 5-126.
The Average command only moves the points, it does not connect them. In order to merge the two selected endpoints into a single anchor point, you must issue the Join command, which will turn the open path (that looks like it is closed) into a closed path.

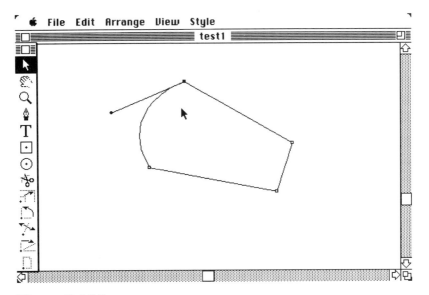

Figure 5-127.
This screen shows the resulting closed path.

set the *x* axis to horizontal and the *y* axis to vertical (this is the preset condition); to rotate both axes so that the *x* axis passes through any two anchor points that you select; or to rotate both axes by a precise angle that you specify. You can only issue the Constrain command when there are either no anchor points selected or when there are only two anchor points selected (see Figure 5-128).

In the Constrain dialog box, the "Horizontal and vertical axes" option, which sets the *x* and *y* axes parallel to the sides of the document, is selected. If you want to reset the *x* and *y* axes to their original settings, make sure no points are selected in the document (or that two points are selected), issue the Constrain command, and select the "Horizontal and vertical axes" option by clicking on it with the mouse. The small dot in the center of the circle preceding the option indicates that it is currently selected.

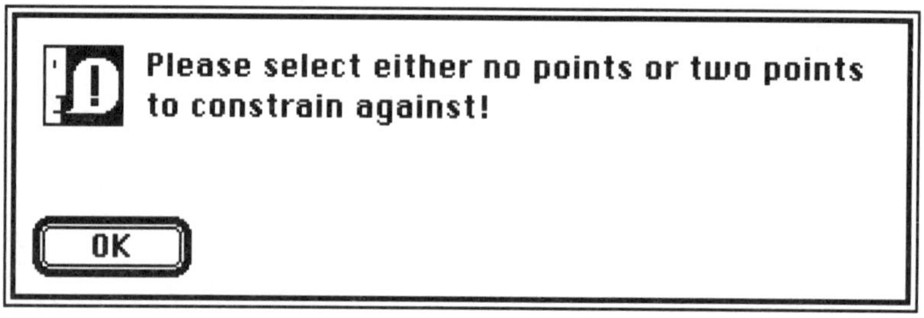

Figure 5-128.
If you try to issue the command when only one point, or three or more points are selected, you will be presented with this error alert box.

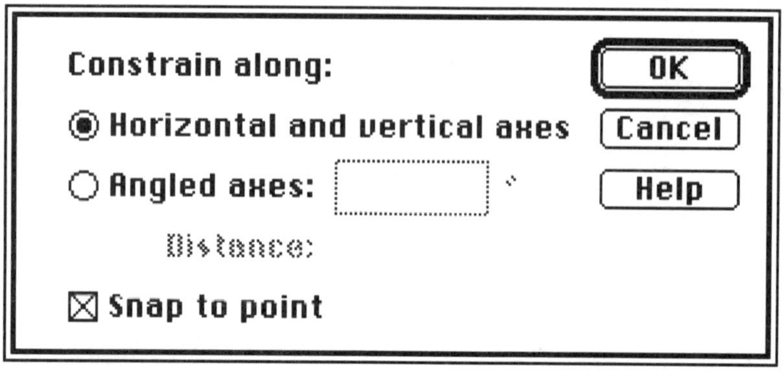

Figure 5-129.
Because no points were selected when the Constrain command was issued, the word "Distance:" is grayed-out. If two anchor points had been selected, the distance between the two points would have been displayed.

When the "Snap to point" option is turned on, an object being manipulated with a pointer moves onto an anchor point whenever the pointer is within two screen pixels of an anchor point. The small x preceding the "Snap to point" option indicates that the option is turned on; to turn it off, click in the box and the x will disappear.

The "Angled axes:" option displayed in Figure 5-130 shows the angle of the line that passes through the two anchor points you selected. This line will become the new *x* axis; both the *x* and *y* axes are rotated counterclockwise from the horizontal origin. The number after the word "Distance:" in the dialog box represents the distance in points (one point = 1/72 of an inch) between the two anchor points.

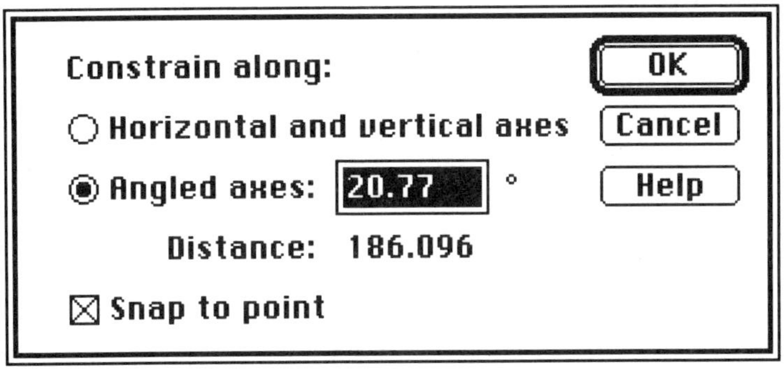

Figure 5-130.
To rotate the x and y axes so that the x axis passes through two anchor points that you have selected, select only the two desired points, then issue the Constrain command. The distance between the selected points is displayed.

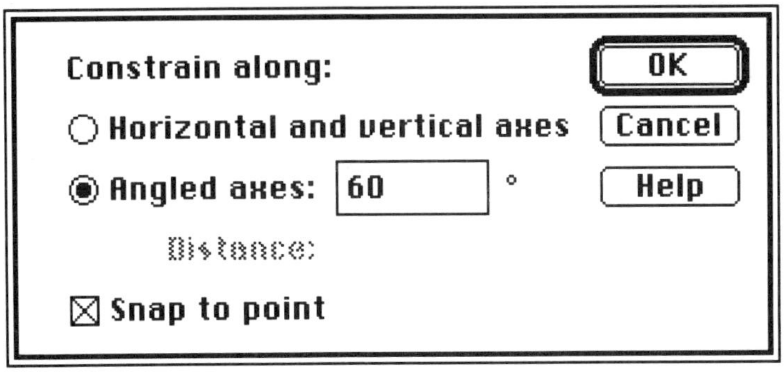

Figure 5-131.
The small dot indicates that "Angled axes:" is currently selected. Type in the number of degrees to rotate the x and y axes (60° counterclockwise).

If you want to rotate the x and y axes by a specific angle, make sure no points are selected in the document (or that two points are selected), issue the Constrain command, and select the "Angled axes:" option by clicking on it with the mouse button.

After you have selected the Constrain options that you desire, you can click on the OK button to implement the Constrain command, click on the Cancel button to void any specified rotations, or click Help in order to request the Help folder with information about the Constrain command (see Figure 5-131).

View Menu

The View menu contains various commands that allow you to alter your view of the Illustrator document. The View commands let you see a preview of the printed artwork; see the artwork and the template together for tracing the template; see the Illustrator artwork only; see the template document only; control the size at which the document is viewed in the active window; create multiple views of a document; and control whether or not the toolbox and rulers are displayed.

Preview

The Preview command creates an approximate view of what Illustrator artwork will look like when it is printed. Select Preview from the View menu (Command-Y), and the Illustrator program removes the Illustrator document (artwork) and the template document from view and uses the current Paint and Type settings to create an approximation of what your artwork would look like if it were printed. You cannot modify the image of the artwork directly in the Preview window.

The only operations you can perform on a Preview image are those that alter your view of the image such as the scroll bars, hand tool, zoom tool, and page tool. However, if you have open windows that represent more than one view of a document, the windows that contain previews of the artwork will be updated automatically when changes are made in other views of the document that do allow alterations of the artwork. Previews of gray-scales and color shades are not accurate, and only serve as a very rough approximation of the final output. Preview is very useful for checking the order in which objects are painted by the program.

Command + Option + C — copies a Preview image to the Clipboard as a PICT file.

Artwork & Template

The Artwork & Template command displays both the Illustrator document and the template beneath it (if any) in the active window. The Artwork & Template view is what is displayed when you first open a document, and it is the view that you will probably use most of the time for creating and working on your artwork (Figure 5-133).

Artwork Only

The Artwork Only command displays only the Illustrator document in the active window, and hides the template document from view. The Artwork Only view is handy for working on the artwork when the template is distracting you from the fine details (Figure 5-134).

Template Only

The Template Only command displays only the template document in the active window, and hides the Illustrator document from view. The Template Only view is useful for inspecting the original scanned image without it being obscured by the artwork (see Figure 5-135).

Actual Size

The Actual Size command displays the document in the active window at the actual size of the Illustrator document; at this size one screen pixel is equivalent to one point (1/72 of an inch). You can issue the Actual Size command by either selecting Actual Size from the View menu, pressing Command-H, or holding down the Option key while double-clicking on the hand tool with the mouse. Issuing the Actual Size command also centers the Illustrator document (and accompanying template, if any) in the active window. In the example below ,the mouse artwork was in view at its actual size when the Actual Size command was issued; the net result was that the document was centered and the primary image was moved slightly out of the active window's display area (see Figure 5-136).

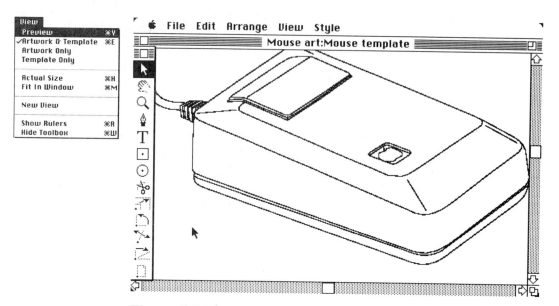

Figure 5-132.
A Preview image.

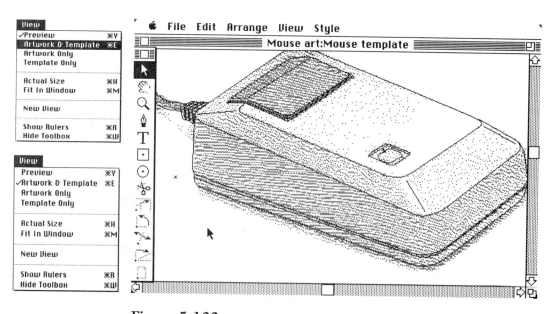

Figure 5-133.
The artwork (i.e. the Illustrator document) and the template (i.e. a MacPaint document or a PICT document) are displayed together.

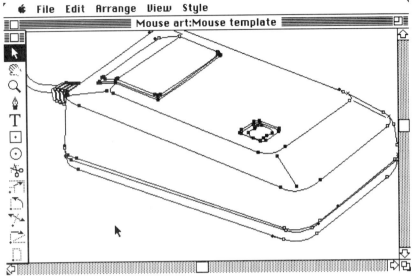

Figure 5-134.
The Artwork Only view.

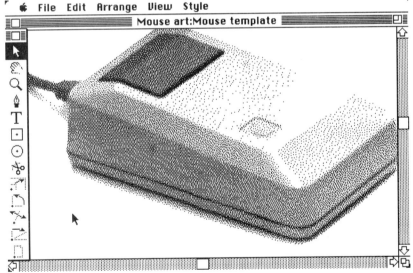

Figure 5-135.
A Template Only view of the original scanned image used for the mouse drawing.

Fit In Window

The Fit In Window command displays the entire 14-by-14-inch Illustrator document in the active window. Select Fit In Window

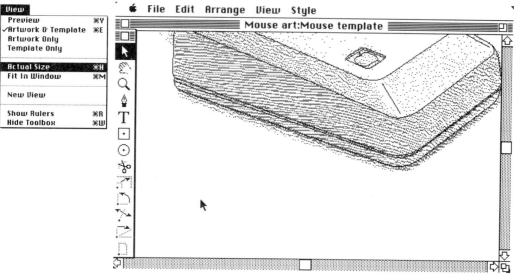

Figure 5-136.
The artwork (i.e. the Illustrator document) and the template (i.e. a MacPaint document or a PICT document) displayed at actual size.

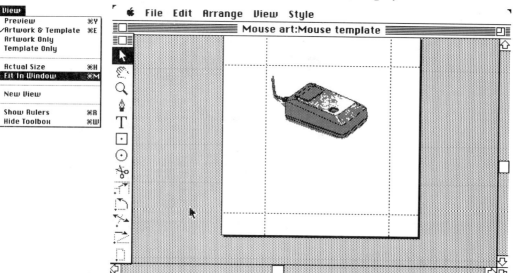

Figure 5-137.
The result of the Fit in Window command.

from the View menu, press Command-M, or double-click on the hand tool in the tool palette with the mouse. The Fit In Window command also centers the Illustrator document (and accompanying template, if any) in the active window (Figure 5-137).

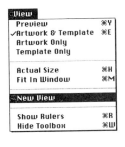
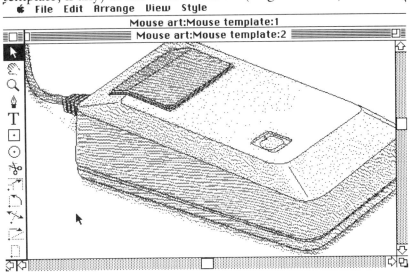

Figure 5-138.
A new window and an old window are automatically numbered and placed one on top of the other.

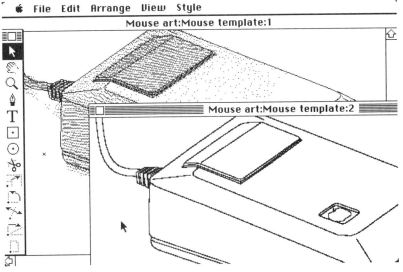

Figure 5-139.
Window number 2 (the Preview view) was selected and moved.

New View

The New View command creates a new window that displays the Illustrator document. The New View command can only be issued by selecting New View from the File menu to create a new active window that is identical to the window that was active when the command was issued. The new window is below and to the right of the window that was active when the New View command was issued. The new window can be manipulated independently of the active window; however, any changes made to the Illustrator document from any active window will affect the document and be displayed in all views of that document. In Figure 5-137 the new window and the old window are automatically numbered by Illustrator and the numbers are placed after a colon that follows the Illustrator document and template document names. Any other new views of the same document that are created will be consecutively numbered in the order in which they were opened. If you close one of the views of a document, the remaining view windows of that document will be automatically renumbered, removing the closed window from the sequence.

Creating new views of a document can be helpful for such purposes as viewing a preview and a regular view of the artwork (as shown in Figure 5-139), for viewing different areas of the artwork, or for viewing the artwork at different magnifications simultaneously.

Creating new views is especially useful when you are using a screen larger than the standard 9-inch video screen of the Macintosh Plus and Macintosh SE. If you are using Illustrator with a larger screen, you will be able to improve Illustrator's performance if the active window does not overlap with the toolbox. You can do this by simply moving the toolbox and the active window apart using the selection tool. Another method is to point to the zoom box in the upper right-hand corner of the active window and click the mouse button while holding down the Option key. This procedure will enlarge the active window until it almost fills the larger screen, while positioning the window so that it does not overlap the normal position of the toolbox. To reduce the window to its original size, repeat the procedure of pointing to the zoom box in the upper right-hand corner of the active window and clicking in the box while holding down the Option key.

Using new views can slow down the system, so one of the accelerator boards available for the Macintosh Plus and Macintosh SE really helps; also Illustrator's performance is greatly enhanced when the program is used with a Macintosh II.

Show Rulers

The Show Rulers command displays two rulers, one along the right-hand side and one along the bottom of the active window. Show Rulers only appears as a menu option if the rulers are not currently displayed in the active window; if the rulers are already displayed, the Hide Rulers command occupies this position in the menu instead (see Figure 5-142). The rulers are useful for precision work where measurements or sizes are important. Every window can have its own set of rulers. When you first create a document or first start the program and open an existing document, the rulers will not be displayed.

To display the rulers, select Show Rulers from the View menu (Command-R).

The rulers use two different units of measurement, points (one point = 1/72 of an inch) and picas (one pica = 12 points or about 1/6th of an inch), depending on the magnification or reduction of the document. In Figure 5-140 the rulers are numbered only in picas. The rulers display picas as large-sized numbers and points as small-sized numbers. When you view the artwork at its actual size (100%), there are tick marks at 3-point intervals and numbered subdivisions

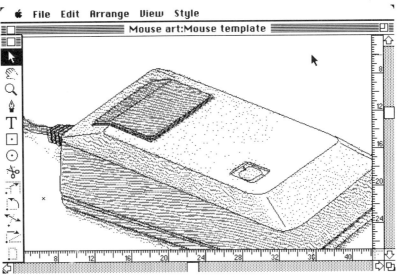

Figure 5-140.
To display the rulers, select Show Rulers from the View menu or press Command-R. Two rulers will appear, one along the bottom of the active window and one down the right side of the window.

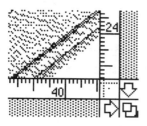

Figure 5-141.
The small black square inside the box where the rulers intersect represents the current size of a 2 pica square.

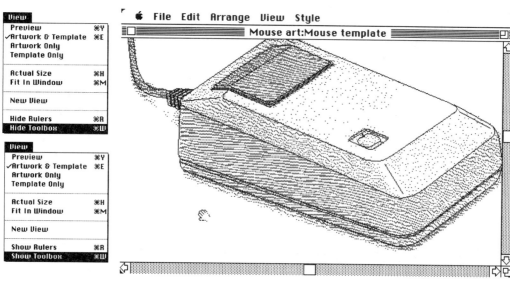

Figure 5-142.
This screen shows the mouse document with the toolbox hidden

on the ruler at 4-pica intervals (2/3 of an inch). As the magnification or reduction of the view changes, the numbering system on the ruler also changes; for example: at the smallest reduction (6.75% of the actual size) there are tick marks at 4-pica intervals and numbered subdivisions at 64-pica intervals, and at the largest magnification (1600%) there are tick marks at 1/4-point intervals and numbered subdivisions at 3-point intervals (see Figure 5-140). It's interesting to note that the Macintosh's video display has a resolution of 72 pixels per inch; this corresponds to pixels being pretty much equal to 1-point squares. Both MacPaint documents and PICT files used for templates have the same 72-dot-per-inch resolution as the Mac's video screen. Therefore, when you are viewing the document at its actual size, one point equals one pixel on the template.

When the rulers are displayed you will notice that as you move the mouse, the pointer's position is indicated by a dotted line on each of the rulers. The point of reference for the rulers (i.e., the zero point) is tied to the document, not the window, so if you scroll, move, or zoom around the document, the numbers on the rulers will change to reflect the document's point of reference.

When the document is created, the point of reference used as the origin for the numbering on the rulers is the upper left-hand corner. If you want to change the point of reference for the rulers' numbering system, position the arrow over the lower right-hand corner of the active window, where the rulers intersect, and a set of dotted cross-hairs appears (see Figure 5-141). Hold down the mouse button (the pointer will change into a plus sign(+) when you move it into the active window), and drag the cross-hairs over the point that you want to become the new origin for the rulers and release the mouse button. (This is also the PostScript origin.)

The rulers provide visual feedback about what size magnification or reduction you are viewing the document at in the active window. A size indicator box is located in the lower right-hand corner of the window, where the horizontal and vertical rulers intersect.

When you view the document at actual size (100%) or larger, the current size of a 1-point-by-1-point square is shown as a black square inside a white square.

When you view the document at a reduced size (smaller than 100%), the current size of a two-pica square is shown as a white square inside a black box. For more information on magnifying (zoom in) and reducing (zoom out) the document view, see the section on the zoom tool.

Hide Rulers

If you want to remove the rulers from view, you can do so by either choosing Hide Rulers from the View menu or by pressing Command-R as a shortcut. The Hide Rulers command only appears as a menu option if the rulers are currently displayed in the active window; if the rulers are not displayed, the Show Rulers command will occupy this position in the menu instead.

Hide Toolbox

The Hide Toolbox command removes the toolbox from view (see Figure 5-142). Hiding the toolbox lets you see more of the Illustrator artwork on the screen at one time. You can issue the Hide Toolbox command by either selecting Hide Toolbox from the View menu, pressing Command-W, or clicking in the small box that is located at the top of the toolbox. When the toolbox is hidden you can still use the tool that was selected when you hid the toolbox. You can also use the selection tool by holding down the Command key; the hand tool by holding down the space bar; and the zoom tool by either holding down the space bar and Command key to zoom in or by holding down the space bar, Command key, and Option key to zoom out. If you want to use any of the other Illustrator tools, you must first bring the toolbox back onto the screen by issuing the Show Toolbox command described below.

Show Toolbox

The Show Toolbox command displays the toolbox after it has been removed from view by the Hide Toolbox command. You can issue the Show Toolbox command by either selecting Show Toolbox from the View menu or by pressing Command-W as a shortcut. When the toolbox is displayed, it cannot be placed behind another window; if you try to place another window on top of the toolbox ,the toolbox will force itself on top of the window. If you are using Illustrator with a screen larger than the standard 9-inch video screen found on the Macintosh Plus and Mac SE, you will be able to improve the performance of the program by making sure that the toolbox and the active window do not overlap. You can do this by either moving the Toolbox and the active window apart with the selection tool, or pointing to the zoom box in the upper right-hand corner of the active window and clicking in the box while holding down the Option key. This will enlarge the active window to almost full-screen size but will position the window so that it does not overlap the normal position of the toolbox. If you want to reduce the window to its original size, repeat the procedure of pointing to the zoom box in the upper right-hand corner of the active window and clicking in the box while holding down the Option key.

Style Menu

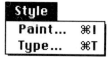

The Style menu contains two commands, Paint and Type, that allow you to specify attributes that determine how the artwork will be painted and how the type will be displayed. Learning to use these commands is critical to creating Illustrator artwork.

Paint...

The Paint command lets you control how regions are filled (with white, black, gray-scale, or color) and how paths are stroked (in white, black, gray-scale, or color; with either solid or dashed lines; and at what line weight). The Paint command also lets you control how corners and ends of strokes are formed, specify the miter limit for strokes, specify the pattern for dashed strokes, and attach text notes, such as PostScript comments to descriptions of objects in the Illustrator document. To issue the Paint command, you can either select Paint from the Style menu or press Command-T as a shortcut. Issuing the Paint command brings up the Paint dialog box shown in Figure 5-143.

Illustrator turns the artwork you draw into the final image that is output to the printer (or displayed on the screen with the Preview command) by painting objects in the document with layers of opaque ink. In Illustrator ink can be black, white, any shade of gray, or any process color (a color created with the four color process which specifies a color as a percentage combination of black, magenta, cyan, and yellow). Illustrator paints objects according to how they are ordered in the document. Illustrator starts painting the backmost object in the document and then paints objects successively until the foremost object is painted. Since the ink that Illustrator paints with is opaque, each layer of ink completely covers any layers under it. Illustrator paints objects in the order that you

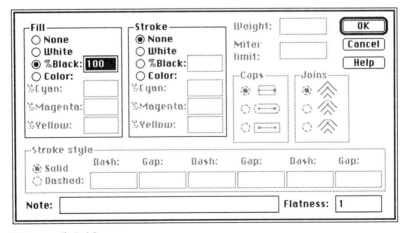

Figure 5-143.
The Paint dialog box shows the default settings the first time the Paint command is issued, provided that no objects are selected.

drew them, with the most recently drawn object painted last. If you want to change the order in which objects are painted (which is often necessary for the artwork to look right) you must use the Paste In Front and Paste In Back commands described earlier in this section. The Group command, along with the two Paste commands, is also handy for controlling the order in which objects are painted. You can use the Paint command to examine (or change) the painting attributes of a particular object by selecting the object and issuing the command; when the Paint dialog box appears, it will display the Paint settings for that object.

When Illustrator paints your document for previewing or printing, all the objects in your artwork, including the type, are treated as paths. Paths consisting of a single point (such as center points) are not painted. Type characters are treated as if each character were a closed path that is filled with black (or another specified shade of gray or color). You use the Paint command to specify which of the paths in your artwork should be filled (with what color ink) or stroked (with what thickness or color of line) or both. If you are using type in your artwork, you can also specify whether the type should be filled (the default setting), or stroked, or both.

If Illustrator is instructed to fill a closed path with no endpoints, Illustrator fills the area inside the path with the type of ink that you specify. If Illustrator is instructed to fill an open path with two distinct endpoints, the program will treat the open path as if it were a closed path by connecting the two endpoints with a straight line; it will then fill the area inside the imaginary closed path. Complex paths that intersect themselves are painted according to a system called the "winding number rule" (see Chapter 6).

If you instruct Illustrator to stroke a path, the path is drawn as a series of connected curves and/or straight lines that are centered on the path. The thickness (line weight), color (white, black, gray, or color), and pattern (solid or dashed) of the line can be examined or specified in the Paint dialog box. If you specify that an object should be filled and stroked, then the object will be filled first, and then the stroke will be placed over the fill (the filled area will be covered by one-half the specified line weight).

When you first start the Illustrator program, the Paint dialog box contains the following default settings: "Fill" is set to 100% Black (the selected areas will be filled with 100% black ink); "Stroke" is set to none (there will be no strokes delineating the paths); "Weight:", which is grayed-out when Stroke is set to none, is set to 1 point (the line weights, or thickness of the line, of any strokes will be 1 point);

"Miter Limit:", which is grayed-out unless a mitered line join is selected, is set to 10 (the length of a miter joint is limited to 10 times the line weight); "Caps", which is grayed-out when Stroke is set to none, is set to "Butt" (the line has squared-off ends); "Joins", which is grayed-out when Stroke is set to none, is set to "Miter" (lines come to a point at corners); "Stroke Style", which is grayed-out when Stroke is set to none, is set to solid (lines that delineate paths will be solid rather than dashed); "Flatness" is set to 0 (curves will be drawn with a medium amount of flatness); and the "Note:" box is empty. When you issue the Paint command for the first time after you start the program, these default settings will be selected and displayed in the dialog box provided that no artwork is selected. If you had selected a single path, or an object consisting of a single path, before you issued the Paint command, the settings for that path or object would be displayed in the dialog box. If you had selected more than one object before you issued the Paint command, the settings common to all the selected objects would be displayed in the dialog box, and any settings that were not the same for all the selected objects would be left unspecified.

The first set of specifications in the Paint dialog box are the Fill options that let you specify what color ink, if any, should be used to fill any objects that were selected when the Paint command was issued. If you select "None" by clicking on it with the mouse button,

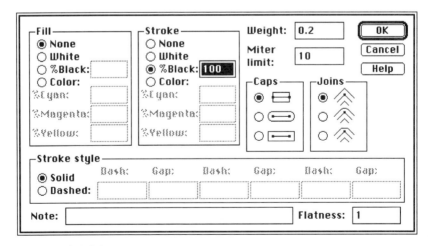

Figure 5-144.
This dialog box appeared after an object that was stroked with a .2-point line weight was selected. With the exception of the line weight, stroke, and fill, all other specifications represent the default settings.

the area will not be filled and will be transparent. A spot will appear inside the small circle preceding the word "None" to signify that the option is selected. If you select "White" by clicking on it, opaque white ink will be used to fill any selected objects. Painting areas with white ink can provide a handy way to erase things; this is analogous to using a bottle of white-out to correct typing errors. If you select "%Black:" by clicking on it, the number in the box following it will be set to 100, indicating that the area will be filled with 100% black ink. If you want to fill the selected objects with a shade of gray, enter the desired shade (as a percentage of black) into the box instead of the number 100. Note that the screen preview does not do a good job of displaying gray-scales; the LaserWriter creates a fair gray-scale, and typesetting machines such as the Linotronic 300 produce the best gray-scales. If you select the "Color:" fill option by clicking on it, the color choices below the option no longer appear grayed-out, and they are all set to a value of 100%. To specify colors for a four-color process (black, cyan, magenta, and yellow), click in the appropriate boxes and type in numbers between 0 and 100 that represent the amount of each of the four colors that you want the selected objects to be filled with. If your printer does not feature color printing capabilities, Illustrator converts the specified color mix into an equivalent shade of gray.

The second set of specifications in the Paint dialog box are the Stroke options. If you select "None," the selected paths will not be stroked. If you select "White," opaque white ink will be used to stroke the paths of any selected objects. If you select "%Black:," the number in the box following it will be set to 100, indicating that the area will be stroked with 100% black ink. If you want to stroke the selected paths with a shade of gray, enter the desired shade (as a percentage of black) into the box instead of the number 100. If you select the "Color:" stroke option, the color choices below the option no longer appear grayed-out, and they are all set to a value of 100%t. To specify colors for a four-color process, click in the appropriate boxes and type in numbers between 0 and 100 that represent the amount of each of the four colors (black, cyan, magenta, and yellow) that you want the selected paths to be stroked with. If you do not have a color printer, Illustrator converts the specified color mix into an equivalent shade of gray.

The next item in the Paint dialog box is the Weight: option that allows you to specify the line weight (thickness) that the selected paths will be stroked with. The Weight: option will appear grayed-out if the Stroke option is set to none. To specify the line weights that will be used to stroke any selected paths, click in the box after the word "Weight:" and enter a number that represents how many points of thickness (one point = 1/72 inch) you want the lines to be. Line weights can be less than 1 point, but very fine lines will appear thicker when printed on the LaserWriter than when printed on a typesetting machine such as the Linotronic.

The next three options, Miter limit, Caps, and Joins, are used to specify how ends of lines and corners should look. The Caps options let you select how you want the endpoints of open paths and the drawn ends of dashed lines to look. In the Caps box are three options; from top to bottom they are: a butt cap, a round cap, and a projecting cap. Butt cap refers to the end of a line which is squared-off and perpendicular to the line; in other words, the endpoint of the path butts up against the squared-off end of the line. Round cap refers to the end of a line that is rounded off; in Illustrator the diameter of the cap is equal to the thickness of the line, and the line that represents the actual path in the artwork ends where the cap starts to curve. A projecting cap is a line-end that has a squared-off end that projects half the value of the line weight beyond the end of the actual path. Since both the round cap and the projecting cap project out beyond the length of the actual path by one-half the distance of the line width, if you choose round caps or projecting caps for dashed lines, the line caps will project into the space between the dashes, half the distance of the line width (e.g. with a 1-point line, the round cap or projecting cap would extend 1/2-point beyond the end of the actual

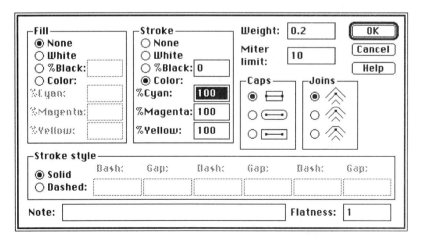

Figure 5-145.
Selecting the color stroke option.

path). Select the type of line cap that you want by clicking on it.

In the Joins box that is adjacent to the Caps box are the three types of corners that you can choose from. From top to bottom they are a miter join, a round join, and a bevel join. A miter join is a sharp corner that ends in a point. The sharper the angle of the corner, the sharper the point that sticks out from the corner. When the miter join option is selected, the Miter limit option is also displayed. The miter limit is the maximum ratio of the length of the sharp corner-point to the width of the line. The default setting for the Miter limit option is 10; this means that the sharp corner-point cannot be more than 10 times longer than the line is wide. You can specify any value for the miter limit that is equal to or greater than one; however, a miter limit of one will make the corner a bevel join (see below). When the round join option is selected, corners will be formed from a circular arc with a diameter equal to the width of the line. It's a good idea not to select round joins and butt caps because the circle at the join may overlap the butt caps. A bevel join is when a sharp point created by a miter join is flattened off; as mentioned above, a bevel join is the same as a miter join with a limit of one.

The Stroke style box lets you specify whether you want a solid line or a dashed line. If you want a solid line, simply choose that option by clicking on it if it is not already selected. If you want a dashed line, click on the word Dashed:; the Dash and Gap boxes will be actively displayed. Click in the first Dash box and type the length, in points, that you want the first dash to be. Then click in the first Gap box and type the length, in points, that you want the first gap to be. Fill in the other four boxes if you want the dash and gap length pattern to vary. Whatever lengths are typed will be repeated and used for the dash pattern of the line. Remember that the type of line cap you select also affects the dash pattern, and that if you select round or projecting caps you should widen the gap width ito accommodate caps that stick out an amount equal to half the current line weight setting.

In the lower right-hand side of the Paint dialog box is the Note: box that allows you to enter a text comment into the PostScript text file that Illustrator uses as its standard means of saving the artwork. The Note option is handy for tagging an object so that you can find it in the PostScript file. The note appears as a comment with the "%%Note" prefix in the PostScript file. For further information about PostScript and Illustrator see Chapter 6.

The last option in the Paint dialog box is the Flatness option. Flatness refers to how smoothly curves will be drawn, and it affects both previewed and printed artwork. The flatness value is measured

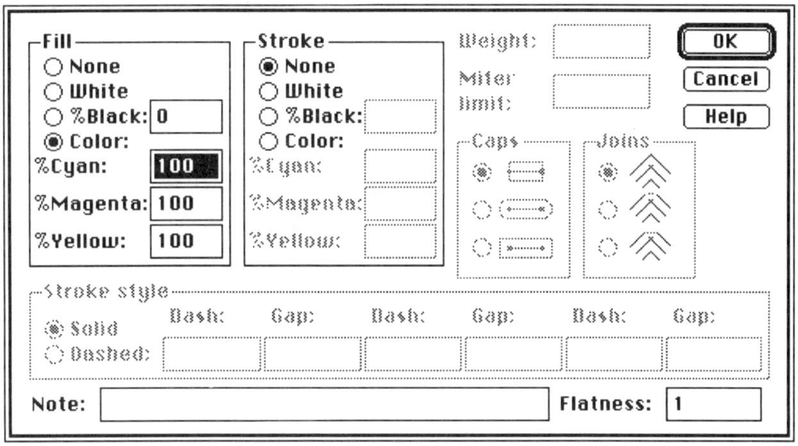

Figure 5-146.
Selecting the color fill option.

in terms of pixels in the output device and corresponds to the distance of any point on the printed curve from any point on the theoretically ideal curve. The value used can be anywhere from 0 to 10; smaller values will produce more accurate curves but will take longer to compute. If you are willing to sacrifice image quality, you can set the value higher than the default value of zero. Printing and previewing will be faster, but the curves in the artwork will not be as smooth. Increasing the flatness value also helps when printing or previewing long paths which can be slow to draw.

Once you have set the paint attributes the way that you want, you can implement them by pointing to the OK button and clicking the mouse button; this sends the dialog box away and places the specified attributes in the document. The double line surrounding the OK button indicates that pressing the Return key can be used as a shortcut for selecting the OK option. To cancel any attribute changes that you have just specified, click on the Cancel button instead to send the Paint dialog box away and leave your Illustrator document unchanged.

Type...

The Type command is used for altering type or changing the specifications for type created with the type tool. For a more detailed description of the type tool and the Type dialog box, see the section on the type tool. Since text cannot be edited directly on the

Illustrator document, if you want to change type that is already in the document, select the type block you want to edit with the selection tool and then choose Type from the Style menu (or press Command-T); this will bring up the Type dialog box and you can edit the text at the bottom of the box.

Some important things to keep in mind about entering text in the Type dialog box: you must put Returns at the ends of lines, and you are limited to 254 characters of text. The text that you enter into the Type dialog box can be edited using the standard Cut (Command-X), Copy (Command-C), Paste (Command-V), or Select All (Command-A) commands found in the Edit menu.

You also use the Type dialog box to set attributes of the type such as typeface, type size, leading, kerning, and alignment. Illustrator's default type attribute settings are Helvetica typeface, 12-point type size, 12-point leading, 0 kerning, and left alignment (Figure 5-148). If you have selected only one block of type, this text is displayed in the bottom section of the Type dialog box and the attributes of the text are displayed in the upper section of the dialog box. If you have selected more than one block of type, only the attributes shared by all the selected blocks are displayed, and the text area at the bottom of the dialog box is blank and cannot be used.

To set the typeface of the selected text, choose a typeface from among those listed in the scroll box located in the upper left-hand region of the Type dialog box (see Figure 5-148). The scroll bar located on the right side of the scroll box lets you scroll through the available typefaces if there are more than will fit into the scroll box. The typefaces listed in the scroll box may have no prefix, or they may have a prefix of either a dot (•) or a question mark (?). If the typeface does not have a prefix, it means it is available in your Macintosh's system file but there is not a proper screen font for displaying the typeface on your screen, and Illustrator uses an alternate screen font and prints with the proper font, if it is available. If the correct font is not available, then Illustrator substitutes an available printer font (usually Courier). If the typeface is prefixed by a dot (•), it means the typeface is available in your Macintosh's system file and there is also at least one proper screen font for displaying the typeface on your screen, and Illustrator loads the proper font to the printer if it is available. If the correct font is not available, then Illustrator substitutes an available printer font (again, usually Courier). If the typeface is prefixed by a question mark (?), it means that you have opened an Illustrator document that uses typefaces not available in your Macintosh's system file, and that the document was created using a

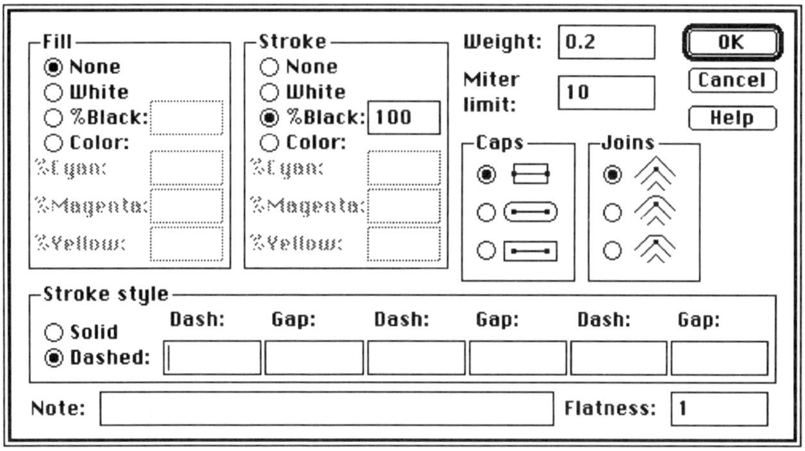

Figure 5-147.
The Stroke Style is set for a dashed line.

different system file. Illustrator will display the type on the screen using a Macintosh system screen font (usually Chicago), but no font will be downloaded to the printer for printing.

To set the type size, point to the small box after the word "Size:," click the mouse button, and type in the number representing the point size that you want the type to be. To set the leading, point to the small box after the word "Leading," click the mouse button, and then type in the leading that you want. Leading is the amount of space between the lines of type, measured from baseline to baseline. Likewise, to set the kerning, point to the small box after the word "Kerning," click the mouse button, and type in the desired amount of kerning. Kerning is the measure of space between characters; by typing a positive number you can add space between characters; by typing a negative number you can bring characters closer together (see Figure 5-148).

To set the alignment of the type, point to one of the small circles in the Alignment area of the dialog box and then click the mouse buttton; a small black dot will appear in the center of the small circle that you selected. Clicking in the first circle (and its accompanying image of a paragraph) selects left alignment (flush left, ragged right); clicking in the second circle selects center alignment (each line centered under the next); and clicking on the third circle selects right alignment (flush right, ragged left).

Once you have set the type attributes, you can implement them by pointing to the OK button and clicking the mouse button; this sends

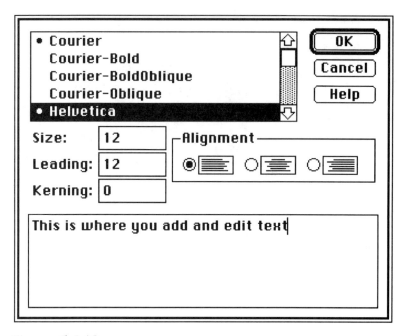

Figure 5-148.
The Type dialog box shows the default type attribute settings. To reset the typeface of the selected text, choose a typeface from the scroll box located in the upper left-hand region.

the dialog box away and places the specified type attributes in the document. Press the return key as a shortcut for selecting the OK option. On the other hand, if you want to cancel any attribute changes that you have specified, click on the Cancel button instead to send the Type dialog box away and leave your Illustrator document unchanged.

It's important to remember that if you have altered the *x* and *y* axes by using the Constrain command on the Arrange menu, the placement of text blocks will be relative to the *x* and *y* axes; this may give the text a different appearance. If you are placing type and it looks a bit slanted or askew, check the alignment of the *x* and *y* axes by looking at the dialog box that appears after you select the Constrain command on the Arrange menu (or Command-K).

You ow know all about the tools, menus and dialog boxes, and you are ready to master the Illustrator program. When you are ready for it, Chapter 6 provides details on PostScript and Illustrator, so that you can create more special effects, such as the weather map in Chapter 2.

CHAPTER

6

PostScript and Illustrator

The PostScript language has emerged as the leading graphics language in use today due to its endorsement by many major computer companies including both Apple and IBM. PostScript is the foundation on which Adobe built the Illustrator program. Illustrator uses PostScript for such purposes as drawing images on the Macintosh video screen, communicating with printers and typesetting machines, and as a format for saving artwork documents. Knowing PostScript will allow advanced Illustrator users to understand Illustrator documents and create special PostScript effects.

What is PostScript?

PostScript is a computer language that is used for describing the appearance of graphics and text on a page. Illustrator documents are PostScript programs saved as ordinary text files. PostScript is used to write programs for computers or printers, or to create special graphic effects.

PostScript describes text and graphics in a standard format that can be understood by other computers, printers, and other output devices. Printers (such as laser printers and typesetting machines) interpret PostScript page descriptions and create bit-mapped representations of the pages for printing. Video displays use PostScript to accurately interpret page descriptions, convert the result into a bit-mapped image, and display the image on the computer screen.

Since graphics and text together convey more information per page than text alone, there is a major trend in computer technology away from the text-only computer screens that have dominated computing since its inception and towards the heavy use of graphic information in both computer documents and operating systems (such as the Macintosh Finder, Microsoft Windows, and IBM's OS/2 Presentation Manager). Data processing and information processing on microcomputers is rapidly becoming document processing, and the documents being processed are using much more graphics to help convey information. PostScript has emerged as the standard language for describing the text and graphics that are on the pages of computer documents.

PostScript allows pages to be described very concisely, which means that PostScript files take up less memory than many other types of page descriptions, including the typical bit-mapped descriptions. For example, a page on the Apple LaserWriter has a printable area of 8-by-10.9 inches for a total of 87.2 square inches; at the LaserWriter's resolution of 300 dots per linear inch (which equals 90,000 dots per square inch) an 87.2 square inch LaserWriter page would have 7,848,000 dots in it. To store this document as a bit-mapped document with no gray-scale (where one dot is represented by one bit of memory) would require 7,848,000 bits of memory, which is just shy of one megabyte. Considering that the standard Macintosh diskette only stores 800K, a full-page bit-mapped image would not fit on a diskette, and you'd be forced to use a hard disk system. If you've ever used a scanner to digitize a page of graphics, you know that the resultant files are usually enormous (sometimes approaching a megabyte). However, a PostScript description of a page usually takes up much less memory.

Not only does PostScript offer a compact way to describe pages, but the PostScript description is also not tied to a particular device. In computer jargon this is referred to as device-independence. What device-independence means in practical terms is that PostScript files created on the Macintosh with Illustrator (or any other application that works with PostScript) can be used on certain computer systems from IBM and other vendors, and these PostScript descriptions can be printed on many different PostScript printers and typesetting machines from a wide array of vendors such as Apple, IBM, DEC, and Linotype. The advantages of PostScript, and its endorsement by both Apple and IBM, has led to its current status as the major industry standard among computer graphics languages.

PostScript was created with graphic arts in mind, and it uses a way of describing images that is modeled after graphic arts. In PostScript an image is created by putting certain types of computer-generated "ink" in specified areas. The ink can be in various forms such as lines, shapes, or spots of ink in a bit-mapped photograph. The computer-generated ink can be black, white, any shade of gray, or any shade of color. PostScript starts building a page by taking a white page and placing the ink in specified areas according to the PostScript description of the page. As ink is placed on the page, any new ink completely covers any ink it is placed on top of; in other words, every type of ink on the page is opaque and keeps its color, rather than being transparent and bleeding colors together.

Some of PostScript's capabilities include the ability to construct arbitrary shapes from straight lines and curves. Shapes may be convex, concave, contain disconnected sections and holes, and can even intersect with themselves. PostScript includes painting commands for further describing shapes; the paint commands allow PostScript to do such things as assign any thickness of line to outline a shape, fill the shape with any color, or use the shape as a clipping path to crop any other graphics or images. PostScript features a general coordinate system that allows all types of graphics to be transformed mathematically in all the possible linear transformations such as scaling, rotating, reflecting, skewing, and translating. Post-

Script also has commands that allow it to be used to describe text alone, or text integrated with graphics. PostScript allows you to specify typefaces, type styles, and type sizes. PostScript treats text as graphic shapes that can be manipulated and operated on by any of PostScripts graphics commands such as painting, scaling, rotating, reflecting, or slanting. PostScript also has commands for working with digitized images that are either scanned or created artificially with a computer. PostScript works with digitized images of any resolution and provides methods for assigning gray-scale and color values to the images.

The main commands used for placing images on a page are fill, stroke, image, and show. The fill command places a filled area on the page. When PostScript calculates how to fill a path, it uses the "Winding number rule." According to this system, the way in which Illustrator determines whether a particular location is inside the path (for the purpose of filling the area) is to draw an imaginary ray from that location that extends to infinity (beyond the edge of the document), and then examine each place that the path of the object being filled crosses that ray. Then, starting with a value of zero, a value of one is added to the total each time the path crosses the ray from the left, and a value of one is subtracted from the total each time the path crosses the ray from the right. After the program either adds or subtracts a unit for all the places that the path crosses the ray, it can determine whether or not to fill the area by examining the total. If right-hand intersections equaled left-hand intersections, then the total would be zero; a zero total indicates that the original location was outside the object because the ray extending from that location entered and exited the object (by crossing the path) the same number of times. If a value other than zero remained as a total, then Illustrator decides that the original location was inside the object and fills the area with the specified type of ink.

The stroke command draws lines on the page, the image command is used for placing a gray-scale halftone digitized image on the page, and the show command places characters on the page. Just as Illustrator uses paths to create artwork, PostScript uses the concept of the "current path" as a way to draw things on the page. Commands used to describe how the path should be drawn include newpath, moveto, lineto, curveto, arc, and closepath. In addition to the current path, PostScript also features a "current clipping path" that represents an outline of the area on the page that will be displayed or printed. Usually the clipping path is the entire printable area on a page. Anything that is drawn outside that area is cut off and discarded. However, by using the PostScript clip command, you can shrink the size of the area that will be displayed or printed down to any desired size or shape. Clipping the artwork can be useful for placing it in a particular layout, or for creating special graphics effects.

In order to draw pages the same way on different types of devices, PostScript uses two different types of coordinate systems, device space and user space, for locating items on a page. Device space is the area that can be displayed or printed on a particular output device. On the Apple LaserWriter Plus for example, the device space is an 8-by-10.9-inch area with 300 dots per linear inch for a total of about 7,848,000 dots. The characteristics of the device space such as image resolution and the shape of the dots used to create images are idiosyncratic to the particular device. PostScript's device space provides an x-axis and y-axis coordinate system that allows any dot to be located. The device space is only a consideration for the PostScript interpreter program in a printer; PostScript programs only need to concern themselves with the user space. The user space provides a standard ideal coordinate system that is always the same for every page, regardless of the characteristics and idiosyncrasies of the output device (printer, typesetting machine, video display, etc.). The PostScript interpreter in the printer automatically converts the items in the user space into points to be printed or displayed in the device space. PostScript starts each user space out as a default user space and sets the point of origin in the lower left-hand corner of the output page, and the length of a unit of space along either the x-axis or y-axis to a default value of 1/72nd of an inch (approximately 1 point). A PostScript program can then modify the user space by using the coordinate transformation commands: translate, rotate, and scale. Translate lets you change the point of origin, rotate lets you turn the axes relative to the point of origin, and scale lets you change the length of a unit of space.

PostScript programs are usually created by other programs such as Illustrator (or any program that works with the LaserWriter). However, it is possible to use PostScript to create special graphic effects that are not feasible to draw with Illustrator program alone, such as wrapping text or graphics around models of solid objects.

PostScript and Output Devices

A PostScript page description can be rendered on a wide variety of output devices such as printers, typesetting machines, and video monitors. The PostScript page description is interpreted by a special controller known as a raster image processor (or RIP) that is connected to the output device. The RIP converts the compact PostScript page description into a very large number of dots that are then printed on a specific printer or displayed on a particular video monitor. Although the primary use of PostScript is to describe pages for printing, it should be noted that Illustrator uses PostScript for drawing your artwork on the Macintosh screen. This is an example of how PostScript is used for displaying images on video monitors. Because video monitors require a very fast transfer of information to keep the screen updated, PostScript has not yet gained wide use for controlling video displays. In order to use PostScript on a video display, you need a very fast processor chip (or group of chips) to handle the conversion of PostScript into dots on the screen. Keep in mind that a large video display such as are available as an add-on to the Mac can have as many as a million dots or more on the screen at any given time, and that the dots need to be updated many times a second. However, with the ever-increasing interest in PostScript, and an ever-increasing number of products that work with it, developers will certainly find future uses for PostScript as a video display control language. One indication that something big is in the works along those lines is the announcement in early 1987 that Microsoft (the creators of MS-DOS) has licensed a software technology called NEWS (Network Extensible Window System) from workstation manufacturer Sun Microsystems. NEWS is a PostScript-derived windowing system for UNIX computers connected by communications networks. Microsoft's licensing of this technology indicates that PostScript may start gaining ground as a video screen description language as well as a printed page description language.

The advantage to desktop publishing of using PostScript as a screen description language as well as a printer language is that what you see on the screen will probably more closely correspond to what is printed on the page. The discrepancy between what you see on the screen versus what prints on the printer is what I call wysiNQwyg (what-you-see-is-Not-Quite-what-you-get). This discrepancy can be especially bothersome when working with certain graphics and page-layout programs. The discrepancy is cause by the fact that most Macintosh applications use a graphics description language called QuickDraw to control the video display; when a document is printed on a PostScript printer, the Macintosh's native QuickDraw is translated into PostScript as part of the printing process. Inherent differences between QuickDraw and PostScript cause a certain amount of precision to be lost in the translation.

In order to solve the problem of the discrepancies between QuickDraw and PostScript, Illustrator uses PostScript to draw artwork on the screen, uses PostScript as the format in which it saves the artwork, and sends a PostScript file directly to the printer. The advantage of this method is that QuickDraw doesn't enter the picture, so to speak, and less precision is lost between the way that the image is displayed on the screen and described to the printer. Also, since the Illustrator file is saved in the PostScript format, no translation is needed between QuickDraw and PostScript, which improves the speed and performance of the printing process.

Since Illustrator files are saved as pure PostScript text files, you can use the standard PostScript language to understand and modify the Illustrator files.

PostScript Tutorial

If you plan on doing any special effects with Illustrator documents, you will need to know the PostScript programming language. In order to help you learn PostScript we have included a tutorial that will give you some basic PostScript skills. If you want to learn even more about the PostScript language, you can either take a PostScript programming class (available at some colleges and universities), or you can read the PostScript Language Tutorial and Cookbook and the PostScript Language Reference Manual, both published by Addison-Wesley. The PostScript Language Tutorial and Cookbook provides an introduction and explanation to PostScript as well as some handy tips and techniques for improving your PostScript programming skills. The PostScript Language Reference Manual is a more technically oriented book.

This introductory PostScript tutorial presents some of the basic principles, structures, and commands you'll need to know in order to understand the way PostScript programs operate. This tutorial assumes that you are already familiar with some other programming language or that you are a fairly experienced computer user. If you have no programming experience and still want to learn PostScript, you should probably have a friend who knows about computer programming help you out with some of the terminology and concepts. If you have access to a LaserWriter or other PostScript printer, with the help of this tutorial, perhaps the PostScript Language Reference Manual from Addison-Wesley, and a bit of experimentation, you will probably be able to write some PostScript routines of your own.

PostScript is a stack-oriented language, keeping its working values, definitions, and intermediary results in a set of ordered lists, known as stacks. That makes it more like Forth than like BASIC or Pascal. In general, values and objects are either used immediately or pushed onto a stack. When the program needs data or encounters acommand to retrieve a value, it pops a value back off the top of the stack again (see Figure 6-1).

PostScript is also an extensible (or 'threaded') language, meaning that you can define routines in terms of basic PostScript operations and then use these new terms as part of further definitions. When the LaserWriter, or other PostScript printer, interprets your PostScript program, it follows each new term back through your definitions until it reaches a description made up of primitive operations that it knows how to perform (see Figure 6-2).

As a complement to the threaded-stack structure of the language, most PostScript operations are written in post-fix — you first list the objects you want to use, and you then say what you want do with them. For example, to add 3 and 4, you write:

```
3 4 add
```

rather than the

```
3 + 4
```

infix form you would use in BASIC or ordinary math. This procedure makes it possible for PostScript to evaluate objects according to a set of simple rules, although it does make the programs harder for beginners to read and write.

In general, PostScript works its way through a program as follows. As the computer reads each set of symbols, PostScript figures out where the breaks are between the words and assigns each group to a logical unit called a token. As soon as a token becomes available, PostScript looks to see what type of object it represents.

If the token is a number, PostScript saves it for later use by pushing it onto the operand stack. It does the same for definitions. Likewise for specially marked command routines intended for later use. If, on the other hand, the token is a name, PostScript checks to see if it represents an executable routine or a primitive operation. If it does, the language executes the statement, pulling as many values off the stack as the operation requests and returning any results back onto the stack.

The basic scheme, then, is first to define any new terms and push them onto the stack. You then supply the values you want the program to work with. Finally, you give the commands that will retrieve the values, do the required arithmetic and logic, and print out the result. In practice, it's slightly more complicated, and you usually alternate between adding values to the stack and popping them back off.

We'll get to a concrete example in just a moment, but first let's take a short detour into the way PostScript handles stack operations. PostScript actually has four distinct stacks: operand, execution, dictionary, and graphic states (see Figure 6-3). A different class of operations affects each stack.

The operand stack is much like a piece of scratch paper or the running total on a calculator. If an operation needs input values, it pops the required number of values from the operand stack. Similarly, any results produced go back on the stack for later use. This holds true for both arithmetic operations and those that handle text.

The execution stack is where PostScript stores away your program. Normally, you don't explicitly work with this stack but let PostScript do the stack management as it works its way through your program.

The dictionary stack lets you create new definitions and save libraries of procedures. PostScript searches this stack for your definitions, then for built-in operations, and flags any terms that it can't find in either.

Finally, the graphics-state stack is a holding area for sets of parameters that define how the PostScript language interfaces to a specific printer or interprets the exact graphic commands in your program. PostScript can keep track of several sets of parameters, which makes it possible to temporarily alter graphics characteristics in order to draw certain objects and then return to the original mode.

The Simplest Possible Program

You have now done enough theory to start with some practical examples, beginning with the simplest useful PostScript routine,

```
copypage
```

a one-line program that tells a PostScript printer to produce a printout of the current page. Because you haven't said to write anything on the page and the printer assumes a blank white page to begin with, this routine will simply eject an empty sheet of paper.

Suppose you want two blank pages. The routine then becomes

```
2 {copypage} repeat
```

and PostScript, as it reads this line, first encounters the 2. Remember, PostScript pushes values it encounters in the input stream are pushed onto the operand stack until they are needed. So the 2 is pushed onto that stack.

Then PostScript finds {copypage}. Curly brackets (braces) tell PostScript that it should save the enclosed commands, rather than execute them. The program treats deferred commands as a special form of text input — as operands to be saved on the operand stack until they're called for. That's what happens to the {copypage} command.

Proceeding along, PostScript then finds the repeat command. Repeat is a word that it understands as an executable command that takes two operands. Going back to the stack, repeat treats the object on the top of the stack as a sequence of commands to execute and the next object on the stack as the number of repetitions to be made.

The object on the top of the stack is copypage, which still prints out the current page. The next object is the repeat factor, which in this case is 2. The LaserWriter responds by printing two blank pages.

To add some text to the page you'll have to gather up some more PostScript tools. To print text, you'll need to use fonts, arrays, and a positioning command.

Before PostScript can place text within a page image, it has to know what style and size you want to use. For this example, use Times Roman.
The first token in the statement is:

```
/Times-Roman
```

which is the name of the font, preceded by a slash. The slash tells PostScript that Times-Roman is a name that it should put on the operand stack, rather than interpreting it. Otherwise, PostScript would look at the name Times-Roman, decide that it wasn't a built-in command or a word already defined, and flag it as an error.

With Times-Roman on the stack, you can then issue a command to select it for use. Your line then becomes

```
/Times-Roman findfont
```

and the findfont command tells PostScript to locate the dictionary of information about the font whose name is on top of the operand stack and push all the information about that font onto the operand stack.

Fonts are generally stored in a reference size, rather than in the actual size of letters that you'd probably want to use. PostScript uses a one-point font as the reference (1/72- inch high), which it can do because it is able to smoothly scale fonts up in size without creating jagged lines.

The operator called scalefont takes the scale factor from the top of the operand stack and the font information from underneath it. You have set the font name, but you need the number. To put a number on the stack, you include it in a command as a separate token. Putting these elements together, the command is now

```
/Times-Roman findfont 12 scalefont
```

Finally, with the font all specified, you add one more command to make it the current font until further notice.

The first line now reads

```
/Times-Roman findfont 12 scalefont setfont
```

Now that you have a font, the next step is to specify where on the page you want the typing to start. The most basic positioning command in PostScript is moveto, which tells the LaserWriter which point on the page to use as the starting point for further graphics or text commands.

Naturally enough, since a page is two-dimensional, moveto takes two numeric values as its inputs. In stack-language form, the two values must already be on the stack already when you execute the moveto command. The command line to start at halfway up the page, about an inch from the left margin, is

```
72 396 moveto
```

0,0 is at the bottom left of the page and there are 72 units to an inch.

In PostScript, the operator to place text on the page image is show, which takes a string for an input, places the characters on the image, and advances the current location point as it goes. The string input, as you've probably guessed, must first be placed on the operand stack.

Strings in PostScript are made up of sequences of characters. You can create these sequences with operators, or as literal elements. First you'll learn to create arrays with literals. You set strings off by enclosing them with parentheses. Therefore your text string is

```
(this page intentionally not left blank)
```

and the command to place the text on the page is

```
(this page intentionally not left blank) show
```

That gets the print on the image, which, as you already know, is put on the paper with showpage.

It took quite a bit of doing, but you now have a complete Postscript program. To print your single line on the page, you run the program

```
/Times-Roman findfont 12 scalefont setfont
72 396 moveto
(this page intentionally not left blank) show
showpage
```

You can now understand that PostScript is a stack-oriented language, and you have worked a little bit with the stacks. You have written a short program and seen the very basics of how to get an image on a page. On the way, you've encountered commands, deferred commands, arithmetic, strings, arrays, and graphics. And you've gotten the printer to actually a print a page.

Next, a closer look at the PostScript graphics commands and what you can do with them. Then, back to text in more detail.

PostScript Graphics Commands

Using a collection of saved values called the current graphics state for the defaults, PostScript creates on a page an image that depends on your commands. Those graphics commands, like all other PostScript commands, are written in post-fix form, with the operators following the values they work on.

In the examples that follow, lines that start with the percent sign are program comments. In these examples the comments usually appear first, then the command lines they explain.

The first operation in most PostScript graphics routines is to save the current graphics state. This operation allows us to change the state as you please without worrying about losing the standard values other routines might need. When we're done, you restore the original graphics state. The first and last operational lines of the program, then, are commonly

```
%save the graphics state
gsave
%restore the saved state.
grestore
```

Further on, you'll change some of the graphics-state values, but right now it's time to consider the blank page you have to work with. The PostScript page is a two-dimensional space with the origin (0,0) point at the bottom left, and a default scale of 72 units to the inch. If you want to switch the drawing point to two inches over and four up, for example, you write

```
144 288 moveto
```

On the LaserWriter, the page is assumed all white unless you have a mark placed upon it.

The most common way to make graphic designs on a PostScript page is to create a "path" of connected lines or curves, which you can then make visible, fill, replicate, or used as a template for filling with colors and shades of gray. This is, in fact, exactly what Illustrator does when it creates a piece of artwork. To create a simple drawing of a house, for example, you might in turn create paths representing the walls, doors, windows, and roof. You tell PostScript when you want to start a path with the newpath command. Your sequence thus far becomes:

```
gsave
144 288 moveto
newpath
grestore
```

If you were to add a showpage command at this point, we'd still get a blank page. Moving to a position or defining a path doesn't actually draw the image. To actually draw the image, you create a path and either use the stroke command (to follow the outline of the path, much like inking in a drawing with a pen) or the fill command (to color in any area completely enclosed by the current path). You may recognize that the concept of either stroking or filling paths is identical to Illustrator's. You now have all the elements to draw a small bar across the paper.

```
%save the state
%move to the initial position
gsave
144 288 moveto

%set up a path,
%draw a line,
%ink it in,
%output the page

newpath
288 288 lineto
stroke
showpage
grestore
```

Now, expand that a bit to make the program draw a simple box and color it black. Tell it exactly where to move for the first point on the box, specify relative movements for three of the sides, and tell PostScript to close up the path to make the fourth side. When you have completed the outline, tell PostScript to fill in the square.

```
%set initial position
gsave
288 288 moveto

%set up a path,
%move up, over, down
%complete path,
%fill it in
newpath
0 144 rlineto
144 0 rlineto
0 -144 rlineto
closepath
fill
```

```
%print out
showpage
grestore
```

Notice that we didn't say explicitly what to fill the box with. PostScript specifies that the fill operator gets the fill color or pattern from the current graphics state, and on the LaserWriter the initial default fill pattern is black.

Can you add a round peg to your square hole? PostScript uses simple arcs and more complex Bezier curves (a class of curves connecting four points). Stick with the arcs in this example, although Illustrator relies mostly on the Bezier curves. To make a circle, you start a new path, specify the origin point, give the radius, and finish with the starting and ending angles. A one-inch circle in the middle of a standard page becomes

```
%save
%create a path
%specify the arc
%ink it in
gsave
newpath
288 360 72 0 360 arc
stroke

%show page, restore
showpage
grestore
```

To make this an outline, follow the arc command with stroke; to make the circle solid, follow it with fill.

You don't have to choose just a white interior or a solid black fill. By setting the color parameter in the graphics state, you can choose any gradation in between. To set a middle-darkness gray, for example, before executing a fill you write

```
0.5 setgray
```

Although in the narrow context it may seem counterintuitive that leaving the image white requires a color value of 1 and filling with black needs a 0, if you remember that PostScript is a general solution that is also designed for working with color printers, having more brightness carry the higher value makes sense. Postscript has still other commands for setting hues (color tones), but naturally they don't do much good on the one-color LaserWriter.

If you want to outline your arc rather than fill it, you also have a wide variety of choices for the stroke pattern and size. In much the way you can set the brush shape and pattern in MacPaint or MousePaint, you can set the stroke width and the shape of the corners. Stroke width is another value saved in the graphics state, but you can change it with the setlinewidth command. For example,

```
5 setlinewidth
```

says to set the width to five units wide. The units start out as points, but you can change them and even make the vertical and horizontal units different. You'll have to pass on the whole topic of user coordinate systems, so check the Postscript manual if you want to find out how to make lines that look as if they came from an italic-nib drawing pen.

Line endings and corners are set by the linecap and linejoin parameters, also part of the graphics state. You can draw a few examples in a moment, but here are the possibilities.

Line caps (the end of lines) can be butt (ending right at the end of the stroke), rounded (semicircles centered at the end of the stroke) or projecting square (boxed with centers at the end of the stroke). Similarly, line joins can be mitered (extended until they meet), rounded (circular with center at intersection) or beveled (flattened connections). You will notice that these are the same choices as are offered in Illustrator's Paint dialog box

Make a series of three half-boxes, each with a different stroke width, line cap, and join. Because your're going to make three identical figures, you'll use PostScript's ability to define a word by pushing a name and deferred procedure onto the stack, followed by the def operator to define the name you specified as invoking the procedure.

```
%define a procedure to start a
%path, move right 1", up 1",
%ink in the result, then move
%over 1"

/halfbox
{newpath
```

```
72 0 rlineto
0 72 rlineto
stroke
72 0 rlineto}
def

%save the state,
%move to the initial position

gsave
144 144 moveto

%set but caps and mitered joins
%set 2 unit line width
%move to an initial position,
%invoke the procedure

0 setlinecap
0 setlinejoin
2 setlinewidth
100 350 moveto
halfbox

%set rounded caps and rounded joins
%set 5 unit line
%invoke the procedure

1 setlinecap
1 setlinejoin
5 setlinewidth
halfbox

%set projecting caps and bevelled joins
%set 10 unit line
%invoke the procedure

2 setlinecap
2 setlinejoin
10 setlinewidth
halfbox

%print the result,
%reset the state
```

```
2 setlinejoin
10 setlinewidth
halfbox

%print the result,
%reset the state

showpage
grestore
```

For the last example, draw an arrow, followed by a closing message. Write

```
%because you are including text
%you need to set a font

gsave
/Times-Roman findfont
12 scalefont
setfont

%start off at the middle of the page
%and mark the start of the figure

newpath
288 500 moveto
%draw a vertical two-inch line
%with no change in horizontal
%position

0 -144 rlineto
currentpoint
stroke
newpath
moveto

%make the triangular head by
%moving a half inch up and right,
%an inch left, and then closing the
%path. Fill in the result.
36 36 rlineto
0 -72 rlineto
```

```
closepath
currentpoint
fill
moveto

%put our text in, make a copy
(That's all, folks) dup

% find the width, throw out
% the height, divide the result
% by two, and make it negative

stringwidth pop 2 div neg

% set -18 points for vertical,
%put the x and y in right order
%on stack, move relative

-18 exch rmoveto

% now save our string, which
% should be on top of stack

show

%finally, you print the page
%and restore the state
showpage
grestore
```

If you have trouble following that last part, you might want to try writing it down step-by-step while making a diagram of what's on the stack.

Text and PostScript

The ability to work with and manipulate text is one of the strong suits of the PostScript language. To PostScript, text is, on the one hand, a special class of graphics shapes, and, on the other, a set of special codes. Thus, all the graphics commands that apply to other shapes in PostScript also apply to text. In addition, text presentation has some special commands and procedures of its own.

As stated earlier, PostScript is a stack-oriented language. Operations get their inputs from this variable-length list of values, and results or other items not immediately needed are pushed back onto the stack until popped back off. PostScript actually has four stacks, but the one you should be most concerned with is the operand stack.

PostScript uses the post-fix form of notation, with the input values expressed first, followed by the operation that acts on them ("3 4 add" rather than "add 3 and 4" or "3 + 4"). Programs don't need a special overall format, but lines starting with a percent sign (%) are treated as comments.

You have already seen how producing a printed line on the page entails picking a font, making it the right size, establishing a position on the page, specifying the string to be printed, and then telling the printer to output the page. The simple program was:

```
% pick a font
/Times-Roman findfont
% scale it to 12 point,
% set it as the current font
12 scalefont setfont
%move over 1 inch, up about 5
72 396 moveto
% image the text at that point
(this page intentionally) show
(not left blank) show
% print out the page
showpage
```

Now, take a look at some of the more special ways PostScript can handle text.

Start by making a family of related typefaces from the ordinary Times-Roman font included in the LaserWriter. Typeface designers would probably say that the results of these digital transformations are not nearly as good as a specifically designed form of the letters, but they'll do for most everyday purposes.

First, make a copy of the Times-Roman font, calling it Yourfont. Remembering that operators and commands get their values from the stack, you have

```
% put a name on the stack
/Yourfont
```

```
% tell PostScript to retrieve a copy of
% Times Roman and put it on the operand stack too
/Times-Roman findfont
% define that copy as Yourfont
def
```

You're now ready to start making variations. Use the makefont command, which both scales and slants a font using a six-element ordered group of numbers called a matrix. Yor can mostly skip over the mechanics of matrix multiplication here. Instead, just follow some simple plug-in formulas for using makefont matrices.

For a start, make a version of Yourfont that's much taller than normal (or much narrow for its height, depending on how you want to think of it). To scale a font, you plug in the scale factor in the x (horizontal) direction as the first value, the scale factor in the y (vertical) direction as the fourth value, and leave the others as zero. Your code thus becomes

```
% define Yourfont as a copy of Times-Roman
/Yourfont /Times-Roman findfont def
% put a copy on the stack, followed
% by the matrix, then create the new font
Yourfont [12 0 0 36 0 0] makefont
% make that new font the current font
setfont
% move to position on the page, write
216 432 moveto
(Tall fonts and) show
% wait to print until the next part
```

In addition to making the font larger or smaller, you can also slant the letters. Again, you use the makefont command, but this time the matrix is a bit more complex. To get a slant to the right, for example, you want the top of the letter to sit further over to the right than the bottom of the letter does, with the horizontal skew proportional to vertical distance (halfway up, the letter should be displaced half as far over as at the top, and so on). The mathematical function that gives that proportionality factor for x as a function of y and the specified angle is the tangent. To slant a letter, you put the tangent, multiplied by the horizontal-scale factor, in the matrix's third position.

There is one small additional complicating factor: PostScript doesn't have the tangent function built in, but instead expects you to find it by dividing the sine by the cosine. So, continuing on with the example, you

```
% put a copy of the font on the stack
Yourfont
% follow it with our matrix
% with the the third position filled with the
% sine of 30 degrees divided by the cosine of 30
% degrees, multiplied by 24 points
[24 0 30 sin 30 cos div 24 mul 24 0 0]
% create the new font, set it as current
makefont setfont
% continue imaging text at our current position
(slanted fonts) show
% print the page
showpage
```

Next, see how you can get PostScript to make text fit into a specified space. You might need to do that, for example, to create justified columns in a report or to label a chart.

The basic strategy will be to measure the length of a text phrase, then subtract the length from the intended measure. Follow that by dividing the remaining distance among the spaces in the line, which you'll then add to the image. Because you want to use several values more than once, but PostScript operations take parameters from the top of the stack, you'll have to use several exchange operations to reorder the pending values on the stack.

```
% save the environment
gsave
% set up a 12-point font
/Times-Roman findfont 12 scalefont setfont
% move in 4 inches, up 8
288 572 moveto
% put two copies of the string on the stack
(All the news that fits in print) dup
% make another copy, use it to count length,
% which uses up the copy and leaves the length
dup stringwidth
% get rid of change in vertical position
% because you just want an even horizontal edge
pop
```

```postscript
% exchange the length and the extra copy of the string
% you left on the stack with the first "dup"
exch
% now, you need to set up the stack to count
% the spaces in a line. First, you
% put a zero on the stack for a counter
0
% pull the string up above the 0 on the stack
exch
% start a procedure to do for each element
% of the string, but mark it for deferred execution;
% the procedure will count how many spaces you have in
% the string
{
% set a flag if the element is a space (code 32)
32 eq
% leave a procedure on the stack to add 1
% to top of stack, which should be our counter
% when this operation is executed
{ 1
add}
% do the add to counter procedure if
% the flag was set true
if
% end of the procedure for each member
}
% tell PostScript to execute the test and
% possibly add to counter procedure for
% each element of the string (which is on the
% stack)
forall
% now exchange so the length is
% on top of the count
exch
% now subtract the leftover space
% from a desired length of 4 inches (72 X 4)
288 exch sub
% do the division, computing length
% to add at each space
exch div
% you now have the excess space that must
```

```
% be added at each space position sitting
% on the top of the stack. You don't want
% any extra vertical increment,
% but you need a y-axis value on the stack to
% be taken off by widthshow
0
% widthshow needs the string at the top of
% the stack, and it's now 3 down,
% so pull the third element to the top and
% roll all the others down
3 -1 roll
% show the string (from the stack),
% adding the increment whenever a space
% (character code 32) is encountered
32 exch widthshow
% show the page, restore the environment
showpage grestore
```

Of course, if you were actually writing a program to justify (even up) lines of text, you might optimize the process so the stack would need less rearranging. For simple text, however, the LaserWriter's built-in computer (or any other PostScript printer's RIP) is much faster than the print mechanism anyway, so optimizing isn't always worth the trouble. Instead, it's more worthwhile to write programs in logical order, with ample comments.

In this section, you saw a few ways to shape your own alphabets and how to make text fit in a defined space. Those processes are a small fraction of what PostScript can do with text, but they serve as an introduction. PostScript can literally write in circles, spirals, up and down steep angles, and even backward and forward.

Matrices in Space

PostScript keeps track of shapes and points as grid locations, but the grid may be different for the individual characters, for the page description, and for the output device. You can also set up temporary grids with new origins (0,0 position) or at an angle to the existing lines. Many of the PostScript operators are concerned with making a transformation from one grid to another.

One effective way to go between grids is by using matrix multiplication. PostScript makes extensive use of these multipliers, from mapping the character space into the user space, to mapping the user space onto the output device itself. Like many of the details of PostScript, you can start off without worrying at all about matrix mathematics and let PostScript automatically calaculate the essential values. If you're curious or ready for more advanced operations, however, this is how graphic matrices work.

Starting with any point value in two dimensions, extend that (X, Y) pair to a triplet matrix of [x y 1]. You can then accomplish the three basic graphic transformations by multiplying by the appropriate three-by-three matrix. For those of you who haven't learned matrix multiplication or have forgotten it along the way, multiplying the matrix

```
A    B    0
C    D    0      by [ X    Y    1]
E    F    1
```

yields a new three-element matrix with

```
first term  = (X*A)+(Y*C)+(1*E)
second term = (X*B)+(Y*D)+(1+F)
third term  = (1*0)+(1*0)=(1*1).
```

To translate (move position sideways), you set the matrix to

```
1    0    0
0    1    0
dx   dy   1
```

which multiplied by

```
[X    Y    1]
```

yields

```
[(X*1)+(Y*0)+(1*dx)   (X*0)+(Y*1)+(1*dy)
 (1*0)+(1*0)+(1*1)],
```

simplifying to

```
X' = X + dx,  Y' = Y + dy,  1 = 1.
```

To scale (move up or down in size), the matrix becomes

```
Sx   0    0
0    Sy   0
0    0    1
```

which multiplied by

[X   Y   1]

yields

[(X*Sx)+(Y*0)+(1*0)   (X*0)+(Y*Sy)+(1*0)
(1*0)+(1*0)+(1*1)],

simplifying to

X' = X * Sx, Y' = Y + Sy, 1 = 1.

Finally, to rotate the axes at an angle, the matrix is

```
cos(a)    -sin(a)    0
sin(a)     cos(a)    0
0          0         1
```

which multiplied by [X Y 1] yields

[(X*cos(a))+(Y*sin(a))+(1*0)
(X*-sin(a))+(Y*cos(a))+(1*0)   (1*0)+(1*0)+(1*1)],

simplifying to

X' = X * cos(a) + y * sin(a)
Y' = X * -sin(a) + Y * cos(a)
1 = 1

Although these matrix operations seem tedious by hand, they're reasonably easy for a computer. More complex transformations can be constructed using combinations of displacement, scale, and rotation in the proper sequence.

If you'd like to try your hand at PostScript programming, you'll need access to a LaserWriter or another PostScript printer hooked up to an AppleTalk or serial connection. You can write the PostScript programs on just about any word-processing program. To send the program to the printer that is connected to your computer via AppleTalk, use the SendPS program included on the Adobe Illustrator Gallery Disk.

If you want to send your program to a printer connected via the serial port, you can use a communications package such as MacTerminal or MicroPhone. Set your communications parameters to 8 data bits, 1 stop bit, no parity, and the X-ON/X-OFF protocol. You can use 1200 bps (set the Mode control on the LaserWriter to 1), 9600 bps (Mode 2), or AppleTalk (Mode 3). Send the LaserWriter a Control-D to stop any current job, a Control-T to have it report the job's status, and the Executive command to tell it to echo back your input. Then, enter your PostScript programs.

The Illustrator Document

An Illustrator document is a PostScript program that describes the appearance of a piece of artwork that you create with the Illustrator program. An Illustrator document is saved as a text file that can be opened and edited using a standard word-processing program such as Word, MacWrite, or WriteNow. The document communicates a description of the artwork to PostScript ouput devices such as the Macintosh screen, printers, and typesetting machines; and to graphics software such as Illustrator program itself.

Illustrator files consist of a prologue and data. The prologue defines the procedures that are used by Illustrator to describe the artwork. The data part of the Illustrator document consists of calls to the procedures defined in the prologue and the associated target groups of data about the components of the artwork such as coordinates and positions of all the lines and curves, their associated line weights, gray-scale or color values, paint and type specifications, and page breaks. The procedures in the prologue relate to many of the functions that are available within the Illustrator program with the notable exception that transformations such as scaling, rotating, reflecting, and skewing are performed within the Illustrator program itself and only the information about the resultant transformation is contained in the Illustrator document. Although commands for performing the transformations are available within PostScript, saving the transformed objects saves time during printing since the PostScript interpreter in the printer (the RIP) doesn't have to be burdened with the task of the transformation, which can be a relatively slow process.

Illustrator can also save a document in the Macintosh Encapsulated PostScript format or the IBM PC Encapsulated PostScript format. These formats contain a reduced resolution image of the artwork in addition to its PostScript description, and therefore, cannot be opened with a standard word processing program. This image provides a 72 dot-per-inch representation of the artwork in either the QuickDraw PICT format (in Macintosh Encapsulated PostScript) and Aldus/Microsoft TIFF format (in IBM PC Encapsulated PostScript.) The representation of the artwork can be used by another program such as a page layout program for placement of the artwork in a layout, or for scaling or cropping the image. The page layout program (such as PageMaker) can use the bit-mapped representation of the image to provide a WYSIWYG screen approximation without requiring the program to understand PostScript.

The PostScript portion of Encapsulated PostScript documents created by Illustrator version 1.0 and 1.01 follows the bit-mapped representation of the artwork and conforms to the Adobe PostScript Document Structuring Conventions, version 2.0, the Adobe Encapsulated PostScript File Format For Apple Macintosh and IBM PC Application, version 1.2, the Aldus Rncapsulated PostScript File Format for PageMaker Import for PC Windows and Macintosh Applications, version 1.2, and the Altsys Encapsulated PostScript File Format for Apple Macintosh and PC-Windows Applications, version 1.2.

Another convention used by all the Illustrator document formats is not to include the PostScript command showpage (or copypage) at the end of the document as is often the case in other PostScript documents. The showpage command causes the PostScript output device to print (or display) the page and clear the page from the printer's memory after the page is printed. The copypage command is similar to the showpage command except that the image of the page is left unchanged in the printer's memory after the page has been printed. Since Illustrator files are usually created for the purpose of becoming a component in another document (such as a page layout), printing the page at the end of the artwork is not usually desirable because it would interfere with the normal printing process of that page by causing it to be printed prematurely. Illustrator temporarily appends a showpage command to the end of the document as part of Illustrator's normal printing process that is invoked by either selecting Print from the File menu or by typing

Command-P as a shortcut. If you want to print an Illustrator document, you can add the showpage command to the end of the document while you are editing it, or you can use the SendPS program described on page 20, which has an option for temporarily appending the showpage command to a PostScript file for the purpose of printing.

The Illustrator Document Structure

Illustrator uses a standard text file format to store its documents. One of the advantages of using the text format is that people can easily read and modify an Illustrator document with just about any word-processing program. On the tutorial disk is is a simple piece of Illustrator artwork (the drawing of a Macintosh mouse in Chapter 5), and below the Illustrator document that was created when the mouse artwork was created. Following the Illustrator document printout is an explanation of what the various elements in the document mean.

```
%!PS-Adobe-2.0 EPSF-1.2
%%Creator:Adobe Illustrator(TM) 1.0
%%For:Fred Davis
%%Title:Mouse art
%%CreationDate:4/25/87 1:39 PM
%%DocumentProcSets:Adobe_Illustrator_1.0 0 0
%%DocumentSuppliedProcSets:Adobe_Illustrator_1.0 0 0
%%DocumentFonts:Courier
%%BoundingBox:27 -366 526 -55
%%TemplateBox:0 -720 576 0
%%EndComments
%%BeginProcSet:Adobe_Illustrator_1.0 0 0
% Copyright (C) 1987 Adobe Systems Incorporated.
% All Rights Reserved.
% Adobe Illustrator is a trademark of Adobe Systems Incorporated.
/Adobe_Illustrator_1.0 dup 100 dict def load begin
/Version 0 def
/Revision 0 def
% definition operators
/bdef {bind def} bind def
/ldef {load def} bdef
/xdef {exch def} bdef
```

```
% graphic state operators
/_K {3 index add neg dup 0 lt {pop 0} if 3 1 roll}
bdef
/_k /setcmybcolor where
{/setcmybcolor get} {{1 sub 4 1 roll _K _K _K
setrgbcolor pop} bind}   ifelse def
/g {/_b xdef /p {_b setgray} def} bdef
/G {/_B xdef /P {_B setgray} def} bdef
/k {/_b xdef /_y xdef /_m xdef /_c xdef /p {_c _m
_y _b _k} def} bdef
/K {/_B xdef /_Y xdef /_M xdef /_C xdef /P {_C _M
_Y _B _k} def} bdef
/d /setdash ldef
/_i currentflat def
/i {dup 0 eq {pop _i} if setflat} bdef
/j /setlinejoin ldef
/J /setlinecap ldef
/M /setmiterlimit ldef
/w /setlinewidth ldef
% path construction operators
/_R {.25 sub round .25 add} bdef
/_r {transform _R exch _R exch itransform} bdef
/c {_r curveto} bdef
/C /c ldef
/v {currentpoint 6 2 roll _r curveto} bdef
/V /v ldef
/y {_r 2 copy curveto} bdef
/Y /y ldef
/l {_r lineto} bdef
/L /l ldef
/m {_r moveto} bdef
% error operators
/_e [] def
/_E {_e length 0 ne {gsave 0 g 0 G 0 i 0 J 0 j 1 w
10 M [] 0 d
/Courier 20 0 0 1 z [0.966 0.259 -0.259 0.966
_e 0 get _e 2 get add 2 div _e 1 get _e 3 get add
2 div] e _f t T   grestore} if} bdef
/_fill {{fill} stopped
{/_e [pathbbox] def /_f (ERROR: can't fill, in-
crease flatness)
def n _E} if}
```

```
  bdef
  /_stroke {{stroke} stopped
  {/_e [pathbbox] def /_f (ERROR: can't stroke,
increase flatness) def n         _E} if} bdef
  % path painting operators
  /n /newpath ldef
  /N /n ldef
  /F {p _fill} bdef
  /f {closepath F} bdef
  /S {P _stroke} bdef
  /s {closepath S} bdef
  /B {gsave F grestore S} bdef
  /b {closepath B} bdef
  % text block construction and painting operators
  /_s /ashow ldef
  /_S {(?) exch {2 copy 0 exch put pop dup false
charpath currentpoint _g setmatrix
  _stroke _G setmatrix moveto 3 copy pop rmoveto}
forall pop pop pop n} bdef
  /_A {_a moveto _t exch 0 exch} bdef
  /_L {0 _l neg translate _G currentmatrix pop} bdef
  /_w {dup stringwidth exch 3 -1 roll length 1 sub
_t mul add exch}  bdef
  /_z [{0 0} {dup _w exch neg 2 div exch neg 2 div}
{dup _w exch neg  exch neg}] bdef
  /z {_z exch get /_a xdef /_t xdef /_l xdef exch
findfont exch scalefont setfont} bdef
  /_g matrix def
  /_G matrix def
  /_D {_g currentmatrix pop gsave concat _G current-
matrix pop} bdef
  /e {_D p /t {_A _s _L} def} bdef
  /r {_D P /t {_A _S _L} def} bdef
  /a {_D /t {dup p _A _s P _A _S _L} def} bdef
  /o {_D /t {pop _L} def} bdef
  /T {grestore} bdef
  % group construction operators
  /u {} bdef
  /U {} bdef
  % font construction operators
  /Z {findfont begin currentdict dup length dict
begin
```

```
{1 index /FID ne {def} {pop pop} ifelse} forall /
FontName exch def dup    length 0 ne
  {/Encoding Encoding 256 array copy def 0 exch {dup
type /nametype    eq
  {Encoding 2 index 2 index put pop 1 add} {exch
pop} ifelse} forall} if pop
  currentdict dup end end /FontName get exch defin-
efont pop} bdef
end
%%EndProcSet
%%EndProlog
%%BeginSetup
Adobe_Illustrator_1.0 begin
n
%%EndSetup
0 g
0 G
1 i
0 J
0 j
0.2 w
    10 M
[]0 d
%%Note:
163.75 -161.25 m
156.75 -165.75 152.75 -171.25 160.75 -174.25 C
344.25 -249.75 l
360.25 -251.75 361.75 -254.25 377.75 -242.75 c
393.75 -231.25 459.75 -185.75 y
464.811 -180.343 457.938 -177.323 452.25 -174.75 c
447.156 -172.445 243.25 -91.75 y
232.625 -88.125 224.25 -88.25 216.25 -93.25 c
208.25 -98.25 104.569 -169.953 102.25 -173.25 c
99.875 -176.625 97.75 -182.75 118.25 -189.25 c
138.75 -195.75 365.25 -291.25 371.75 -294.25 c
378.25 -297.25 393.75 -307.25 421.75 -284.75 c
449.75 -262.25 507.75 -217.75 y
513.25 -212.75 513.75 -206.75 502.75 -200.75 c
491.75 -194.75 457.625 -177.25 y
S
101 -176.625 m
98.5 -209.625 99.25 -239.25 99.25 -242.25 C
```

```
99.75 -251.5 102.625 -251.25 113.75 -255.25 c
130.714 -261.349 376.25 -345.25 y
384.75 -347.25 399.75 -351.5 420.75 -335.75 c
444.19 -318.169 516.75 -260.25 y
523.625 -253.312 521.25 -247.75 520.25 -242.25 c
519.25 -236.75 515.75 -216.25 y
514.75 -210.875 509.875 -206.375 y
S
103 -251.25 m
98.5 -253.75 102.25 -254.75 107.25 -256.75 c
112.25 -258.75 377.75 -348.25 y
389.75 -352 401 -350 410.75 -344.75 c
419.421 -340.08 519.75 -260.25 y
521.875 -258.187 520.937 -253.937 y
S
521.187 -256.937 m
518.25 -275.312 510.255 -279.244 507.25 -282.25 c
503.75 -285.75 416.75 -351.5 y
404 -362 388.75 -363.75 374.75 -359.25 c
360.75 -354.75 116.25 -269.25 y
106.375 -265.25 101.5 -264.625 101 -253.125 c
S
85 -181 m
83 -167.5 l
96 -159.75 l
199.75 -160 l
86.5 -167.75 l
88.5 -182.5 l
85 -181 l
s
89.899 -182.811 m
88.014 -168.234 l
101.639 -160.26 l
105.642 -160.525 l
91.75 -168.5 l
93.634 -184.403 l
89.899 -182.811 l
s
95.076 -185.032 m
93.036 -169.254 l
107.784 -160.622 l
112.117 -160.909 l
```

```
97.079 -169.541 l
99.119 -186.755 l
95.076 -185.032 l
s
100.392 -187.333 m
98.309 -170.254 l
114.274 -160.91 l
118.464 -161.221 l
102.686 -170.565 l
103.02 -172.323 l
S
90.25 -163 m
71.5 -161 48 -168 42.25 -115.5 c
36.5 -63 35.75 -57 y
S
83.5 -172 m
70 -170.75 41 -174 35.5 -124.5 c
29.668 -72.009 29 -66 y
S
147.125 -154.25 m
145.125 -155.875 145.125 -156.25 144.25 -158.5 C
158.25 -157.5 162.25 -157.75 163.75 -158.75 c
165.25 -159.75 216.492 -180.796 217.75 -180.25 C
220.562 -182.187 296.375 -127.562 296.375 -126.062
c
S
144.25 -158.625 m
144.5 -160.375 144.875 -161 y
S
104.25 -176.25 m
152.75 -170.75 l
S
226.75 -90.75 m
248.75 -99.75 l
S
218.312 -177.125 m
217.875 -179.75 l
S
294.19 -126.316 m
283.092 -134.798 234.443 -168.174 221.228 -175.821
C
218.228 -177.446 217.009 -176.519 214.384 -176.144
```

```
C
  202.719 -171.863 166.924 -157.366 165.25 -156.25 c
  163.991 -155.41 159.772 -155.025 150.615 -155.595
C
  145.365 -156.22 145.838 -155.079 148.588 -152.829
C
  166.414 -141.471 215.09 -106.17 220 -105 c
  223.715 -104.114 243.875 -101.625 246 -103 C
  294.299 -123.469 L
  295.486 -124.219 295.253 -125.441 294.19 -126.316
C
  s
  294.687 -123.75 m
  295.564 -124.353 296.125 -124.812 296.375 -126.062
C
  S
  296.375 -126.125 m
  296.5 -127 296.625 -128.437 y
  S
  144.125 -159.375 m
  142.375 -160.375 141.187 -160.812 142.312 -161.062
  C
  156.312 -160.062 162.25 -160.25 163.75 -161.25 c
  165.25 -162.25 214.75 -182.25 217.75 -182.75 c
  220.75 -183.25 298.149 -128.899 297.812 -127.437 c
  297.625 -126.625 296.875 -126.687 296.5 -126.5 c
  S
  368.25 -255.25 m
  392.25 -293.25 l
  S
  465.25 -186.25 m
  505.25 -207.25 l
  S
  322.5 -220.75 m
  338.5 -210.75 l
  340.25 -209.5 343.5 -209 346.25 -210 c
  351.45 -211.891 371 -219.5 y
  373 -221 372.25 -222.25 370.25 -224 c
  365.984 -227.732 353.75 -235.25 y
  352 -236.25 349.5 -236.5 346.75 -235.5 c
  341.844 -233.716 322.5 -226 y
```

```
319.5 -225 318.75 -223.25 322.5 -220.75 C
S
321.25 -224.75 m
338.75 -213.5 l
340.5 -212.25 343.75 -211.75 346.5 -212.75 c
351.7 -214.641 371.25 -222.25 y
S
339.687 -220.375 m
335.687 -220.75 332.125 -222.125 331.875 -224.5 c
331.625 -226.875 332.375 -230 338.25 -231.875 c
344.125 -233.75 347.936 -233.396 351.375 -232.25 c
354 -231.375 353.462 -229.617 354.5 -228.75 c
356.463 -227.107 359.564 -227.437 361.5 -225.625 c
365.411 -221.963 354.219 -216.578 348.5 -215.625 c
347 -215.375 346.319 -215.056 344 -215.875 c
342.024 -216.572 341.375 -217.125 341 -218.125 c
340.625 -219.125 341.125 -221.5 340.25 -219.25 c
339.375 -217 339.125 -215.25 338.25 -215.25 C
337.875 -216.75 337.937 -219.75 339.687 -220.375 C
338.812 -220.375 339.687 -220.375 y
S
167.25 -155.25 m
245.125 -103.875 l
S
217.812 -180.375 m
217.125 -181.812 217.875 -182.562 y
S
%%Trailer
_E end
```

The Document Structure Explained

As stated earlier, the document consists of two major sections, a prologue followed by a script. The prologue contains a set of specific definitions that are used by the script. These definitions describe Illustrator's output functions in PostScript language primitives. The script describes the component graphic elements that are used to create the artwork. The description consists of references to the definitions made in the prologue, interspersed with operands and the data required by those operations. Below is an overview of the Illustrator document's component sections and subsections, and the order in which they appear in the document. Following the overview is a more detailed description of the prologue definitions and the component descriptions within script.

The following describes an Adobe Illustrator document, focusing primarily on the document's overall structure as defined by a set of PostScript comments. Comments can be recognized by the percentage sign (%) that precedes them. Comments are totally ignored by a PostScript interpreter. However, they convey structural information about the document to other programs that operate on the document. Some comments serve primarily to mark the boundaries between the various parts of the document (the prologue and the script). Others provide information such as a bounding box that encloses all the marks painted as a result of executing the document and the set of fonts that may need to be down-loaded to a PostScript printer before the document can be printed.

The Prologue Section of an Illustrator Document

The document's prologue section is subdivided into header and definition subsections.

Prologue Header Subsection

```
%!PS-Adobe-2.0 EPSF-1.2
```
is the first line in the document and indicates that the document conforms to version 2.0 of the PostScript Document Structuring Conventions and version 1.2 of the Encapsulated PostScript Document Format.

```
%%Creator:Adobe Illustrator(TM) version serial
```
indicates that the document was created by the specified version of Adobe Illustrator optionally serialized with the specified serial value. The version value and the optional serial value consist of arbitrary text delimited by white space.

```
%%For:name organization
```
indicates that the document was created by a version of Adobe Illustrator personalized for the specified name and organization. The name and organization values consist of arbitrary text, including white space. Organization is terminated by a newline.

`%%Title: name`

indicates the title of the document. The name value consists of arbitrary text terminated by a newline.

`%%Creation Date: date time`

indicates the date and time at which the document was created. The date and time values consist of arbitrary text, including white space. Time is terminated by a newline.

`%%DocumentProcSets: Adobe_Illustrator_version level revision` indicates that the document requires the specified prologue procedure set. The version, level, and revision values consist of arbitrary text delimited by white space.

`%%DocumentSuppliedProcSets: Adobe_Illustrator_version level revision`

indicates that the document supplies the specified prologue procedure set. The version, level, and revision values consist of arbitrary text delimited by white space.

`%%DocumentFonts: font...`

indicates that the document uses the specified fonts. These fonts may need to be downloaded to the PostScript printer before the document is sent. The font values consist of PostScript font names delimited by white space.

`%%+font ...`

when following the %%DocumentFonts comment, this comment indicates that the document uses the specified fonts, in addition to those given by the %%DocumentFonts comment. The font values consist of PostScript font names delimited by white space.

`%%BoundingBox: llx lly urx lry`

indicates the bounding box that encloses all the marks painted as a result of executing the document. All four values are either integers or reals; (llx, lly) and (urx, ury) are the coordinates of the lower left and upper right corners of the bounding box, respectively. The coordinates are specified in the default user coordinate system in which the unit length along both axes is 1/72 of an inch. The value urx - llx, which must be an integer, provides an upper bound on the width of the illustration. The value ury - lly, which must be an integer, provides an upper bound on the height of the illustration.

`%%TemplateBox: llx lly urx lry`

indicates the bounding box that encloses all the samples in the document's template. All four values are either integers or reals: (llx, lly) and (urx, ury) are the coordinates of the lower left and upper right corners of the bounding box, respectively. The coordinates are specified in the default user coordinate system in which the unit length along both axes is 1/72 of an inch. Adobe Illustrator assumes that the size of each sample is 1/72-by-1/72- inch. The value urx - llx, which must be an integer, equals the number of rows of samples. If the document has no template, llx equals urx and lly equals ury.

When Adobe Illustrator opens the document, the illustration is placed on the drawing area in such a way that the coordinate ((llx +urx)/2), (lly +ury)/2) is centered in the drawing area.

```
%%EndComments
```
explicitly ends the prologue header subsection and marks the beginning of the prologue definition subsection.

Prolog Definition Subsection

```
%%BeginProcSet:Adobe_Illustrator_version level
revision prologue definitions
  %%EndProcSet
```

The %%BeginProcSet and %%EndProcSet comments explicitly delimit the prologue definitions of the document. These definitions are used by the script section to match the Adobe Illustrator's output functions to the capabilities and primitives that PostScript supports. The entire prologue is packaged as a single procedure set identified by the version, level, and revision values, each of which is delimited by white space.

```
%%EndProlog
```
The %%EndProlog remark explicitly ends the prologue section and marks the beginning of the script section.

The Script Section

The document's script section is subdivided into setup, body, and trailer subsection.

Script Setup Subsection

```
    %%BeginSetup
    script setup
    %%End Setup
```

The %%BeginSetup and %%EndSetup comments explicitly delimit the script setup, which performs various graphics state and error recovery initialization and font reencoding operations required by the document's prologue and script.

Script Body Subsection

`script body`
The script body describes the set of component graphic elements that define the illustration. The script consists of references to definitions made in the prologue, interspersed with operands and data required by those operations.

`%%Trailer`
The %%Trailer remark explicitly ends the script body subsection of the document and marks the beginning of the script trailer subsection.

Script Trailer Subsection

`script trailer`
The script trailer performs various cleanup and error recovery operations required by the document's prologue and script.

Illustrator Document Prologue Definitions

This section specifies and defines the operations provided by the prologue of an Adobe Illustrator document. These operations are used within the script to match Adobe Illustrator's output functions to the capabilities and primitives provided by PostScript.

Graphic State Operations

The prologue maintains a graphics state that establishes a context in which its graphic operations execute. The graphics state inherits most of its functionality from the underlying graphics state supplied by the PostScript interpreter. Many of the prologue's graphics state operations have a one-for-one mapping into a single PostScript primitive, and hence they simply provide a set of abbreviated primitive names or aliases.

The primary difference between the prologue's graphics state and that of PostScript is in the handling of color state and font metric information. The prologue maintains two separate current color parameters: a filling color and a stroking color. These two parameters determine the color of subsequently filled and stroked shapes, respectively (see g, G, k, and K). They are provided to match Adobe Illustrator's capability of filling and stroking a single path with different colors.

The font metric information included in the graphics state, in addition to the current font, consists of the kerning adjustment to the x width of each character, the leading distance between each successive line of text, and a specification of the alignment method that aligns each line of text. These parameters are provided to support Adobe Illustrator's text-block painting operators.

Several of PostScript's graphic state parameters are not directly accessible through prologue operators. These parameters include the current transformation matrix, the clipping path, the halftone screen, the transfer function, and the output device. Values for these parameters are inherited by the prologue when the prologue is executed and remain unchanged throughout the execution of the rest of the document. (This statement may not be strictly true if the document's script contains embedded documents. However, the graphics state may be restored and all printer virtual memory recovered by embedding the document itself within a save/restore context.)

    d   array offset d -

sets the dash pattern parameter in the graphics state which determines the dash pattern of subsequently stroked paths (see s and S). The array and offset parameter values have meaning identical to those of the PostScript setdash operator. That is, if array is empty, normal unbroken stroked lines are produced. If array is not empty, dashed lines, whose pattern (in user space) is given by the elements of array, which must all be non-negative and not all zero, are produced. The offset parameter, which must be non-negative, is interpreted as a distance (in user space) into the dash pattern at which the pattern should be started.

    g   gray g -

sets the current filling color parameter in the graphics state which determines the color of subsequently filled paths (see f and F). The gray parameter value has a meaning identical to that of the PostScript setgray operator. That is, the filling color is set to a gray shade corresponding to gray, which must be a number between 0 and 1, where 0 corresponds to black, 1 corresponds to white, and intermediate values correspond to intermediate shades of gray.

G   gray G -

sets the current stroking color parameter in the graphics state which determines the color of subsequently stroked paths (see s and S). The gray parameter value has a meaning identical to that of the PostScript setgray operator. That is, the stroking color is set to a gray shade corresponding to gray, which must be a number between 0 and 1, where 0 corresponds to black, 1 corresponds to white, and intermediate values correspond to intermediate shades of gray.

i   flat i   -

sets the current flatness parameter in the graphics state which determines the accuracy with which curved path segments are to be rendered on the output device. A positive flat parameter value has a meaning identical to that of the PostScript setflat operator. That is, its value gives the maximum error tolerance (in output device pixels) of a straight line segment approximation of any portion of a curve. If flat is 0, the flatness is set to the flatness value in effect when the document's prologue section is executed, which normally equals the device's default, built-in flatness.

j   join j -

sets the current line join parameter in the graphics state which determines the shape to be placed at the corners of stroked paths (see s and S). The join parameter value has a meaning identical to that of the PostScript setlinejoin operator. That is, the value 0 establishes miter joins, 1 establishes round joins, and 2 establishes bevel joins.

J   cap J -

sets the current line cap parameter in the graphics state which determines the shape to be placed at the ends of open stroked paths and at the ends of dashed line segments (see s and S). The cap parameter value has a meaning identical to that of the PostScript setlinecap operator. That is, the value 0 establishes butt caps, 1 establishes round caps, and 2 establishes projecting caps.

k   cyan magenta yellow black k -

sets the current filling color parameter in the graphics state which determines the color of subsequently filled paths (see f and F). The cyan, magenta, yellow, and black parameter values have meaning identical to those of the PostScript setcmybcolor operator (contact Adobe Systems Technical Support for a definition of this operator). That is, each value must be a number between 0 and 1, where 0 corresponds to no contribution at all of that color, 1 corresponds to maximum intensity of that color, and intermediate values correspond to intermediate intensities.

If the setcmybcolor operator is not known in any of the dictionaries on the current dictionary stack when the document's prologue section is executed, then the current filling or stroking color parameter is set to the color obtained by the following operation

```
red green blue setrgbcolor
```
where
red = 1 - min(1, cyan + black)
green = 1 - min(1, magenta + black)
blue = 1 - min(1, yellow + black)

That is, the black component is added to each of the other three components, and the resulting values are converted to a color specified by the red-green-blue color model.

On most existing black-and-white PostScript printers, the setrgbcolor operator is implemented as if the following operation were performed

```
gray setgray
```
where gray is an NTSC weighed average of the three color components given by

```
gray = .3* red + .59* green+.11* blue
```

Of course, page composition systems and other printing managers may produce color separations on black-and-white printers by redefining the setcmybcolor and setgray operators and establishing the appropriate halftone screens and transfer functions before sending the document.

```
K      cyan magenta yellow black K -
```
sets the current stroking color parameter in the graphics state which determines the color of subsequently stroked paths (see s and S). The cyan, magenta, yellow, and black parameter values have meaning identical to those of the PostScript setcmybcolor operator. That is, each value must be a number between 0 and 1, where 0 corresponds to no contribution at all of that color, 1 corresponds to maximum intensity of that color, and intermediate values correspond to intermediate intensities of that color.

See the k operator for a discussion of the setcmybcolor operator.

```
M      miter M -
```
sets the current miter limit parameter which determines when the objectionably long spikes produced at the corners of stroked paths by mitered joins should be cut off with bevels (see j). The miter parameter value has a meaning identical to that of the PostScript setmiterlimit operator. That is, miter specifies the maximum desired

ratio between the miter length at the corner and the line width.

    w   width w -

sets the current line width parameter in the graphics state which determines the thickness of stroked lines (see s and S). The width parameter value has a meaning identical to that of the PostScript setlinewidth operator. That is, all points whose perpendicular distance from the current path (in user space) is less than or equal to one-half of width are painted. As usual, a value of 0 is permitted: it is interpreted as the thinnest line that can be rendered on the output device.

    z   font scale leading kerning alignment z -

sets the current font parameter in the graphics state which establishes the font dictionary to be used by subsequent text-block painting operators (see a, e, o, and r). The positive scale factor scale is applied to the font dictionary given by the literal name font, producing a new font whose characters are scaled by the positive number scale (in both x and y). The resulting font is established as the current font.

This operator also sets the current leading, kerning, and alignment method parameters in the graphics state. The kerning parameter, given by the number kerning, specifies a value (in user space) that is added to the x width of each character in the scaled font, thus modifying the horizontal spacing between the characters. The leading parameter, given by the non-negative leading, specifies the vertical spacing (in user space) between successive lines of text composing the text block. The alignment method parameter, given by the integer alignment, specifies how the lines of text are aligned with one another. That is, an alignment value of 0 specifies align left (flush left, ragged right), 1 specifies align center (ragged left and right), and 2 specifies align right (ragged left, flush right).

    Z   array newfont font Z -

creates a new reencoded font, whose name is given by the literal name newfont, that is a copy of an existing font, whose name is given by font, except that portions of the new font's encoding vector have been modified as specified by the array parameter value. Array is an array of encoding numbers and literal character names organized as follows:

```
[code1 name11 name12...name1m1
code2 name21 name22....name2m2
....
coden namen1 namen2...namenmn]
```

where codei for $1 <= i <= n$ are encoding numbers between 0 and 255, and nameij for $1 <= i <= n$, $1 <= mi$ are literal character names.

The encoding vector of the new font is identical to that of the existing font except that the element at index codei + j equals nameij for 1 <= i <= n, 1 <=j <= mi. It is assumed that all of the encoding numbers codei + j are distinct. In addition, n may be equal to 0, in which case array is an empty array, and the encoding vector of the new font is identical to that of the existing font.

Path Construction Operations

A path is built up by executing one or more path construction operations that append a sequence of connected straight or curved line segments onto the path. Once a path is completely built up, it is painted with one of the path painting operations.

Only one path may be built up at a time. This path is called the current path. The current path is initially empty and is reset to empty by all of the path painting operations.

The trailing endpoint of the most recently appended segment is referred to as the current point. All of the path construction operations that append a segment start at the current point. Each segment is specified by a set of coordinates specified in user space. A new path is begun by executing a special operation that establishes a current point on an otherwise empty path.

As the path is built up, each point that joins two segments is marked a smooth point or a corner point. If the point is marked smooth, then the point and the two associated Bezier direction points of the segments that the point connects are assumed to be colinear. If the point is marked corner, then no constraint is assumed. (A straight line segment can be thought of as a degenerate Bezier curve whose direction points are coincident with its endpoints).

```
c     x1 y1 x2 y2 x3 y3 c   -
```
adds a Bezier curve segment to the current path between the current point and the point (x3, y3), using (x1, y1) and then (x2, y2) as the Bezier direction points; (x3, y3) then becomes the current point. The new current point is marked a smooth point.

```
C     x1 y1 x2 y2 x3 y3 C   -
```
adds a Bezier curve segment to the current path between the current point and the point (x3, y3), using (x1, y1) and then (x2, y2) as the Bezier direction points; (x3, y3) then becomes the current point. The new current point is marked a corner point.

```
l     x y l   -
```
appends a straight line segment to the current path. The line extends from the current point to the point (x, y); (x, y) then becomes the

current point. The new current point is marked a smooth point.

L   x y L −

appends a straight line segment to the current path. The line extends from the current point to the point (x, y); (x, y) then becomes the current point. The new current point is marked a corner point.

m   x y m −

starts a new current path by setting the current point to (x, y) without adding any segment to the path. Initially, the path must be empty and have no current point.

v   x2 y2 x3 y3 v −

adds a Bezier curve segment to the current path between the current point and the point (x3, y3), using the current point and then (x2, y2) as the Bezier direction points; (x3, y3) then becomes the current point. The new current point is marked a smooth point.

V   x2 y2 x3 y3 V −

adds a Bezier curve segment to the current path between the current point and the point (x3, y3), using the current point and then (x2, y2) as the Bezier direction points; (x3, y3) then becomes the current point. The new current point is marked a corner point.

y   x1 y1 x3 y3 y −

adds a Bezier curve segment to the current path between the current point and the point (x3, y3), using (x1, y1) and then (x3, y3) as the Bezier direction points; (x3, y3) then becomes the current point. The new current point is marked a smooth point.

Y   x1 y1 x3 y3 Y−

adds a Bezier curve segment to the current path between the current point and the point (x3, y3), using (x1, y1) and then (x3, y3) as the Bezier direction points; (x3, y3) then becomes the current point. The new current point is marked a corner point.

Path Painting Operations

The prologue provides a set of painting operations that can convert the current path to represent marks on the current page. All of these operations are based on combinations of the underlying PostScript primitives closepath, fill, and stroke. The results of these painting operations are controlled by the prologue's current graphics state.

All of the painting operations assume that the current path has been previously built-up by a sequence of path construction operations. After the painting operation is completed, the current path is initialized to be empty.

b   - b-
indicates that the current path should be closed and then first filled (see f and F) with the current filling color and then stroked (see s and S) with the current stroking color.

B   - B -
indicates that the current path should be first filled (see f and F) with the current filling color and then stroked (see s and S) with the current stroking color.

f   - f -
closes the current path and then paints (fills) the area enclosed by the current path with the current filling color. The inside of the current path is determined by the normal PostScript non-zero winding number rule. Any previous contents of that area on the current page are obscured.

F   - F -
paints (fills) the area enclosed by the current path with the current filling color. The inside of the current path is determined by the normal PostScript non-zero winding number rule. Any previous contents of that area on the current page are obscured.

n   - n -
closes the current path and then neither fills (see f and F) nor strokes (see s and S) the path.

N   - N -
neither fills (see f and F) nor strokes (see s and S) the current path.

s   - s -
closes the current path and then paints (strokes) a line following the path with the current stroking color. This line is centered on the path, has sides parallel to the path segments, and has a width given by the current line width parameter (see w). The joints between connected path segments are painted with the current line join (see j). The ends of the line's dash segments, if any, are painted with the current line cap (see J). The line is either solid or broken according to the current dash pattern (see d).

S   - S -
paints (strokes) a line following the path with the current stroking color. This line is centered on the path, has sides parallel to the path segments, and has a width given by the current line width parameter (see w). The joints between connected path segments are painted with the current line join (see j). The ends of the path and the ends of the line's dash segments, if any, are painted with the current line cap (see J). The line is either solid or broken according to the current dash pattern (see d).

Text Block Painting Operations

The prologue provides a set of text block painting operations that paint the successive lines of text composing the text block, using the current font, kerning, leading, and alignment method parameters in the graphics state.

    a   matrix a -

indicates the start of a text block whose character outlines should be neither filled (see e) nor stroked (see r). Matrix specifies a matrix that is concatenated with the current transformation matrix to define a new user space whose coordinates are transformed into the former user space according to matrix. This new space establishes an origin for the first line of text.

    e   matrix e -

indicates the start of a text block whose character outlines should be filled with the current filling color. Matrix specifies a matrix that is concatenated with the current transformation matrix to define a new user space whose coordinates are transformed into the former user space according to matrix. This new space establishes an origin for the first line of text.

    o   matrix o -

indicates the start of a text block whose character outlines should be first filled (see e) with the current filling color and then stroked (see r) with the current stroking color. Matrix specifies a matrix that is concatenated with the current transformation matrix to define a new user space whose coordinates are transformed into the former user space according to matrix.. This new space establishes an origin for the first line of text.

    r   matrix r -

indicates the start of a text block whose character outlines should be stroked with the current stroking color. The stroked line is centered on the character's outline, has sides parallel to the outline's segments, and has a width given by the current line width parameter (see w). The joints between connected outline segments are painted with the current line join (see j). The ends of the line's dash segments, if any, are painted with the current line cap (see J). The outline is either solid or broken according to the current dash pattern (see d). The width and dash parameters' lengths are interpreted in terms of the user space in effect prior to the start of the text block. Matrix specifies a matrix that is concatenated with the current transformation matrix to define a new user space whose coordinates are transformed into the former user space according to matrix. This new space establishes an origin for the first line of text.

      t   string t -

prints the characters of string starting at the point (Sx, Sy) in the user space established by either the a, e, o, or r operator at the start of the text block or by the prior t operator. The characters are printed using a combination of the outline filling and stroking methods as specified by the a, e, o, or r operator. The characters are painted using the current font. While painting, the width of each character is adjusted by adding the current kerning to its x width.

The starting point (Sx, Sy) is defined as follows:

alignment method	(Sx, Sy)
align left	(0, 0)
align center	(-wx/2, -wy/2)
align right	(-wx, wy)

where wx and wy are the sum of the x and y widths of all the characters printed, respectively (where the x widths have been adjusted by the kerning parameter value).

After painting, the origin of user space is translated by the current leading in the negative y direction to establish an origin for the next line of text.

      T   - T -

indicates the end of a text block and restores the user space in effect prior to the start of the text block.

Group Construction Operations

The prologue provides two group construction operators that support Illustrator's ability to combine several objects into groups that are then treated as one composite object. These operators have no affect on the graphics state, nor do they place marks on the page. They provide structural information only.

      u   - u -

indicates that the subsequent objects (paths, text blocks, and groups), up to the next matching U operator, are to be grouped together as a single object.

      U   - U -

when matched with a previous u operator, indicates the end of a group of objects.

Prologue Implementaton

The following is a complete listing of the version 1.1 PostScript implementation of the prologue's definitions. Indented descriptions are included throughout the listing to provide additional documentation.

```
%%BeginProcSet:Adobe_Illustrator_1.1 0 0
% Copyright (C) 1987 Adobe Systems Incorporated.
% All Rights Reserved.
% Adobe Illustrator is a trademark of Adobe Systems
Incorporated.
```

The entire prologue is packaged as a single procedure set identified by the %%BeginProcSet comment. Copyright and trademark information are also included.

```
/Adobe_Illustrator_1.1 dup 100 dict def load begin
/Version 0 def
/Revision 0 def
```

All of the prologue's definitions are placed within a dictionary created just for this purpose. This definition dictionary is associated with the key Adobe_Illustrator_1.1 in the current dictionary. The new dictionary is then placed on the top of the dictionary stack so that all of the following definitions will be defined within it.

The Version and Revision keys specify that the dictionary contains the version 0, revision 0 procedure set definitions. The version and revision fields are both 0 since version information is included in the dictionary's name.

In some environments, the entire prologue may be permanently down-loaded. The following program tests for its presence. The program writes true to the standard output file if the proper version and revision of the prologue are present and writes false otherwise.

```
Adobe_Illustrator_1.1 where
{begin Version 0 eq Revision 0 eq and end}
{false} ifelse = flush
% definition operators
/bdef {bind def} bind def
/ldef {load def} bdef
/xdef {exch def} bdef
```

These three definition operators all associate a key with a value in the current dictionary. They are provided to conserve virtual memory within the printer and to reduce the execution time required by the operators.

```
% graphic state operators
/_K {3 index add neg dub 0 it {pop 0} if 3 1 roll} bdef
/_k /setcmybcolor where
{/setcmybcolor get} {{1 sub 4 1 roll _K _K _K se-
trgbcolor pop} bind}     ifelse def
/g {/_b xdef /p {_b setgray} def} bdef
```

```
/G {/_B xdef /P {_B setgray} def} bdef
/k {/_b xdef /_y xdef /_m xdef /_c xdef /p {_c _m
_y _b _k} def} bdef
/K {/_B xdef /_Y xdef /_M xdef /_C xdef /P {_C _M
_Y _B _k} def} bdef
```

The four variables _c, _m, _y, and _b maintain the component cyan, magenta, yellow, and black color values, respectively, that represent the current filling color, and the execution of p establishes the current filling color as the current color in the PostScript graphics state. The five[[should be four?—is "P" a variable or an operand?]] variables _C, _M, _Y, _B and P perform a similar function with respect to the current stroking color. When executed, the four operators g, G, k, and K update the values of the appropriate subset of these eight variables.

The operators _k and _K provide an interface to the setcmybcolor operator. See the k operator for a discussio of their behavior.

```
/d /setdash ldef
/_l currentflat def
/l {dup 0 eq {pop _l} if setflat} bdef
/j /setlinejoin ldef
/J /setlinecap ldef
/M /setmiterlimit ldef
/w /setlinewidth ldef
```

These are implementations of several of the simpler graphics state operators.

```
% path construction operators
/_/R {.25 sub round .25 add} bdef
/_r {transform _/r exch _R exch itransform} bdef
/c {_r curveto} bdef
/C /c ldef
/v {currentpoint 6 2 roll _r curveto} bdef
/V /v ldef
/y {_r 2 copy curveto} bdef
/Y /y ldef
/l {_r lineto} bdef
/L /l ldef
/m {_r moveto} bdef
```

Although path coordinates are specified in a device-independent user space, this independence leads to slight variations in stroke weight due to differences in the device subpixel location of the coordinates. For example, if a vertical line is drawn with a width of 2.5 device pixels, then the line will overlap 3 pixel columns if its center is at a .5 subpixel location, while it will overlap 4 columns if its center is at a .0 location. To eliminate this plus or minus one variation in stroke weight, the endpoints of each path segment are moved to a uniform subpixel location of .25. This operation is called path phase locking.

The choice of .25 as opposed to other possible subpixel locations for phase locking is based on a desire that the location should not produce more even stroke weights than odd ones, and vice versa. For example, a choice of .0 would never produce an odd stroke width, while .5 would never produce an even width. The choice of .25 provides an unbiased balance of these two extreme behaviors.

All the path construction operations are based on the PostScript primitives: moveto, lineto, and curveto. Before executing these primitives, however, the segment's endpoints are phase-locked by executing the _r operator. The Bezier direction points are not phase-locked, unless they are coincident with the segment's endpoints.

```
% error operators
/_e [] def
/_/E {_e length 0 ne {gsave 0 g 0 G 0 1 0 J 0 j 1 w 10 M [] 0 d
/Courier 20 0 0 1 z [0.966 0.259 -0.259 0.966
_e 0 get _e 2 get add 2 div _e 1 get _e 3 get add 2 div] e _f t T    grestore} if} bdef
/_fill {{fill} stopped
{/_e [pathbbox] def /_f (ERROR: can't fill, increase flatness) def n _E} if}
bdef
/_stroke {{stoke} stopped
{/_e [pathbbox] def /_f (ERROR: can't stroke, increase flatness) def n
_E} if} bdef
```

The _fill and _stroke operators provide an error recovery method for the PostScript fill and stroke primitives, respectively. If the filling or stroking of the current path would cause some limit to be exceeded within the PostScript interpreter, these operators will catch the error, display an appropriate error message, and then allow the execution of the document to continue.

When an error is caught by the stopped primitive, _e is set equal to a four-element array containing the bounding box of the current path, and _f is set equal to the string containing the error message. The operator _E is then invoked to display the message. Since the error message may be obscured by the painting of subsequent elements, _E is defined so that it may be called in the document's trailer subsection. If any errors occurred, the message associated with the last occurring error is redisplayed.

```
% path painting operators
/n /newpath ldef
/N /n ldef
/F {p _fill} bdef
/f {closepath F} bdef
/S {P _stroke} bdef
/s {closepath S} bdef
/B {gsave F grestore S} bdef
/b {closepath B} bdef
```

The path painting operators are easily implemented by calling the appropriate PostScript fill and stroke primitives. When the current path must be filled as well as stroked, it is preserved across the fill via the PostScript gsave and grestore primitives. Before the primitives are called, however, the current color in the PostScript graphics state is established by executing either p or P, which are defined by the implementations of g, G, k, and K.

```
% text block construction and painting operators
/_s /ashow ldef
/_S {(?) exch {2 copy 0 exch put pop dup false charpath currentpoint       _g
  setmatrix
  _stroke _G setmatrix moveto 3 copy pop rmoveto} forall
pop pop pop n} bdef
```

The _s and _S operators are used to fill and stroke the outlines of the characters in an argument string, respectively. Both of these operators expect three arguments on the stack like the PostScript primitive ashow: the x and y width displacement values and the string.

Filling the outlines is especially easy: ashow is simply executed. Stroking the outlines involves a loop that enumerates each character of the string. The primitive charpath is executed to obtain the character's outline, which is stroked by the primitive stroke.

Before the outline is stroked, however, the user space that was in effect prior to the start of the text block is restored. This must be done so that the width and dash parameter lengths are interpreted properly. The matrix _g contains the transformation matrix that defines this space. After the outline is stroked, the matrix _G is used to reestablish the prior user space. It is the responsibility of the a, e, o, r, and t operators to define and maintain proper values for these matrices.

A special property of the charpath primitive is used to establish the proper spacing between each character in the string and the next: charpath leaves the current point displaced from its initial position by the width of the character. Before the outline is stroked, this displaced current point is placed on the stack. Afterwards, a current point is reestablished by executing moveto, which takes its arguments from the stack. The rmoveto primitive is then used to emulate the width adjustment performed by ashow.

```
/_A {_a moveto _t exch 0 exch} bdef
/_L {0 _l neg translate _G currentmatrix pop} bdef
```

The _A and _L operators are used just prior and just after a single line of text is painted. _A takes the line of text as a string argument and returns x and y width displacement values and the string, in preparation for the ashow operator. In addition, it sets the current point equal to the line's starting point. This is accomplished by executing the alignment method associated with the operator _a, which expects a string argument and leaves the string along with the starting point on the stack. Then a moveto is executed. The x width displacement value is defined by the current kerning value, associated with _t. The y width displacement value is 0. It is the responsibility of the z operator to define _a and _t properly.

After the line is painted, the origin of user space is translated by the current leading in the negative y direction to establish an origin for the next line of text. The current leading is associated with _l. After the translation, the matrix _G is updated to reflect the new translated user space.

```
/_w {dup stringwidth exch 3 -1 roll length 1 sub _t
mul add exch}    bdef
/ z [{0 0} bind {dup _w exch neg 2 div exch neg 2 div}
bind {dup _w    exch neg exch neg} bind] def
/z {_z exch get /_a xdef /_t xdef /_l xdef exch
findfont exch scalefont setfont} bdef
```

The three variables _l, _t, and _a maintain the current leading, kerning, and alignment method parameters, respectively. The alignment method is implemented as an operator "t" takes the line of text as a string argument and returns the string along with the x and y coordinates of the line's starting point in the current user space. The computation of the starting point is based on the PostScript primitive stringwidth, along with the current kerning value.

The three different alignment methods are implemented as elements of the array associated with _z. When z is executed, the appropriate element is selected from the array and bound to _a.

```
/_g matrix def
/_G matrix def
/_D {_g currentmatrix pop gsave concat _G currentmatrix pop} bdef
 /e {_D p /t {_A _s _L} def} bdef
 /r {_D P /t {_A _S _L} def} bdef
 /a {_D /t {dup p _A _s P _A _S _L} def} bdef
 /o {_D /t {pop _L} def} bdef
 /T {grestore} bdef
```

The a, e, o, and r operators all begin by executing the operator _D to establish the user space associated with the text block. _D saves the transformation matrix associated with the current user space in the matrix _g, concatenates its argument matrix with the current transformation matrix to define the new user space, and then saves the transformation matrix associated with the new space in the matrix _G. These two matrices are used by the character stroking operations as described above.

Then the t operator is bound to the appropriate character filling and stroking method. In general, t first establishes the current filling or stroking color by executing the p or P operator, respectively. Then the _A operator is executed to establish the line's starting point. Next, the _s or _S operator is invoked to fill or stroke the line, respectively. Finally, the _L operator is executed to translate the user space for the next line of text.

At the end of the text block, the T operator executes the primitive grestore to restore the user space prior to the start of the text block. This grestore matches the gsave executed by the _D operator.

```
 % group construction operators
 /u {} bdef
 /U {} bdef
```

These operators provide structural information within the script, hence their implementations do nothing.

```
 % font construction operators
 /Z {findfont begin currentdict dup length dict begin
 {1 index /FID ne {def} {pop pop} ifelse} forall /
FontName exch def dup
```

```
length 0 n e
{/Encoding Encoding 256 array copy def 0 exch {dup
type /nametype
 eq
 {Encoding 2 index 2 index put pop 1 add} {exch
pop} ifelse} forall} if pop currentdict  dup end
end /FontName get exch definefont pop} bdef
```

The Z operator builds the reencoded font by first copying all the entries in the base font dictionary to the new dictionary, except for the FID field. Then, the new font name is installed. Next, the elements of the argument array are enumerated to update the new font's character encoding vector. Finally, the definefont primitive is executed to create the new font.

```
e n d
%%EndProcSet
```

The %%EndProcSet comment defines the end of the prologue's definitions. The definition dictionary is removed from the dictionary stack.

The Illustrator Document Script Subsection

The Adobe Illustrator script section was designed to meet two goals. First, it must be executable by a PostScript interpreter, and second, it must be easily parsable so that it is possible to obtain a complete description of the illustration's graphic elements without having to directly interpret the PostScript program. These goals resulted in a script consisting of a sequence of tokens that conforms to a very strict syntactic form.

Syntax Notation

In the syntax notation used to describe the script, syntactic categories are indicated by italic type, and literal names by bold type. Alternative categories are listed on separate line. Occurrences of the newline character are explicitly included as instances of the category newline. The category text specifies an arbitrary sequence of characters excluding a newline character. The category arbitrary_text specifies an arbitrary PostScript program consisting of a sequence of characters possibly including newline characters. Prologue operator argument categories, such as pattern, offset, gray, and so forth, are left unspecified. Consult the section on Adobe Illustrator Document Prologue Definitions beginning on page XX.

Script Syntax

```
script:
  script_setup script_body script_trailer

script_setup:
  script_setup_begin     script_setup_init
script_setup_encode

script_setup_begin:
  %%BeginSetup newline

script_setup_init:
  arbitrary_text newline

script_setup_encode:
  font_encode
  font_encode script_setup_encode

script_setup_end:
  %%EndSetup newline

font_encode:
  font_encode_begin font_encode_body font_encode_end

font_encode:begin
  %%Begin Encoding:newfont font newline

font_encode_body:
  array newfont font Z newline

font_encode_end
  %%EndEncoding newline

script_body:
  script_element
  script_element script_body

script_element:
  state_element
  object_element

state_element:
  pattern offset d newline
  gray g neline
  gray G newline
```

```
            flat i newline
            join j newline
            cap J newline
            cyan magenta yellow black k newline
            cyan magenta yellow black K newline
            miter M newline
            width w newline
            font scale leading kerning alignment z newline
            %%Note: text newline

        object_element:
          path
          text
          embed
          group

        path:
          path_begin path_body path_end

        path_begin:
          x y m newline

        path_body:
          path_segment
          path_segment path_body

        path_segment:
          x1 y1 x2 y2 x3 y3 c newline
          x1 y1 x2 y2 x3 y3 C newline
          sx y l newline
          x y L newline
          x2 y2 x3 y3 v newline
          x2 y2 x3 y3 V newline
          x1 y1 x3 y3 y newline
          x1 y1 x3 y3 Y newline

        path_end:
          b newline
          B newline
          f newline
          F newline
          n newline
```

```
    N newline
    s newline
    S newline

text:
  text_begin text_body text_end

text_begin:
  matrix a newline
  matrix e newline
  matrix o newline
  matrix r newline

text_body:
  text_line
  text_line text_body

text_line:
  string t newline

text_end:
  T newline

group:
  group_begin script_body group_end

group_begin:
  u newline

group_end:
  U newline

embed:
  embed_begin embed_body embed_end

embed_begin:
  %%BeginDocument: text newline

embed_body
  arbitrary_text newline

embed_end
  %%EndDocument newline
```

```
script_trailer:
  script_trailer_begin script_trailer_body

script_trailer_begin:
  %%Trailer

script_trailer_body:
  Marbitrary_text newline
```

Other Illustrator Document Resources

On the Macintosh, the resource fork of an Adobe Illustrator document contains several ancillary resources that are described here.

```
PICT ID = 256
```

An Adobe Illustrator document may have a graphical screen representation provided so that a preview of the illustration may be manipulated on the screen by a page composition system. On the Macintosh, this representation is saved as a QuickDraw PICT picture resource within the resource fork of the document. The resource is given a resource type of PICT and a resource number of 256.

The pictures picFrame bounding box matches the bounding box of the illustration, as specified by the %%BoundingBox comment. That is, the width and height of picFrame equals the width and height of the bounding box, respectively.

The picture resource is composed of two bit-map images: the image itself and its mask. If a particular bit is set in the mask, then the illustration has actually painted the corresponding bit in the image; otherwise, the corresponding bit has not been painted and hence should be transparent.

The mask is placed in the picture first in the QuickDraw srcBic mode. It punches a white hole in just those areas that are painted. Then the image is placed in the QuickDraw srcOr mode, which fills in the punched areas but leaves the other areas unaffected.

```
P A G E  ID = 256
```

This resource contains the x and y coordinates of the document's page origin, as specified by the page tool, in the default user coordinate system in which the unit length along both axes is 1/72 of an inch. The resource consists of two 32-bit fixed point numbers; the first specifies the y coordinate, the second the x coordinate. The resource is given a resource type of PAGE and a resource number of 256.

```
P R E C  ID = 256
```

This resource contains the standard 120-byte Macintosh Printing Manager print record. It describes the document's user-specified printing preferences selected from the Page Setup and Print dialog boxes. The resource is given a resource type of PREC and a resource number of 256.

T E M P ID = 256

This resource identifies the name of the document's template file, if it has one. It consists of a 32-bit integer containing the directory identifier of the folder containing the template file, followed by a Pascal string containing the name of the volume on which the template file resides, followed by a Pascal string containing the name of the template file itself.

If the document has no template, then the directory identifier integer is zero, and both strings are empty. The resource is given a resource type of TEMP and a resource number of 256.

Index

A4 Letter, 200
About Illustrator, 181
active window, 13
Actual Size command, 227
AIGA symbols, 96
airbrush effect, 71, 87
Alarm Clock desk accessory, 183
alignment, 142, 245
Alignment points, 128
Alternative categories, 302
anchor, 127
anchor point, 117, 131, 138
anchor points, 28, 112, 115
angled axes option, 225
angled shear, 175
Apple icon, 11
Apple LaserWriter, 4
Apple menu, 181
AppleTalk, 20, 273
arc, 250
Arrange menu, 30, 40, 103, 112, 214, 215
array newfont, 290
array offset, 287
arrays, 256
arrow, 106
Artwork & Template command, 13, 227
artwork document, 10
Artwork Only command, 15, 227

Average command, 112, 218, 220
axes, 99
axis, 52
BASIC, 254
BeginProcSet, 285
BeginProcSet comment, 295
Bezier curves, 89, 261, 291
Bezier direction, 291
Bezier direction points, 297
bit-mapped graphics, 76
black, 87
body, 285
boundary, 28
bounding box, 44, 283
BoundingBox, 285
BoundingBox comment, 306
Butt, 239
CAD/CAM, 5
Calculator desk accessory, 183
calligraphy, 68
Cancel button, 196
cap, 288
Caps, 239, 241
center point, 128, 143
character width, 6
charpath primitive, 300
Chooser desk accessory, 20, 184, 202
circle, 9, 24
circle tool, 146

Clear command, 210
Clipboard, 28, 33, 139, 207, 208, 210, 211
clipping, 249
clipping path, 286
Close command, 192
closed path, 129
closepath, 250
color, 87
color printer, 7
color separation, 5
color state, 286
Command key, 7
Command-D, 40, 49, 64
commands, 266
comments, 266
constrain, 7, 9, 226
constrain axis, 7, 103
Constrain command, 49, 103, 222, 246
  axes, 52
Constrain dialog box, 112, 224
Control Panel desk accessory, 184
Copies option, 204
copy, 40, 64, 205
Copy command, 209
copypage, 274
CORA, 4
corner point, 128, 131, 138, 291
Creation Date, 284
current, 250
current path, 250, 290
current point, 290
curved segments, 28
curveto, 250, 297
Cut command, 208
cyan magenta yellow black, 288
data, 273

def operator, 262
default scale, 259
default type attribute, 140
default user, 251
deferred commands, 256
deferred procedure, 262
definefont primitive, 302
desk accessories, 181
Device, 251
device-, 297
device-independence, 249
dictionary stack, 255
digitized image, 250
direction point, 44, 115, 127
document processing, 248
Document Structure, 275, 282
DocumentFonts, 284
DocumentProcSets, 284
DocumentSuppliedProcSets, 284
dots-per-inch, 1
download PostScript file, 20
drawing area, 6, 42
drive button, 195
duplicate, 40, 45, 68
Edit, 214
Edit menu, 207, 208, 209, 212
editing type, 99
eject, 195
ellipse, 9, 149
Ellipses, 148
Encapsulated PostScript format, 5, 10, 195, 274
enclosed path, 28
EndComments, 285
endpoints, 33, 115, 127
EndProcSet, 285, 302
enlargement, 44
EPS, 6
EPSF, 195

execution, 296
execution stack, 255
extensible (or 'threaded') language, 254
FID field, 302
File menu, 11, 189, 190, 194, 232
files, 10
Fill options, 239
filled paths, 68
filling, 260
filling color, 286
film recorder, 4
Fit In, 17
Fit In Window command, 230
Fit In Window option, 42
fixed resolution, 1
flat, 287
flatness, 239
folders, 10
font, 6, 28, 286
font substitution, 45
Font Substitution option, 201
Forth, 254
four-color, 5
FullWrite Professional, 195
Gallery disks, 19
general coordinate system, 249
Get File, 11
Get File dialog box, 190
graphic matrices, 271
graphics description language, 252
graphics-state stack, 255
gray, 287
gray scale, 74, 250
gray shades, 78
gray-scale, 250
grestore, 301
Group, 28, 56
Group command, 33, 108, 215, 238
grouped paths, 83
halftone, 78, 286
hand tool, 7, 119, 124
Help command, 181, 183
Hide Clipboard command, 214
Hide Rulers, 235
Hide Rulers command, 235
Hide Toolbox command, 235
horizontal axis, 96
horizontal printing, 20
ImageWriter, 198, 199, 202
ImageWriter printer, 203
infix form, 254
international-sized sheets of paper, 200
italic-, 262
Join, 112, 287
Joins, 239, 241
kerning, 6, 142, 245
Key Caps desk accessory, 185
Key Caps menu, 185
landscape mode, 20, 42
LaserWriter, 4, 6, 42, 44, 46, 88, 200, 248, 256, 261, 262, 266, 270, 272
LaserWriter Plus, 201
LaserWriter printer, 205
leading, 6, 141, 142, 245
legal-sized sheets of paper, 200
Line caps, 262
line weight, 90, 103
line weights, 24, 90
linear, 249
linecap, 262
linejoin, 262
lineto, 297
Linotronic, 4, 5, 83, 88
Linotronic typesetters, 44
Linotype, 4
literal, 258

literal names, 302
locus point, 40
MacDraw, 2, 11
Macintosh, 248
MacPaint, 2, 11
MacTerminal, 273
magnify, 28
makefont command, 267
marquee, 8, 62, 87
matrix, 270, 293
matrix multiplication, 271
menu selection, 181
MicroPhone, 273
Microsoft Windows, 248
miter, 289
Miter Limit, 239, 241
More, 195
Move dialog box, 110
moveto, 250, 257, 297, 300
Network Extensible Window System, 252
New View command, 75, 232
New command, 189
newline, 284
newpath, 250
newpath command, 259
NEWS, 252
No, 199
Non-uniform scale, 160
Note Pad, 213
Note: box, 239
open path, 129, 131
Open command, 190
operand stack, 255, 266
Operations, 266
operators, 266
Option key, 7, 28, 30, 46
Orientation, 199, 201
OS/2, 248
output device, 286
ovals, 24
page, 44, 200

enlargement, 44
reduction, 44
page boundary, 44
page description language, 4
page orientation, 42
Page Range options, 203
Page Setup command, 20, 42
Page Setup dialog box, 44, 56, 154, 177, 179, 180, 202
page setup settings, 45
Page Setup command, 197, 198
Page Setup dialog, 197
Page Setup dialog box, 199
Page Setup options, 202
page tool, 42, 177
page-layout, 195
PageMaker, 4, 6, 195
Paint attributes, 65
Paint command, 76
paint defaults, 76
Paint menu, 34
paint-type graphics, 76
Paint, 238
Paint command, 237
Paint dialog box, 239
painting operations, 293
Pantone Matching System, 5
Paper, 198, 199, 200
Paper Cassette, 206
Paper Feed options, 204
Paper Source, 206
Pascal, 254
Paste command, 209, 210
Paste In, 38, 68, 87, 238
Paste In Back, 8, 238
Paste In Back command, 87, 212
Paste In Front, 68
Paste In Front command, 28, 30, 65, 211
path, 56, 129

path painting operators, 298
pen tool, 24, 28, 126, 131
phase-locked, 297
picas, 233
PICT, 10, 11, 213, 274, 306
PICT file format, 188
PICT format, 196
PICT ID = 256, 306
PICT-format, 210
pixels, 76, 112
plate maker, 4
PMS, 5
point size, 141
pointer tool, 49
points, 127, 233
polygons, 24
portrait mode, 20, 42
post-fix, 254
post-fix form of notation, 266
PostScript, 4, 5, 9, 20, 249, 292
PostScript comments, 283
PostScript files, 195
PostScript interpreter, 273
PostScript Language Reference Manual, 253
PostScript Language Tutorial and Cookbook, 253
PostScript printer, 202, 272
precise movement, 49
precise scale, 92
Presentation, 248
preview, 7
Preview command, 75, 226
Preview option, 15, 37
Print command, 42
Print dialog box, 178
Print command, 202
Print dialog box, 202, 203
Print options, 204
printed page, 42

printer, 45
Printer Effects, 201
printing, 44
process colors, 5
prologue, 273, 282, 283, 292, 293
prologue definition subsection, 285
Prologue Header, 283
prologue header subsection, 285
quality, 203
QuickDraw, 196, 202, 252, 274, 306
Quit command, 19, 206
Ragtime, 195
RAM, 215
range of pages, 205
raster image processor, 4, 251
ReadySetGo! 3, 4
ReadySetGo3, 195
rectangles, 24
Redo command, 208
Reduce or Enlarge, 200
reduction, 44, 93, 199
Reflect dialog box, 168, 170
reflect tool, 168, 169, 170
reflecting, 57
reflection, 56, 97
reflection tool, 83, 96
resolution, 2, 4
RIP, 251, 273
rmoveto, 300
Rotate dialog box, 162, 166
rotate tool, 162, 166
rotating, 45
rotation, 7, 42, 64
rotation dialog box, 93
rotation tool, 40, 64, 84, 93
rulers, 233, 235
Save As, 32

Save As command, 10
Save As, 196
Save As command, 194
Save As dialog box, 194
Save command, 32, 193, 194
Save document as:, 195
Scale dialog box, 154, 159
scale tool, 124, 154, 156
scalefont, 257
scaling, 6, 45
scaling dialog box, 90
scaling line, 104
scaling options, 161
scaling tool, 68, 90
scaling tool, 71
scanned templates, 90
scanner, 249
scanners, 5
scissors tool, 9, 83, 115, 149, 153
Scoop, 195
Scrapbook, 213
Scrapbook command, 209
Scrapbook desk accessory, 187
screen driver, 5
script, 282
segment, 56, 129
segments, 28, 33
Select All command, 211
selecting objects, 8
selecting path, 8
selection marquee, 109, 117
selection rectangle, 8
selection tool, 106, 108, 110, 112
SendPS, 275
SendPS program, 19, 20, 273
serial connection, 273
setgray, 288
setlinewidth, 262
setup, 285

shadow, 32
Shear Angle, 175
Shear dialog box, 174
shear tool, 50, 52, 172, 174
shearing, 52, 57
shearing tool, 50
Shift key, 7, 28, 46
Show Clipboard, 208
Show Clipboard command, 212
Show Rulers command, 233
Show Toolbox command, 236
showpage, 20, 274
showpage command, 259
size, 6
size-indicator box, 125
slant an image, 50
slide makers, 5
smooth point, 127, 291
smoothing effect, 45
Smoothing option, 201
Snap to Point feature, 112
Snap to Point option, 222, 225
space bar, 7
Special Effects, 199
square tool, 142
squares, 24
stack-oriented, 258
stack-oriented language, 254, 266
stat camera, 154
straight segments, 28
string, 294
stringwidth, 301
Stroke, 238, 239
stroke command, 250
Stroke Style, 239
stroked type, 7
strokes, 65
stroking, 260
stroking color, 286

Index 315

style, 6
Style menu, 34
syntactic, 302
TEMP ID=256, 307
Tall Adjusted, 199
tangent function, 267
template, 2, 90
Template Only command, 227
Template Only option, 15
TemplateBox, 285
templates, 11
text, 6
text placement cursor, 139
Text tool, 6, 28, 99
text-block painting operators, 286
The New York Times, 2
threaded-stack structure, 254
TIFF, 274
Title, 284
title bar, 108
token, 254
trailer, 285
trailing endpoint, 290
tranformation, 56
transfer function, 286
Transform, 49
Transform Again, 40, 71, 161
Transform Again command, 42, 64, 87, 214
transformation, 46, 56, 64, 71, 78, 84, 87, 93
translate, 271
transparent object, 68

triplet matrix, 271
type attributes, 245
type characteristics, 84
Type dialog box, 139, 140, 213, 244
type size, 141
type tool, 138, 139, 243
Type command, 243
Type dialog box, 243
typesetter, 4
typesetters, 83
Undo command, 208
Undo Cut, 209
ungroup, 9, 143
Ungroup command, 216
uniform scaling, 6, 90, 160
user, 262
user space, 251
vertical axis, 96
vertical spacing, 6
View menu, 13, 15, 34, 75, 226, 227
virtual memory, 296
Weight, 238
width, 289
winding number rule, 238, 250, 292
window's size box, 107
Word, 195
working, 254
wysiNQwyg, 252
WYSIWYG, 274
XPress, 195
zoom, 107
zoom tool, 17, 28, 120, 124